Socialist Joy in the Writing of Langston Hughes

University of Missouri Press
Columbia and London

Socialist Joy in the
Writing of **Langston
Hughes**

Jonathan Scott

Library of Congress Cataloging-in-Publication Data

Scott, Jonathan, 1968–
  Socialist joy in the writing of Langston Hughes / Jonathan Scott.
     p.   cm.
  Summary: "Explores Hughes's intellectual method and its relation
to social activism. Examines his involvement with socialist movements of the 1920s and 1930s and contends that the goal of overthrowing white oppression produced a "socialist joy" expressed
repeatedly in his later work, in spite of the anti-communist crusades
of the cold war"—Provided by publisher.
  Includes bibliographical references and index.
  ISBN-13: 978-0-8262-1677-9 (alk. paper)
  ISBN-10: 0-8262-1677-3 (alk. paper)
  1. Hughes, Langston, 1902–1967—Criticism and interpretation.
2. Hughes, Langston, 1902–1967—Political and social views.
3. Socialism in literature.   4. Socialism and literature—United
States—History—20th century.   5. African Americans in
literature.   I. Title.

PS3515.U274Z78 2007
818'.5209—dc22

2006024593

♾ This paper meets the requirements of the American
National Standard for Permanence of Paper for
Printed Library Materials, Z39.48, 1984.

Designer: Jennifer Cropp
Typesetter: The Composing Room of Michigan, Inc.
Printer and binder: The Maple-Vail Book Manufacturing Group
Typefaces: Palatino, Typewriter, and Courier

For Deedee

and in memory of
Ruth Scott

There is more of a concentration today on the affirmation of identity, the need for roots, the values
of one's culture and one's sense of belonging. It's
become quite rare to project one's self outward.

                                    -Edward Said

Contents

Acknowledgments

I've been obsessed by the relation between the individual and the collective. In writing about Langston Hughes, the subject became even more interesting to me, both because of my topic and because of the writing and researching itself. A writer's work is solitary, but without other people no writer can survive for long. The first person I'd like to thank is Tim Brennan—a truly great thinker, writer, and teacher who has been my mentor and friend for the past two decades, whose central place in my life has been constant despite many changes in each of our lives. It's been impossible for to me to think about this book without also thinking of him and his influential work.

Amiri Baraka graciously agreed in 1992 to be a member of my doctoral examination committee at the State University of New York at Stony Brook, and his guidance during that formative period of my life left a lasting mark on me. Besides being one the world's most important poets and intellectuals, Amiri is the purest spirit I'll ever know.

Melba Joyce Boyd and I share the same place of origin—the southwest side of Detroit. She has not only read my manuscript with patience and care but before that gave me a wonderful welcome-back present in 1996 by offering me several courses to teach in African American literature and culture at Wayne State University, where she was the chair of Africana studies.

Before returning to Detroit, while I was still a graduate student in New York, I met Tony Medina—a genius poet and now an inspiring professor at Howard University. Through our lasting friendship, my ideas about Langston Hughes have grown immensely. His book for children, *Love to Langston*, is a gem.

Heidi Kleedtke, to whom this book is dedicated, is a Detroit sister who embodies the best of our never-say-die hometown. Wherever I've been she's been by my side, supporting everything I've ever done. Without her unreflecting love, writing and teaching would never be as much fun.

My father, Gerald Scott, and my brother, Joel Scott, who is a public school teacher at McKenzie High in Detroit, have been constant emotional supports—they have been loyal friends and the best family a person could be born to.

In 2000, my mom, Ruth Scott, passed away. This book is offered in her memory for so many reasons. One is that she was always asking me to recite another Langston Hughes poem. He was her favorite poet.

Kam Hei Tsuei has been a wonderful friend, a close reader of my writing, and a serious student of Langston Hughes. Her enthusiasm for literature is always enlivening, and her contagious laughter usually to keep from crying.

Three people who shaped my thinking during the writing of this book passed away before its publication: Harold Cruse, Michael Sprinker, and Theodore Allen. When I was an undergraduate student at the University of Michigan, Professor Cruse spent many generous hours schooling me over coffee and cigarettes. Michael was my mentor during my Ph.D. work at Stony Brook, and Ted my political soul mate from Brooklyn and one of my closest friends for more than ten years. I hope in these pages I'm able to keep their iconoclastic spirits alive.

I'd also like to thank other friends whose intelligent love of books and ideas has contributed to the development of my thinking. Anamaría Flores is the best comrade and coworker a person could ask for and a good friend. Tony López has been a steady source of intellectual joy. José Henriquez is an irreplaceable comrade and a kindred spirit. By his example, Nabeel Abraham showed me about the life of the independent intellectual. Thank you Sameeh Hamad for making me your brother, Omar Hamad for the comradeship, Susan Suliman for your clarity of mind and unshakable conviction, and Ron Hayduk for your warmth and commitment to justice. Charles Johnson I thank for sharing with me his brilliant thesis called "White Capital." Rodney Foxworth always inspires me with his energy and optimism, and Hank Williams with his everyday love of teaching. Thanks to Javier Lee for growing up with me, and to Joyce Dukes for her elegant mind. To George Farnhum for all his Bajan wisdom and Javy Genoa for his militancy. Thanks to Miriam Delgado, Vanessa Shannon, Andrea Alonzo, Danny Sexton, Roger Sedarat, Margie White, and Hyacinth Martin for being wonderful colleagues. Thanks to Garfield Phillips for a long and supportive friendship, and to Elliot Podwill for all the political humor. To Holly Martis for being a close friend and insightful reader of my work.

Although there are many years between us now, Anton Shamas helped me to think clearly about literary theory in his graduate seminar at the University of Michigan. His masterpiece, *Arabesques*, remains one of my favorite novels.

Rudy Lewis, the editor-in-chief and publisher of *ChickenBones*, has been important to me because he is important to so many others. His tireless labor of love at the fine African American journal he founded is unpaid and underappreciated. He has helped me with several essays and is always engaged at the highest level of intellectual work. The same is true of Glen Ford at the *Black Commentator*, who has published several essays of mine and has always encouraged more. Hazel Waters and A. Sivanandan at *Race and Class* and Victor Wallis and Yusuf Nuruddin at *Socialism and Democracy* have been superb editors of my writing and helpful guides in the writing I continue to do. Much thanks also to Kostas Myrsiades, editor of *College Literature*, for the same reasons.

Professor Basem Ra'ad is the chair of the English Department at Al-Quds University in Jerusalem and a new friend I'm honored to have. He recently offered me a teaching position in Palestine that will take my work in a different direction.

And thank you to Kathy Christison for your interest in my scholarship and for being a kindred soul.

Special thanks to Beverly Jarrett, editor-in-chief of the University of Missouri Press, not just for her interest in *Socialist Joy* and in seeing it published, but far more important for seeing through to the end the publication of all sixteen volumes of *The Collected Works of Langston Hughes*—one of the greatest revolutionary triumphs in the history of U.S. academic publishing. Thanks also to Jane Lago, managing editor, University of Missouri Press, for her helpful guidance on my manuscript.

I'm in the debt of Isabel Planas and Elba Peña for all their helpful and underpaid labor in the English Department at the Borough of Manhattan Community College.

And to all the students I've taught at BMCC over the past six years, you have also been teaching me—about keeping your head up through the worst of times, including a lot of unnecessary grief put on working people by their remarkably inefficient "superiors." You've also taught me how to teach by being in class every day with active, open minds, lots of laughter, genuine humility, and a great determination to be free. You'll always be with me.

Finally, thanks to all the hardworking people of the city of Detroit for bringing me up.

Socialist Joy in the
Writing of Langston
Hughes

Introduction

The Blood of Others

Alive, I read the poems of the dead,
I who laugh and cry and can shout
"¡Patria Libre o Morir!"
on the back of a flatbed truck
the day we enter Managua.

I read the poems of the dead,
watch the ants in the grass,
my bare feet, your straight hair,
the curve of your back
after hours of meetings.

I read the poems of the dead
and fear this blood that fuels our love
does not belong to us.

—Gioconda Belli

One of the consequences of American formalism and New Criticism is that the writing of literary and cultural history has been assigned to the biographer rather than to the critic. Students of Langston Hughes feel this more than most, since the striking imbalance between the biographical writings devoted to him and the critical scholarship that seeks to understand the aesthetic choices he made as a writer, and the circumstances in which he made them, poses a series of vexing problems.[1] In a similar way, students of Hughes are impressed by the quantity of work devoted to him by scholars and critics completely outside the orbit of American studies. One of the first appreciations of Hughes's poetry was penned by a Cuban essayist and translator, José Antonio Fernández, and published in the Cuban press. And, as I learned from a Russian émigré, the saga of Jesse B. Semple was required reading in the old Soviet common school curriculum. In fact, a great diversity of Hughes's writing has been translated into Russian and Spanish. According to Hughes scholar Richard Jackson, when Hughes died in 1967 "his writings had been translated more than those of any other living American poet."[2] That Hughes spent several years living and traveling in Latin America and the Caribbean, as well as in the Soviet Union, explains much of this. Indeed, his lifelong interest in the Bolshevik Revolution and in Latin American and Caribbean music and poetry, exemplified in the work he did as a professional translator and anthologist, has made Hughes a household name around the globe. To put it simply, in U.S. society, where the main cultural export to the rest of the world is anticommunist action movies, the dynamic and undeniable ties among Hughes, the Bolshevik Revolution, and Latin America and the Caribbean go a long way in explaining why so little has been written about these connections in the U.S. academy.

Another side of the triangular relationship among Hughes and "non-American" traditions such as the Bolshevik Revolution and Latin American and Caribbean music and poetry is communist ideology, which plays a central role in the present study. In Hughes's writing, the popular struggles in Europe against the rise of fascism, in Latin America and the

---

1. The biographical scholarship on Langston Hughes is rich and diverse, whereas the book-length aesthetic criticism is thin in comparison. The biographical texts are James Emanuel's *Langston Hughes* (1967), Milton Meltzer's *Langston Hughes: A Biography* (1968); Charlemae Hill Rollins's *Black Troubadour: Langston Hughes* (1970); Alice Walker's *Langston Hughes, American Poet* (1974); Faith Berry's *Langston Hughes: Before and Beyond Harlem* (1983); Arnold Rampersad's two-volume *The Life of Langston Hughes* (1986, 1988); Jack Rummel's *Langston Hughes: A Poet* (1988); James Haskins's *Always Movin' On: The Life of Langston Hughes* (1993); Floyd Cooper's *Coming Home: The Life of Langston Hughes* (1994); Tony Medina's *Love to Langston* (2002); Martha Rhynes's *I, Too, Sing America: The Story of Langston Hughes* (2002); Robert Burleigh's *Langston's Train Ride* (2004); and Laurie F. Leach's *Langston Hughes: A Biography* (2004).

2. "The Shared Vision of Langston Hughes and Black Hispanic Writers," 89.

Caribbean for decolonization and national independence, in Russia for socialism, and in the United States for the overthrow of white racial oppression made possible a new international common ground from which new concepts of writing and politics could be advanced and popularized. While each side of this triangle needs detail and definition—for example, the literary and cultural criticism on Hughes's relations to "non-American" traditions is, in American studies, embarrassingly meager— the nexus between the historical and the aesthetic is the focus of this work. My aim is to take into account both aspects of Hughes's life and art by dwelling on a single facet of his work, his creative method.

Exploring the character of "American studies" in light of the Hughes scholarship is an obvious line of inquiry yet one that is beyond the purview of my project here. What needs to be said, I think, is that the situation in regard to Hughes appears to be a representative fragment of the whole, in which the revolutionary strides made to desegregate the U.S. academy in the 1970s and early 1980s have been countered over the last twenty years by a motley group of distinctly racialist and reactionary ideologies, whose effect on American studies should not be underestimated. Researchers examining the journal articles and dissertations written on Hughes cannot help but notice two things. The first is that the emergent scholarship on Hughes that accompanied the establishment of black studies programs during the 1970s, such as the important work of R. Baxter Miller, Faith Berry, Steven Tracy, Martha K. Cobb, Melvin Dixon, James Presley, Arnold Rampersad, Dellita Martin-Ogunsola, Eloise Y. Spicer, Richard Jackson, Edward O. Ako, and Edward Mullen, was never "integrated" into American studies.[3]

In the main, American studies remained resistant to Hughes and

3. The major works on Hughes published in academic journals during the 1970s and 1980s are Cobb's "Concepts of Blackness in the Poetry of Nicolás Guillén, Jacques Roumain, and Langston Hughes" (1974); Presley's "Langston Hughes, War Correspondent" (1976); Miller's "'Even After I Was Dead': The Big Sea-Paradox, Preservation, and Holistic Time" (1977); Martin-Ogunsola's "Langston Hughes's Use of the Blues" (1978) and "Langston Hughes and the Musico-Poetry of the African Diaspora" (1986); Jackson's "Shared Vision" (1981) and "Langston Hughes and the African Diaspora in South America" (1986); Tracy's "To the Tune of Those Weary Blues" (1981), Rampersad's "The Origins of Poetry in Langston Hughes" (1985); Eloise Y. Spicer's "The Blues and the Son: Reflections of Black Self-Assertion in the Poetry of Langston Hughes and Nicolás Guillén" (1984); Ako's "Langston Hughes and the Négritude Movement: A Study in Literary Influences" (1984); and Faith Berry and Maurice A. Lubin's "Langston Hughes and Haiti" (1987). In 1995, Michael Thurston published important new research on Hughes's relationship to the American communist movement, "Black Christ, Red Flag: Langston Hughes on Scottsboro."

Hughes scholarship the same way it has remained resistant to every major ideological challenge to its most deeply cherished and socially patrolled belief: its "racelessness." In 1992, for instance, Toni Morrison found it necessary to explain to white Americanists, once again, that in U.S. society "American means white" and, more to the point, "The act of enforcing racelessness in literary discourse is itself a racial act."[4] In American studies, this enforcement of racelessness with respect to Hughes can be seen in the strong emphases constantly placed on Hughes's faith in American democracy, the possibilities of interracial cooperation, and so on. In other words, there are quite a few critical treatments in American studies of Hughes's "Theme for English B," "I, Too," and "The Negro Speaks of Rivers," but nothing on his poems "White Man," "A Christian Country," "Ballads for Lenin," or "Letter to the Academy."

Second, most of the high-quality critical scholarship on Hughes has been published in just three or four academic journals, and much of this scholarship, despite its perspicacity, originality, and brilliance, never made its way into expanded book-length studies, which is standard practice in other academic disciplines. The exceptions to this pattern in Hughes scholarship are Martha Cobb's *Harlem, Haiti, and Havana: A Comparative Critical Study of Langston Hughes, Jacques Roumain, Nicolás Guillén* (1979), Faith Berry's *Langston Hughes: Before and Beyond Harlem* (1983), Arnold Rampersad's two-volume *The Life of Langston Hughes* (1986 and 1988), Steven Tracy's *Langston Hughes and the Blues* (1988), and R. Baxter Miller's *The Art and Imagination of Langston Hughes* (1989). These five eminent Hughes scholars were there at the very beginning of what we can call the Langston Hughes episteme, and their books are founding texts. One would expect many other books of criticism and interpretation on Hughes given both the quantity and the quality of journal articles and dissertations published during the 1970s and 1980s. Yet somehow most of them never happened.

Established in 1982, the *Langston Hughes Review* has published a splendid variety of scholarly articles on Hughes. Unfortunately, these articles are not available electronically, which limits access to them on the part of students and teachers whose schools do not subscribe to the journal. The other academic journals that have published a host of excellent articles on Hughes are *Callaloo* and *Black American Literature Forum/African American Review;* these are available electronically. Especially important is *Callaloo's* special issue in the fall of 2002, "Langston Hughes, 1902–1967: A Centen-

---

4. Morrison, *Playing in the Dark: Whiteness and the Literary Imagination,* 46.

nial Celebration," which offers more than just critical essays on Hughes's writing.[5] But one will be hard-pressed to find anything of substance on Hughes in such journals as *American Literature, American Literary History, PMLA,* and *American Quarterly.*

The problems of Hughes scholarship begin with the fact that the first book-length study of his poetry, Onwuchekwa Jemie's *Langston Hughes: An Introduction to the Poetry,* did not appear in the United States until 1976, almost ten years after Hughes's death. That nothing of substance in American studies was published during Hughes's own lifetime or in the immediate aftermath of his passing is less telling than the fact that current Americanists have found this issue unworthy of critical investigation, creating the misleading impression that the Langston Hughes story is basically complete and codified, needing only refinement and reiteration. American studies today resembles U.S. society as a whole: a militant denial on the part of white America that white racial oppression persists and the notion—repeated ad nauseam in the mainstream media—that African Americans would be better off "moving forward" with the rest of the white nation rather than always dwelling on their "unfortunate past."

In February 2001, the University of Missouri Press announced a great turning of the tide for Langston Hughes scholarship. It had located Hughes's major works and would publish them as they had originally appeared during his literary career. As *The Collected Works of Langston Hughes,* the texts would be published in sixteen volumes. The press had spent twelve years acquiring the rights to publish the collection and locating first editions of Hughes's works. A paradise on earth for Hughes scholars, as well as for teachers and students of American literature and culture, the *Collected Works* brought an end to the long period of neglect and marginality imposed on Hughes's writing, in particular on his prolific literary output during the height of the cold war—the bulk of which had remained out of print.

At the risk of sounding deluded, it seems to me that the sixteen-volume *Collected Works* will have the same kind of effect on American literature

5. Notable among the essays are David Chioni Moore's "'Colored Dispatches from the Uzbek Border': Langston Hughes's Relevance, 1933–2002"; Seth Moglen's "Modernism in the Black Diaspora: Langston Hughes and the Broken Cubes of Picasso"; Jeff Westover's "Africa/America: Fragmentation and Diaspora in the Work of Langston Hughes"; and James Smethurst's "'Don't Say Goodbye to the Porkpie Hat': Langston Hughes, the Left, and the Black Arts Movement." Each of these articles emphasizes rethinking the conventional notion of Hughes as a "folk poet," instead treating him as a world-class intellectual.

and culture that Dr. Martin Luther King's program of nonviolent direct action had on U.S. society in the 1960s, in which—as King famously put it in his "Letter from Birmingham Jail"—the task is "to foster such a tension that a community which has constantly refused to negotiate is forced to confront the issue." In Hughes's case, the issue is that for more than thirty years the U.S. academy felt no need to officially canonize and properly preserve the literary legacy of one its greatest writers, who "happens to be black." In this study, I will show that Hughes's blackness was precisely such that it is still fostering the creative tension that Dr. King wrote about so eloquently in his essay from prison: "the kind of tension in society that will help men rise from the dark depths of prejudice and racism to the majestic heights of understanding and brotherhood."

Mindful of the transparent resegregation of the Hughes canon within the U.S. academy, as well as the absence of any book-length studies that consider his aesthetic theory and intellectual practice as a whole, I will approach Hughes's creative activity on three levels. First, I will critique recent criticism—poststructuralist (or French theory) in particular, but other forms of cultural theory also—that posits timeless and unsurpassable contradictions between historical determination (social being) and art and literature (ideology). Second, I will explore old "truths" about Hughes in a way that allows them to be understood from new perspectives. And, third, I will suggest possibilities for programmatic research projects on his writing: for projects that have as their object the consciously dialectical twists and turns that Hughes was always making in his writing between the historical and the aesthetic.

The tendency to want to claim writers and artists for one's own "professionalist" or academic discipline has been accelerated by cultural theory. Hence, criticizing poststructuralist theory is a way of saying that this book's starting point is not a critique of ideology or cultural politics (or "cultural production") but instead an exploration of the contradictory relations between them, which I consider the correct approach of secular criticism. Moreover, putting the first level of inquiry into contact with the second and third levels is premised on an object of study that itself shifts between the realms of ideology and cultural production.

Perhaps because Hughes's own career was characterized by such an iconoclastic series of excursions between partitioned and segregated worlds—white America and African Americans, Spanish-speaking America and the United States, socialism and "pluralism," "proletarian literature" and literary Négritude—the biographical research on Hughes, where his own life is the object of study, has come to outweigh heavily the literary criticism, in which the object is the cultural artifacts he produced, artifacts that cannot be easily assessed and evaluated with the tools of American formalism and New Criticism. Hughes's travels around the globe were mirrored by his travels around art and literature. Thus, the scholar of Hughes needs to cease being a formalist to appreciate the full scale of his literary output, much less to adequately critique it. In Hughes scholarship the aporia is between the pace and trajectory of his hectic life and the scattered and disorganized nature of the research and writing devoted to his remarkably streamlined creative activity.

Indeed, whereas the life and art of Hughes have often turned the literary biographer into an adept cultural critic, they have afforded the formalist scholar a rare indulgence: being able to choose selectively from a dazzling array of forms and genres, such as translation, journalism, short fiction, song writing, folklore, poetry, drama, children's literature, musicology, the novel, and travel writing. This formalist indulgence, however, has come at the expense of a generalist approach to Hughes's writing, for hardly ever has formalism been able to appreciate the intriguing overlaps in his writing: overlaps between his writing for the African American press and his short fiction, for instance, or between his writing for young people and his experiments with avant-garde literary aesthetics.

A solution, I think, lies in the question of method. It was not only Hughes himself who was "always movin' on," to borrow the title of James Haskins's excellent biography; his creative method as well was always ranging across racially segregated worlds of art and literature and continually seeking out new points of contact for the building of new, popular-democratic forms of American art and literature. This is the unifying theme of this book, in which my strategy is to follow Hughes's method just as the literary biographer has followed his life and times. At the same time, I am careful to avoid slipping into an undialectical account of method: what Margaret Walker referred to shrewdly as the tendency in American literary criticism to offer "either an intrinsic analysis of the genre or an extrinsic analysis of the author's life and background."[6] As she says, undialectical approaches to criticism are felt disproportionately when it comes to African American writers. In analyzing Hughes's creative method, I follow Walker's advice.

The outstanding feature of the extant scholarship on Hughes is that

6. Walker, *Richard Wright: Daemonic Genius*, 6.

Arnold Rampersad, an accomplished literary biographer, has written the definitive account of how Hughes responded as an artist and an intellectual to the epochal moments of the twentieth century. This study treats Rampersad's exhaustive research and writing on the life of Hughes with due respect. At the same time, my aim is not to retell the official Hughes story through recourse to Rampersad's empirical work, or for that matter the perspicacious scholarship of Faith Berry, R. Baxter Miller, and Steven Tracy. Rather, I hope to present empirical research and to follow the important lead of two literary scholars who have reanimated critical reflection on and appreciation of Hughes's legacy in American art and culture—Christopher C. De Santis and Donna Akiba Sullivan Harper.

De Santis has done a great service to students and scholars of Hughes by excavating twenty years of his newspaper columns for the *Chicago Defender*, published as *Langston Hughes and the "Chicago Defender": Essays on Race, Politics, and Culture, 1942–62* (1995). Likewise, Harper's excellent *Not So Simple: The "Simple" Stories by Langston Hughes* (1995) provides a finely nuanced account of Hughes's construction of Simple, an account based on original research and investigation. Yet the difference between the present study and De Santis's and Harper's scholarly work is that this work is more about method than about literary genre or form. The study of method, however, is indebted to both Harper's and De Santis's scholarship, since their work revisits precisely what Amiri Baraka once called "the solemn ghost town of aesthetics," a place where "the need for definitions . . . even if there already are many," is the order of the day so that the view from the top of the hill is never confused with that from below.[7]

Harper's and De Santis's scholarship is premised on the dynamic relations between Hughes's reading base (the view "from below") and his development as a writer and an intellectual (that from "above"). I will trace the unfolding dialectic of writer and reading public in Hughes's writing during the 1950s and 1960s, the high period of the cold war, by concentrating on his method. Three moments in his career are essential for gaining this kind of appreciation and understanding: (1) his early experimentations with the blues aesthetic in his poetry of the 1920s and 1930s, which helped Hughes negotiate masterfully the tensions among the American communist movement, Du Boisian equalitarianism, and black cultural nationalism; (2) his newspaper writing for the *Chicago Defender* in the 1940s and 1950s, which enlarged Hughes's reading base and gave birth to the

7. Baraka, "Expressive Language," 170.

Simple stories; and (3) his sundry interventions in American popular culture, which include a series of popular histories for young people, writing workshops, a mass-market poetry anthology, and an avant-garde book of photojournalism.

Chapter 1 reexamines Hughes's relations with twentieth-century liberatory anticolonialism in Latin America, the Caribbean, and Africa so that one of his most compelling "travels" between partitioned worlds—an upstart U.S. empire and the decolonizing world—can be explored from the standpoint of today's "postcolonialist" moment. The aim here is twofold: first, to show how valuable Hughes was to Latin American and Caribbean artists and intellectuals, such as Nicolás Guillén and Claude McKay, who were enabled by Hughes's direct involvement with liberatory anti–white supremacist cultural resistance in the United States; and, second, to break apart the static conception of Hughes's writing that prevails today in the U.S. academy—a conception that, in the main, is blind to the links he forged during his life with those involved in African, Latin American, and Caribbean decolonization struggles. The "backward glance" is a way of grounding historically Hughes's writing so that the international scale of his aesthetic contributions can be felt.

Chapter 2 takes up the issue of method by considering a specific instance in Hughes's writing where two dominant aesthetics clash, those of poetry and of the blues. Hughes revised one of the main symbols of the American communist movement—white and black hands gripped together in a laboring-class struggle—by utilizing a blues aesthetic and a blues way of making poetry. The image—ubiquitous in American Communist Party culture and politics during the 1930s, enabled by the CPUSA's application of Lenin's thesis on national self-determination to the Black Belt—received a radical overhauling by Hughes in his chapbook *A New Song*, published in 1938 by the International Workers Order. I argue that in place of the Communist Party's trope of interracial solidarity Hughes proposed the concept of the North American mestizo, an idea far ahead of its time even today, for despite the visibility of the terms *multiculturalism* and *biracialism* in the U.S. mass media, especially in advertising, recent surveys indicate that only a handful of Americans actually know what they mean and even less wish to identify themselves in such a way. I argue that Hughes relied on the blues in order to rephrase the tone and shape of this archetype and to persuade the multiethnic American working classes that their salvation might be found through an embracing of it. In keeping with the theme of the backward glance, I will suggest that today's advocates of multiculturalism could do well by returning to Hughes for a successful political language and an advanced aesthetic style.

Chapter 3 explores the transition Hughes made from creative writer to journalist, focusing both on the articles he wrote for the *Chicago Defender* covering the Bolshevik Revolution and on the historical origin of his Jesse B. Semple saga. Focusing on the idea that Hughes's relationship to communism is far more complex than it has been made out to be, I demonstrate that while Hughes clearly distanced himself from the American Communist Party during the high period of the cold war, he never renounced the Marxist tradition as the best solution for fighting white racial oppression. In fact, his newspaper articles on the Bolshevik Revolution made the case that only through a seizure of state power by a multiethnic popular-democratic party of the American working classes could racial oppression be finally abolished in the United States. Chapter 3 also examines Hughes's methodology as a newspaper writer: precisely how and for whom he communicated the lessons of the Bolshevik Revolution. In addition, the origin of his *Defender* column "Here to Yonder" is explored, as is his changing relationship to African American readers during the 1940s and 1950s. A careful reading of his *Defender* articles suggests that the foundation of his Simple stories was his everyday writing for the African American press. It was through the *Defender* that Hughes returned to Harlem and through Simple that he reestablished strong ties to a growing African American reading public. The beginnings of Simple are inseparable from Hughes's reemergence in the 1940s and 1950s as one of black America's most beloved writers.

Chapter 4 visits Hughes's interventions in American popular culture during the high period of the cold war in order to show another aspect of his creative method, which found its fullest expression in three very different writing projects. Divided into three sections, this chapter examines the circumstances in which Hughes wrote and his different creative responses to them. Two antagonistic historical movements took hold during the 1950s: the rapid consolidation of U.S. anticommunism and the transformation of local anti–Jim Crow activism in the American South into a powerful national civil rights struggle. During this conjuncture Hughes produced a history of the NAACP, *Fight for Freedom* (1962), yet his most ambitious projects of the period had already been completed by the end of the decade: an exhaustive and international anthology of liberationist poetry, *The Poetry of the Negro*, coedited with his comrade Arna Bontemps; a writing workshop project, *The First Book of Rhythms*, whose goal was the intellectual-moral development of American youth; and a photo essay of Harlem life in the 1940s and 1950s, *The Sweet Flypaper of Life,* coarranged with the great Brooklyn photographer Roy DeCarava. All three enterprises anticipated the eradication of white racial oppression and in fact depended on it.

A return to the work of Dr. Du Bois was a logical and necessary undertaking as the start of America's second reconstruction appeared for Hughes and many others to be just around the corner. Hence, the first part of Chapter 4 seeks a return to Du Bois in the structure and form of Hughes and Bontemps's *Poetry of the Negro* anthology. The second section examines the teaching method Hughes employed to prepare young people for popular-democracy in post–racial oppression America, while the third assesses his fascinating collaboration with DeCarava. *The First Book of Rhythms* was just one of many texts Hughes wrote for children during the 1950s. Its particular significance is that it was a product of Hughes's close involvement with the Chicago Laboratory School in 1949, where he directed a series of writing workshops for city youth. Although his ideological vantage point was that of a utopian, post–white supremacist future, the strategies he used in the workshops were geared specifically to first- and second-generation city dwellers whose roots were in the Mississippi Delta. In this way, again, the backward glance is the animating principle, since writing instruction in the 2000s has devolved into competing and contradictory theories and pedagogical approaches, each a response—conscious or unconscious—to the presence of American students who do not speak standard English and prefer not to. Therefore, Hughes's teaching method in the Chicago writing workshops is not only instructive in an immediate, pedagogical sense but educative in social and political terms as well. What he lays out in *The First Book of Rhythms* is a blueprint for teaching young people how to write by learning first how to think dialectically. The burden of Chapter 4 is to show how he achieved this task.

That the Italian communist writer and organizer Antonio Gramsci proposed in the 1920s a similar plan for Italian public school education helps illuminate the impressive scale of Hughes's teaching method in the workshops. For Gramsci, fighting fascism in Italy and building a new, democratic society on its ruins required establishing a national education program that would produce a "dynamic conformism," as he termed it, in Italy's common schools. Rather than being the *object* of planning and development, as in reactionary ideologies, national unity was instead the *outcome* of a different object altogether: the abolition of reactionary bourgeois systems of social control, those based on forms of national, racial, gender, and class oppression. "Dynamic conformism" occurs when an individual of the nation speaks for the whole of that nation precisely by seeking self-emancipation for all its laboring-class members, beginning from the bottom up. As Gramsci and Hughes both believed, at the level of public school education the way to working-class self-emancipation lies in "a mastery of the method." Gramsci wrote: "To discover a truth oneself, without external suggestions or assistance, is to create—even if the truth is an old one. It demonstrates a mastery of the method, and indicates that in any case one has entered the phase of intellectual maturity in which one may discover new truths."[8]

Putting this principle into practice was Hughes's goal in the workshops as it is in this book generally. Thus, the book's first two chapters look back in order to understand where Hughes's method came from, while the last two treat his method in terms of its own logic and direction. In form, the study tries to thematize rather than classify and chronicle. It aims to reflect upon, appreciate, and understand rather than to assign meaning or overintellectualize. What I offer is a generalist approach to Hughes's writing: generalist in the sense of nonspecialized or cross-disciplinary. I am not concerned solely with genre or form, literary and cultural history, or formal artistic technique. Like the object itself—the writing of Langston Hughes—the critical method I use moves across all these fields of study without resting on one in particular. If there is a departure point, it is the question of method itself: how to evaluate and appreciate a writer and intellectual such as Hughes who cannot in the end be understood by critical approaches that depend on equilibrium, completion, and continuity. Those cannot account for dialectical movement and change in an artist's creative life and in the art and literature that is its product and testament.

The somewhat cryptic epigraph that began this chapter needs a brief explanation. Written by the Nicaraguan Gioconda Belli, the poem "The Blood of Others" is referenced here to capture the same feeling for Hughes that she expresses in her poem for the Nicaraguan poets of her generation—especially for "Sandino's daughters," to borrow Margaret Randall's eloquent phrase. In Randall's words, "The Blood of Others" evokes "a place she inhabits with explosive joy and profound sorrow, with a frank smile and the intimate dignity of a woman who knows that the battle lost is worth infinitely more than the battle never fought."[9] The "battle lost"

---

8. Gramsci, "On Education," 33.
9. Margaret Randall, *Sandino's Daughters Revisited: Feminism in Nicaragua*, 168–69.

is an allusion to the collective Nicaraguan struggle for national independence during the 1970s and 1980s. It was a struggle crushed externally by the U.S. government and, as Randall shows, held back internally by unsolved national contradictions.

What might have been is a leitmotif in this study of Hughes, as is the emphasis on "the blood of others": on the many lives lost in the struggle for an equalitarian American society. This idea is built into this book's title: that those to whom Hughes devoted himself as a writer and an intellectual, and on whose behalf Belli herself continues to write, be seen not merely as "fuel" for creative activity but as writing's locus, that place where writing makes its most prophetic contribution to socialist joy.

1

The Backward Glance

My country in my memory
and I in Paris on display
like a harmless bat.
Oh,
for the plane
to take me with four motors
on a single flight!

—Nicolás Guillén, "Exilio"

In the discourse of postcolonialism, exile has been often sublimated. Perhaps because of its inherent limitations as an official state ideology, exile has functioned more as a rhetorical trope, set in opposition against the nation. At the same time, exile continues to stand, undeniably, at the crossroads of neocolonialism and national independence. More important, it no longer belongs exclusively to the time-honored European and Euro-American expatriate traditions. In all events, through postcolonialist discourse's sublimation of exile, the historical circumstances and social conditions of exile's emergence as a key term have been overintellectualized to an extent that a range of unhistorical interpretations now stand in for the capitalist colonial origins of the experience itself. Much has been said

14

about the ambiguous nature of exile and, by extension, about the radical divergences between certain postcolonial and colonial structures of thinking. This notion has led to the maxim that *all* traditions are dangerous. The problem is that this culturalist concept of exile tends to ignore its own history, for the special scale of exile—its radical *in-betweenness*—derives its staying power from a much older tradition, the African tradition in the New World. The Afro-American figures of the Signifyin' Monkey and Anancy the Spider, for instance, are based on the divine trickster figure of Yoruba mythology, Esu-Elegbara. As Henry Louis Gates Jr. has shown in his classic work *The Signifying Monkey,* the African trickster's New World figurations include Exú in Brazil, Echu-Elegua in Cuba, Papa Legba in Haiti, and Papa La Bas in the United States. "These trickster figures," Gates suggests, "all aspects or topoi of Esu, are fundamental, divine terms of mediation: as tricksters they are mediators, and their mediations are tricks."[1] When the history of exile is taken for granted, it is usually this aspect—exile as a site of black liberatory cultural resistance—that tends to suffer most.

The postcolonial critic as mediator between antagonistic traditions—Western versus Eastern or non-Western; cosmopolitanism versus revolutionary nationalism—is a distinguishing feature of the discourse. But as Timothy Brennan has noted wisely in "The National Longing for Form," because the politics of exile are hostile to all nationalisms, including the anticolonial revolutionary nationalisms of the decolonizing world, this mediating role has tended to support the consolidation of imperialism in the postwar period. He argues, in this light, that in postwar fiction nationalism has been replaced by the *topos* of exile, its opposite. Consequently, the division between exile and nationalism "presents itself as one not only between individual and group, but between winner and loser, between a mood of rejection and a mood of celebration."[2] Hence, the strategy of keeping exile historical (or collective) and imaginatively real (or dialectical) in the "national" sense—one of the main goals of the New World African trickster—has been weakened.

Despite exile's ascendancy within an explicitly nationalist U.S. discipline poised, paradoxically, against every nationalism other than its own, the origins of the figure clearly go back to the early period of decolonization in which the struggles for national liberation in the decolonizing world had reached a decisive stage. It was in 1960, for example, that Ba-

1. *The Signifying Monkey: A Theory of African-American Literary Criticism,* 6.
2. "The National Longing for Form," 60–61.

jan writer George Lamming published in London his seminal book of essays, *The Pleasures of Exile.* Writing in exile during the formation of the first nationalist West Indian political parties, Lamming describes exile as the search for a dialectical inversion rather than a sublimation of "the national question." Not a flight from national culture, which has been the conservative ethnic emigrant story of exile in Europe and the U.S., the experience of exile in the Caribbean inspired an antagonistic redefinition of nationalism itself and a celebration of exile's possibilities for the future. "The pleasure and the paradox of my own exile," Lamming wrote eloquently, "is that I belong wherever I am."[3]

As Perry Anderson has shown in his perspicacious and influential analysis of nation forming and emigration, "Components of the National Culture," it was exactly this kind of opaque worldliness that the exiles of Europe were desperately trying to elude. "The wave of emigrants who came to England in this century," he argued, "were by and large fleeing the permanent instability of their own societies—that is, their proneness to violent, fundamental change." Anderson's apt metaphor of "natural selection" to describe the nature of this historically conservative middle-class emigration is especially provocative alongside Lamming's ironic phrase "the pleasures of exile." For Lamming's immigration to England was based not on the likelihood of unhappy revolutionary social upheaval in his native land but rather precisely on its political postponement by the British government. Anderson argued that, whereas the Polish, Hungarian, Austrian, German, and Russian émigrés "gravitated" to an English national culture "dying of inanition" in order to feel safe from any popular-democratic advances in their own countries, Lamming and his fellow Caribbean emigrants found themselves in England for the opposite reason. For Lamming, they were there not to reinforce the existing orthodoxies of English nationalism by exploiting so-called moral weaknesses as the reactionary émigrés had done, but rather to prepare the way for national liberation at home by rejecting in England "the degradation of a society which is just not colonial by the actual circumstances of politics, but colonial in its very conception of its destiny." The European émigrés had asked of England the chance to restore the old bourgeois order of things: to return to that concept of an unbroken ruling-class "national

---

3. *The Pleasures of Exile*, 51. In *Race against Empire: Black Americans and Anticolonialism, 1937–1957*, Penny M. Von Eschen analyzes the historical moment of Caribbean decolonization in direct relation to the African American civil rights struggle; see, in particular, "The Making of the Politics of the African Diaspora," 7–22.

destiny" that had been lost to them in their own countries, a loss they had blamed on the vicissitudes of class struggles. In contrast, what the Caribbean émigrés demanded was that England renounce this imperial destiny and be "transformed, rejuvenated, and ultimately restored" to its "original condition" as an equal and whole nation among nations also equal and whole.[4]

Lamming argued poignantly that his own exile and that of his fellow West Indian émigrés could have been avoided by successful socialist nation building in the Caribbean. At the time of Lamming's exile in England, Caribbean writers and intellectuals, such as C. L. R. James and Eric Williams, were working toward this goal. Lamming, however, saw the nationalist project in the Caribbean as premature given the cultural distance between the West Indian laboring classes and their new "national" political leaders. Having functioned as intermediaries under British colonial rule, the West Indian middle classes were eager under decolonization to rule the islands themselves. The problem for Lamming was that their apprenticeship under the British had ill prepared them to think about national culture and political independence through structures of their own making. In response, Lamming inverted the question of exile by placing it directly in the context of neocolonialism, raising once again the old contradictions of revolutionary nationalism and European imperialism, but this time from a third position: that of the "archetypal middle-man," to use Jan Carew's felicitous phrase, "part saint, part trickster" who "periodically renewed contact with communal wellsprings of rhythm, creation and life."[5]

In Lamming's and Carew's new conception, the exilic Caribbean "middle-man" does not proceed from a state of social alienation to personal emigration and flight. Ironically, the pleasures of exile derive from the fact that under neocolonialism the situation has been inverted: immigration to the metropolis flows not from a condition of the alienated individual but rather from the collective circumstances of a whole alienated people, where exile is the general rule rather than the individual exception. Rather than a reversal of colonialism, as some critics have maintained, the Caribbean experience of exile reveals the total scale of its multiple and opaque relationships. As Carew formulated the problem in *Fulcrums of Change:* "The Caribbean writer today is a creature balanced be-

4. Anderson, "Components of the National Culture," 231; Lamming, *Pleasures of Exile*, 178.
5. Carew, *Fulcrums of Change: Origins of Racism in the Americas and Other Essays*, 91.

tween limbo and nothingness, exile abroad and exile at home, between the people on the one hand and the colonizer on the other. . . . The Caribbean writer by going abroad is, in fact, searching for an end to exile."[6]

One of Edward Said's most cited essays is on exile, and his *Culture and Imperialism* is, by Said's own account, an "exile's book." But some post-colonial scholars and critics have seemingly misunderstood Said, for there are many signs today that exile has achieved a disciplinary status in the U.S. academy, a development that is anathema to Said's whole project, since exile for him is a *traveling theory*, not a discipline. In his study of Iranian television in Los Angeles, for example, *The Making of Exile Cultures*, Hamid Naficy organizes his analysis around a set of terms based on exile: "exilism," "exile discourse," and "exilic popular culture." For Naficy, exile is postcolonialism's point of departure because, in this interregnum, culture—no longer "just a trivial superstructure"—becomes "life itself." Naficy's thesis is that through its complex mediating institutions "exilic subculture is protected temporarily from the seemingly hostile dominant cultures." In contrast, for Said exile enables a perspective that is "fully sensitive to the reality of historical experience." It is a method or strategic location, not a subculture, subdiscipline, or political identity. Neither does exile mark the emergence of a new category. Rather, it is a path leading to the end of exile itself.[7]

Studies of nation building during the nineteenth century, such as Benedict Anderson's *Imagined Communities*, have stressed the need for a new definition of exile that situates alongside nation building the historical experiences of the geographically exiled and collectively dispossessed. The logic of postcoloniality, then, is for exile to reveal a structure of interdependency between the emergent nationalist discourses of marginality and exclusion on one side and on the other the cosmopolitan centers of academic-cultural production in Europe and the United States. Yet as Lamming has argued, by their very colonial circumstances the terms of exile are political: their proponents must either accept neocolonialism by making it into a universal condition or show the dialectical antagonisms and transformations of exile that have come from class-conscious mass challenges to colonial rule. The latter stance toward exile calls for an assertion of the oppressed group's determination "not to disappear from the

6. Ibid.

7. For Said's definition of exile, see *Culture and Imperialism*, xxv; for his reference to *Culture and Imperialism* as an "exile's book," see xxvi. In "Exile Discourse," the first chapter of *The Making of Exile Cultures: Iranian Television in Los Angeles* (1–30), Naficy provides a series of nuanced definitions of exile.

world scene," as Edouard Glissant has put it, "and on the contrary to share in its diversification."[8]

In this sense, the figure of exile is a metaphor for the situation that post-colonialist discourse currently faces. It has become the centrist position, or site of negotiation, between empire and the decolonizing world. More-over, this "in-between" space has been radically decentered, and con-sequently its broad analogical possibilities scaled back. On the one hand exile is a historical process connected organically to the emergent and ongoing mass political struggles in the decolonizing world against European and Euro-American colonialism: the occasion, for instance, of Nicolás Guillén's poem "Exilio," written in Spain on the eve of the Cuban Revolutionary Army's overthrow of the U.S.-backed dictatorship of Ful-gencio Batista. On the other hand, exile is a symptom of imperialism's de-nial, disregard, and illegalization of the original forms of social identity among the disparate peoples forced under European colonial rule. This is evident in V. S. Naipaul's caustic notion of the "mimic" societies of the Caribbean, or the absent community.[9] This space is an ambiguous one, ex-isting neither for empire—the position of the ex-colonial intellectual—nor for the many millions directly subjugated by colonialism. The ques-tion, however, is not so much *why* this "in-betweenness" is so ambiguous and indeterminate but rather how it could be finally overcome, and how its transformation into an anticolonial liberatory discourse could be put into play. How, in other words, or under what conditions, is "un solo vue-lo" from *exilio* to *patria* to be made? And what name do we give to the method that reveals the historical depth and antagonistic logic of this epic inversion—this momentous process in literature and culture of decolo-nization and national independence?

In *Culture and Imperialism*, Said proposed a compelling solution, what he terms a "contrapuntal analysis" of imperialist domination and anti-colonial resistance. For Said, to challenge politically and finally break free

8. Rob Nixon's "London Calling: V. S. Naipaul and the License of Exile" is a good example of the U.S. critic's close focus on exile in the study of Caribbean literature. For Anderson's considerations on exile see *Imagined Communities: Reflections on the Origin and Spread of Nationalism*. Glissant, *Caribbean Discourse*, 99.

9. In an interview, Naipaul describes exile in terms of the psychic traumas of the dis-placed colonial writer: "One must make a pattern of one's observations, one's daily distress; one's lack of representation in the world; one's lack of status. These, for me, are not just ideas; when I talk about being an exile or a refugee I'm not just using a metaphor, I'm speaking literally. . . . Because one doesn't have a side, doesn't have a country, doesn't have a community; one is entirely an individual" (Adrian Rowe-Evans, "V. S. Naipaul," 59).

mentally of the structures of colonialist oppression, the method of engagement must be dialectical and involve an awareness of "both processes, that of imperialism and that of resistance to it." In Said's project, the strategies of contrapuntal analysis are based on the ideas of "counterpoint, intertwining, and integration." These concepts, he suggests,

> reaffirm the historical experience of imperialism as a matter first of interdependent histories, overlapping domains, second of something requiring intellectual and political choices. . . . And to consider imperial domination and resistance to it as a dual process evolving toward decolonization, then independence, is largely to align oneself with the process, and to interpret both sides of the contest not only hermeneutically but also politically.[10]

In this way, *Culture and Imperialism* makes possible a detour or "backward glance" from within the discourse of exile.

First, Said refuses to accept the standard equation advanced in English cultural criticism between exile and homelessness. The opposition presupposes a social condition of complete cultural alienation on the part of the transplanted exile, as if the imperial metropolis were a foreign place of social unrest where exiles are an exception and not the rule. As Said remarks in his introduction, New York City is the exilic city par excellence. His experience as an exile in New York "made it possible for me to feel as if I belonged to more than one history and more than one group." This is a crucial departure point for Said in his attempt to realign exile with the international politics of national liberation struggle—a profound desublimation of exile—and a subject I will take up in the ensuing chapters on the writing of Langston Hughes. Second, Said redefines exile to mean not simply a personal condition but also a collective historical experience. In *Culture and Imperialism*, exile is not equated with deprivation, impotence, or rootlessness. "On the contrary, belonging, as it were, to both sides of the imperial divide enables you to understand them more easily." Exile becomes in *Culture and Imperialism* what Said termed in *Orientalism* a "strategic formation": "a way of analyzing the relationship between texts and the way in which groups of texts, types of texts, even textual genres, acquire mass, density, and referential power among themselves and thereafter in the culture at large." It is this move that allows him to discuss to-

---

10. *Culture and Imperialism*, 366. The term *contrapuntal analysis* is in the index; it does not appear in the body of his main argument. Instead, *contrapuntal reading* (66) and *contrapuntal perspective* (32) are Said's phrases of choice.

gether C. L. R. James's *The Black Jacobins* and George Antonius's *The Arab Awakening*—books that are separated on the surface by language, geography, and cultural tradition yet are linked on a much deeper level by the revolutionary nationalist politics of exile, world decolonization struggle, and socialist internationalism.[11]

As a strategic formation, exile is understood in *Culture and Imperialism* to mean the experience of struggling peoples and not the condition of radically displaced middle-class individuals. When we refer to exile, Said argues, rather than citing Conrad and Joyce we could think instead of "the uncountable masses for whom UN agencies have been created, or refugees without urbanity, with only ration cards and agency numbers." As I will show, Said's political return to exile provides an excellent beginning for the study of what June Jordan has called "New World writing," specifically the overlapping or "intertwined" poetry traditions of Caribbean, Latin American, and African American literatures and cultures.[12] Hence, my argument acknowledges a different trajectory in postcolonial studies, an alternative line of critical inquiry and writing that rejects the despair and sense of loss typically associated with European exile precisely by welcoming exile's collective political possibilities and realigning them with the process of liberatory cultural resistance in the hemisphere as a whole.

As might be expected given the situation today facing undocumented workers in U.S. cities—the passing of new and more punishing versions of California's Propositions 187 and 209, as well as the political Right's incessant campaign for "English only" laws—the future of postcolonial studies is anything but secure. In the United States another "reinvention of the 'white race,'" to use historian Theodore Allen's important concept, is underway, produced and managed by the political and cultural representatives of the ruling class.[13] The reprojection of whiteness in the mainstream media, for instance, through the criminalization of African American youth culture and the endorsement of a hostile, cynical view of the fate of the civil rights agenda, is symptomatic of postcoloniality's ambiguous status in the U.S. academy. As many among the liberal Left have learned, "ambiguity" and "indecideability" no longer carry the same optimistic connotations in political culture, for the Right has successfully

11. Ibid., xxvi; *Orientalism*, 20.
12. Said, "The Mind of Winter: Reflections on Life in Exile," 50; Jordan, "For the Sake of People's Poetry: Walt Whitman and the Rest of Us," 6.
13. Allen, *The Invention of the White Race, Volume One: Racial Oppression and Social Control*, 1.

linked the political in-between with "flip-flopping"—a curse it deserves but one that will surely be used against any class-conscious politics of cross-cultural exchange.

In other words, if the negotiation of "cultural difference"—"the consolation prize for those who were not and could not be assimilated," as John Hope Franklin has nicely put it—is today no longer the favored strategy of U.S. ruling elites as it was in the 1960s and 1970s, in the current conjuncture postcolonial studies faces a serious dilemma. Either it too must go the route of some form of "essentialism" by distancing itself as a discipline from the much maligned and basically useless terms of identity politics and "cultural difference," which would amount to a repudiation of its own basic assumptions, or it will be forced to stake an even greater claim for itself as the best solution to enduring problems of underdevelopment, "Third World" immigration, globalization, and so on, but under a new name, without the systemic machinations of late imperialism in the conception. Whatever direction the new discipline takes, it remains the case that, as a politics, postcoloniality has failed to challenge the doctrines of U.S. empire. By repudiating the "national ideal," in Edouard Glissant's articulation, postcolonialist discourse has cut from underneath itself the only basis on which it could confront the U.S. nation-state's aggressive expansion and consolidation throughout the colonial and postcolonial worlds. A notable symptom of this failure is the sublimation of exile to the level of cultural theory, as yet another in a long line of hybridic and everlasting human conditions. Pushed aside, as a consequence, has been the quest for a national literature among those who have been denied one.[14]

The embrace of exile from the standpoint of postcolonialism, in terms of "border crossings," "deterritorialization," "liminal hybrids," "syncretic multiples" and the like, can be better understood, I think, in the context of the recent emergence of the United States as the world's dominant imperialist power. As topoi of postcolonialism, "exile" and "difference" are actually *outcomes* of U.S. world military hegemony, not factors of "liberationist anti-imperialism," to borrow Said's phrase. To be factors of anticolonial cultural liberation, and thus to have real bearing on what has become a national discourse in the U.S. academy, "exile" and "difference" must be organically linked to ongoing mass political struggles. Without being in solidarity with such a mass movement, those putting forth the concepts advanced in exile's name are easily vulnerable to co-optation

14. Franklin, "Ethnicity in American Life: The Historical Perspective," 330; Glissant, *Caribbean Discourse*, 97.

and "democratization." Thus, not only has the celebration of "difference" in the U.S. academy turned "bland," as Amitava Kumar suggests—a situation probably related to the swift passing of NAFTA and GATT legislation by the Clinton administration back in 1994—but "difference" itself is far from having a home in the world.[15]

Consequently, the delocalized discourse of exile confronts today a re-centralized system of "Sameness"—Glissant's useful term for European and U.S. cultural imperialism—consolidated around a deeply felt constellation of national-popular myths and white imaginary presences, which can be delineated in the following way.

Communism: Marx; marxism; socialism; "insurgents"; Fidel Castro; the Sandinistas; Hugo Chavez; dogmatism; "political correctness."

Liberalism: big government; feminism; labor unions; taxes; public education; aid to the "Third World"; environmentalism; affirmative action; social spending; "illegal immigrants"; bilingualism; welfare; crime.

Anti-Americanism: "anti-Semitism"; "global terrorism"; the Palestinians; Islam; Iran; "politicizing"; anything anti-corporate.

Blacks: "racial quotas"; gangs; "failing schools"; "inner-city"; "cycles of poverty"; "black teenage mothers"; "reverse racism."

To put it differently, exile—because it occupies no place in U.S. popular culture, partly because postcoloniality itself has rejected all nationalisms—is in no position today to defend the very social constituencies that postcolonialist discourse has always claimed to represent: displaced ex-colonials, "minorities" (or nonwhites), refugees, and immigrants from the Caribbean, Latin America, and the former European colonies of Africa and Asia. Because in the discourse of U.S. postcolonialism there is supposedly no overriding imperial project, distinctions are seldom made between middle-class exiles and undocumented workers, for example, or African Americans and "people of color"—distinctions that are built into postcolonialist discourse, as Said has observed. For exile to become counterhegemonic it must first speak to questions of everyday class struggle and define itself in opposition not merely to a new U.S.-dominated late

15. For these various terms, see Naficy, *Making of Exile Cultures.* But Naficy argues effectively that "exilism" is doomed to failure "unless it is rooted in some specificity and locality, even essentialism of some strategic sort. This distinguishes exile from other cultural expressions that are based on difference. Without such rootedness, exile discourse, like all other oppositional or alternative discourses, will be co-opted and commodified through diffusion. In the cultural domain, as in literature and film, specificity, locality, and detail are all" (3). Said, *Culture and Imperialism,* 278; Kumar, "Postcoloniality: Field Notes," 271.

imperial world order but to the particular capitalist class under which the postcolonial world is now being reorganized, the counterrevolutionary U.S. bourgeoisie.

This same idea about the sundry political valences of exile was advanced by Lamming more than three decades ago in *The Pleasures of Exile*. "Awareness is a minimum condition for attaining freedom," he wrote, "the confession of unawareness is a confession of guilt." The question for Lamming was how to avoid exile by becoming aware of its root causes and social effects, since the experience was both a product of colonialist oppression and part of what he termed "the old blackmail of Language": empire's "language gift" of parliamentary democracy to its former colonial possessions. In the closing paragraphs, he offers a solution:

> To be colonial is to be in a state of exile. And the exile is always colonial by circumstances: a man colonised by his incestuous love of a past whose glory is not worth our total human suicide; colonised by a popular whoredom of talents whose dividends he knows he does not deserve; another's distress through a process of affection called justice; colonised by the barely livable acceptance of domestic complaint; colonised, if black in skin, by the agonising assault of the other's eye whose meanings are based on a way of seeing he vainly tries to alter; and ultimately colonised by some absent vision which, for want of another faith, he hopefully calls the Future. . . . But the mystery of the colonial is this: while he remains alive, his instinct, always and for ever creative, must choose a way to change the meaning and perspective of this ancient tyranny.[16]

Historical awareness for Lamming is the first stage of nation building, which is at the same time a rejection of the "Destiny" of history imposed by a narrow-minded European colonialism. "If Caliban once contributed to his own colonisation," Lamming argues, "he has no intention, at this stage of his awareness, of conspiring against himself. The century is at once too old and too young to fear this kind of camouflage, to spend its energy arguing against this kind of blackmail." The turn Lamming advocates is toward a West Indian form of "awareness," the Haitian ceremony of the Souls, which he describes eloquently in the opening paragraphs of his introduction to *The Pleasures of Exile*. In his second novel, *Season of Adventure* (1960), Lamming refers to this collective practice as "the backward glance." The backward glance is a metaphor for the love of reality. It is a

16. Lamming, *Pleasures of Exile*, 12.

call for engagements with the past on behalf of the present, or what C. L. R. James once called "facing reality." This gesture can be made only "by the dead and the living who are free."[17]

This concept is consonant with John Berger's idea of dialectical, as opposed to art-historical, "ways of seeing." "Fear of the present," Berger wrote, "leads to mystification of the past." For Lamming, "It is not important to believe in the actual details of the ceremony. What is important is its symbolic drama, the drama of redemption, the drama of returning, the drama of cleansing for a commitment towards the future."[18] What Lamming stresses is the need to think past the overintellectualized or academically specialized terms and problems of exile by replacing them with a new, case study–like political concept of exile and a new episteme: *the collective repossession of the past.* As I want to show briefly, collective repossession is an alternative concept in postcolonialist discourse that resonates through three overlapping New World literary and cultural traditions: the Caribbean, the Latin American, and the African American. Further, the detour or backward glance that this concept offers postcolonial studies is a critical method whose purpose is to reappropriate the terms and concepts of exile for the sake of creating the conditions—ideological and political—for hemispheric laboring-class self-emancipation.

For New World writing, the collective repossession of history registers on several levels. In the Caribbean context, Edouard Glissant has written: "For us, the repossession of the meaning of our history begins with awareness of the real discontinuity that we no longer passively live through."[19] Using Glissant's terminology as a starting point, three primary lines of inquiry into questions of history and literature enable an alternative approach to the discourse of postcolonialism.

The first line of inquiry involves the collective repossession of history as an analytical concept, enabling a qualitative shift in how questions and problems of history and culture are formulated and answered. Jean Franco's 1975 "Dependency Theory and Literary History: The Case of Latin America" is a key text in postcolonial theory because of her reconfiguring of conceptual categories from dominant European and Euro-American methods. The shift is implicit in Glissant's formulation and in the premise of his major theoretical work, *Caribbean Discourse.* In the Latin American context, Franco urges a new approach to literatures based on the

17. Ibid., 158.
18. Berger, *Ways of Seeing,* 11; Lamming, "The West Indian People," 64–65.
19. Glissant, *Caribbean Discourse,* 92.

awakening of historical consciousness or the awareness, to paraphrase Glissant, of the real discontinuity that the peoples of the Americas no longer passively experience.

For Franco, the problem with teaching Latin American literatures from the standpoint of Anglo-American studies is the standard ideological practice of making these literatures "assimilable" to European and U.S. cultural traditions to which they were originally "alien and antagonistic." For anyone approaching literature "from outside the European or North American context," she argues, "the very 'ideal order' (to use T. S. Eliot's word) which Western literature constitutes is also an ideological order which conceals the real relations between the culture of the metropolis and that of the dependent countries." What is needed, then, "is a theory of literature which takes into account both terms of the dialectic—that is, both the dominant cultures of the world and their dependencies." In closing the essay, she cites the work of Nicaraguan poet Ernesto Cardenal to support her argument that a new form of collective consciousness has begun to flourish in Latin America, stimulated by the awakening in the immediate postwar period of popular resistance movements to U.S. imperialism—in particular, the October Revolution in Guatemala in 1945–1954, which soon crystallized in the triumph of the Cuban Revolution in 1959 and was reasserted in 1961 at the Bay of Pigs with the first military defeat of U.S. imperialism in the hemisphere. These historic events had the effect of bringing to the surface the ideology of "American Literature" by forcing onto the center stage of literature and culture the old terms and problems of politics and history—terms that had been separated from the literary work by the cold war ideology of American New Criticism.[20]

As Aijaz Ahmad has argued convincingly, after World War II, when New Criticism appeared on the scene, "with its fetishistic notions of the utter autonomy of each single literary work," its practice of reified reading

> proved altogether hegemonic in American literary studies for a quarter-century or more, and it proved extremely useful as a pedagogical tool in the American classroom precisely because it required of the student little knowledge of anything not strictly "literary"—no history which was not predominantly literary history, no science of the social, no philosophy—except the procedures and precepts of literary formalism, which, too, it could not entirely accept in full objectivist rigour thanks

20. Franco, "Dependency Theory and Literary History: The Case of Latin America," 65.

to its prior commitment to squeezing a particular ideological meaning out of each literary text.[21]

What followed was the myth criticism of Northrop Frye, who, as Franco says, "offered an account of change without resorting to extrinsic criteria." Writing nearly twenty years later, Ahmad reiterated the same point: "The first dissent against New Criticism retained the conception of Literature as a special language yielding a special kind of knowledge, but insisted also that individual literary texts simply could not be discussed outside some larger narrative." This larger narrative was not a narrative of history but rather a "formalist narrative of all-encompassing genres and literary modes."[22]

In this same mode of criticism—thinking about thinking—Amiri Baraka has argued that these strategies of American literary studies in the high period of the cold war also involved a reinvention of white supremacy:

> Afro-American literature as it has come into view, fragmented by chauvinism and distorted by the same reactionary forces that have distorted American literature itself, has indeed been laid out in the same confusing and oblique fashion. A method intended to hide more than it reveals, a method that wants to show that at best Afro-American literature is a mediocre, and conservative, reflection of the mediocre and conservative portrait that is given of all American literature. . . . The development of a *specifically* Afro-American culture must wait for the emergence of the Afro-American people, the particular nationality composed of Africans transformed by the fact and processes of slavery into an American people of African descent.[23]

At this moment, then, when history has been accelerated, forcing literature's hand by enabling it to be openly subversive and resistant to Empire's history, literary theory in the United States became, to use the Peruvian theologian Gustavo Gutiérrez's excellent formulation, "superversive."[24]

The concept is important for several reasons. First, it indicates a radical turn in New World writing away from rhetorical rereadings of history in which the object of history is still another overarching projection of what

21. Ahmad, *In Theory: Classes, Nations, Literatures*, 53.
22. Franco, "Dependency Theory and Literary History," 65; Ahmad, *In Theory*, 53.
23. Baraka, "The Revolutionary Tradition in Afro-American Literature," 312.
24. *The Power of the Poor in History*, 202.

already happened, that is, the notion of "the return of history"—as in the idea that oral narratives and poetry are "folklore" and that their logic is "spontaneous." This is a form of "super-version" because the method assumes a dead link between the past and the present, graspable only by the technicist procedures of historicism. But if oral poetry is really "folklore" and therefore of the past, the seer in the present always has the advantage of a kept audience, since any challenge to the speaker's argument that points to the fact that "folklore" is actually the popular base of many of the most exalted literary forms and genres in world history also belongs to the past and has as its object this same nostalgic past. But if oral narrative and poetry are given their rightful historical determination, they become subjects of their own making and demand recognition as antagonistic cultural forms, dependent neither on the print culture that reduces their scale in order to control them nor on the methods or processes of rejection and assimilation that keep the distinction between the written and the oral in place. In Franco's words, "the most significant feature of colonial culture is this differentiation within the production process itself, between an oral culture dependent on a community and written culture, which was overwhelmingly associated with domination." Hence, in the colonial context the written word is "a mark of cultural superiority." Franco argues: "Whereas in Europe the expanding readership provided writers with a base which was not confined to the middle class, in Latin America the very possession of books served as a mark of cultural superiority and divided the writer from the illiterate."[25]

Second, the term *super-version* is just as appropriate for U.S. literature as it is for the decolonizing literatures of Latin America and the Caribbean. From the beginning of chattel bond-servitude in Anglo-America, Baraka notes, "black life has contributed to and animated Anglo-American life and culture. But a formal, artifact-documented presence could easily be denied slaves." The effects of the illegalization of literacy on African American bond-laborers in the continental colonies were felt as well by laboring-class European Americans, creating the same schism between the writer and the masses that Latin American writers had to face. Lacking a reading base among the laboring classes, composed of illiterate poor whites and African American lifetime bond-laborers, white American writers in the first half of the nineteenth century contributed little more to world literature than, in Baraka's view, "embarrassing satires." On the other hand, the oral narratives produced by African American slaves and

25. "Dependency Theory and Literary History," 68, 74.

ex-slaves had a vital link to a whole people or "living culture," in Franco's concept. "Beside this body of strong, dramatic, incisive, democratic literature," argues Baraka,

> where is the literature of the slavemasters and mistresses? Find it and compare it with the slave narratives and say which has a clearer, more honest, and ultimately more artistically powerful perception of American reality. . . . Yes, there are William Gilmore Simms, John Pendleton Kennedy, Augustus B. Longstreet, and George Washington Harris, touted as outstanding writers of the white, slave South. But their writing is unreadable, even though overt racists like Allen Tate and the Southern Agrarians prated about the slave South as a "gracious culture despite its defects." Those defects consisted in the main of millions of black slaves, whose life expectancy at maturity by the beginning of the nineteenth century in the deep South was seven years.[26]

Baraka's position in this 1979 essay had been anticipated in the immediate postwar period by C. L. R. James in his *American Civilization.* James argued that the only rival among nineteenth-century world literatures to the African American antislavery narratives, the poetry of Walt Whitman, the novels of Melville, and the political writings of Wendell Phillips is Russian literature. The analogy between Russian literature and African American literature emphasized by James is not only intellectually rich but also strategic. The historical conditions of underdevelopment in nineteenth-century Russia, in which the forms of social oppression facing the Russian peasantry were both cause and effect of the consolidation of wealth and power in the metropolitan centers of manufacture and trade— in "White Russia"—are analogous to those experienced by poor whites and African Americans in the United States. As James maintained, the two situations produced analogous literatures: in the case of the latter, a lasting revolutionary democratic literature based on the antislavery movement, and its corollary—a weak and imitative literature of erudite slave masters and their shameless "white race" apologists in the North.[27]

What both James and Baraka propose is to revalue this democratic tradition of U.S. literature by forcing an ideological break with Anglo-American ruling-class literary culture—a culture of rule and social control predicated on a vigilant patrolling of oral poetry and narrative: the solid base of the popular traditions. For this backward glance they look

26. "Revolutionary Tradition," 313, 314.
27. "The American Intellectuals of the Nineteenth Century," 50.

directly to oral narratives and poetry: the "natural elements," in the elegant words of José Martí, of American civilization. Writing about this detour in the context of the emergence of Latin American liberation theology—the specific source of Cardenal's heroic return to the Indian roots of Nicaraguan rebellion—Gutiérrez suggests:

> It is impossible to reread history except in the midst of the successes and failures of the struggles for liberation. Remaking this history, redoing it, means we have to "subvert" it, turn it around, *make it flow backward*— make it flow not from above but from below. The established order has inculcated in us the pejorative concept of subversion: subversion is dangerous to the established order. But from the other viewpoint, the great wrong is to become—or, perhaps, to continue to be—a "super-versive," a bulwark and support of the prevailing domination, someone whose orientation of history begins with the great ones of this world. But a subversive history is the locus of a new faith experience, a new spirituality, and a new proclamation of the gospel.[28]

In postcolonialist discourse, the importance of Franco's essay has been duly noted, but what has been often taken for granted is the prophetic quality of her analysis, of the kind expressed in Gutiérrez's definition of the "remaking" of history. It is not only that the writers she discusses in this early essay are today canonical figures in postcolonial literature (Alejo Carpentier, Jorge Luis Borges, Gabriel García Márquez, Carlos Fuentes, Mario Vargas Llosa), but that the writer she concludes with, who has yet to be canonized (Cardenal), was the one to make Franco's theorizations historically concrete. Four years after the essay's publication, Cardenal was named minister of culture in Nicaragua. He immediately transformed his cultural work at Solantiname (1965–1977)—the period in which Cardenal's Nicaraguan *comunidades de base* movement (Christian base communities) was first tried on the island of Mancarron in Lake Nicaragua—into a national literacy campaign of the revolutionary Sandindista government. More, his poetry workshops (*talleres de poesía*) of the early 1980s forced to the level of national culture what has remained aporetic for bourgeois cultural theory.[29]

<hr>

28. *Power of the Poor,* 202.

29. For a good history of Cardenal's poetry project, see *A Nation of Poets: Writings from the Poetry Workshops of Nicaragua,* which includes a lengthy interview with Cardenal on the ideology of the *talleres de poesía.* In 1977 Solantiname was destroyed by Somoza's National Guard and Cardenal was forced into exile. Also see Mayra

In *Poets of the Nicaraguan Revolution,* Dinah Livingstone notes that Cardenal's main focus at the Ministry of Culture was to "socialize the means of poetic production." The rupture in colonial society between the writer and the community, and thus between art and politics, was healed by Cardenal's workshops at the level of national-popular culture. By 1982, Cardenal had set up more than sixty workshops throughout Nicaragua. At this stage in the project, less than a year before the launching of an aggressive campaign within the Sandinista National Liberation Front to discontinue the workshops, the Ministry of Culture could boast of having one workshop for every three thousand Nicaraguans, as well as a poetry journal devoted exclusively to publishing their work, *Poesía Libre*—a tremendous accomplishment given the extreme shortages of writing supplies and publishing equipment in Nicaragua during the reconstruction period (1979–1984). In a speech given to UNESCO in 1982, Cardenal identified the *talleres de poesía* as the primary site of Nicaragua's "cultural liberation"—just the point Franco had insisted on in her argument for new conceptual categories in the study of Latin American literature, categories that challenge the view of Latin American culture as some "continuous and unresolved opposition between the universal and the regional." Cardenal's cultural work was a deliberate rejection of this false opposition, for the deeper he dug into the local history of colonialism in Nicaraguan society, the more universal did the scale of his poetry project become. As Eduardo Galeano has argued, the *talleres,* alongside the *testimonio* (a major genre in Latin American letters), represent one of the two most significant innovations in modern Latin American literature.[30]

The poem by Cardenal that Franco cites in her essay—*Homenaje a los indios americanos* (1968)—is a product of his personal immersion in Mayan Indian history and culture, as well as his rigorous studies of pre-Columbian Amerindian society. In *Literature and Politics in the Central American Revolutions,* John Beverley and Marc Zimmerman point to Cardenal's new concept of history as the link between his early poetry and the dynamic and internationally influential forms of Latin American poetry that would emerge in the 1970s and 1980s:

Jiménez's invaluable *Poesía campesino de Solantiname,* which contains a variety of writing from the workshops. Jiménez was invited to Solantiname by Cardenal in the early seventies to help organize the poetry workshops.

30. Livingstone, trans., *Poets of the Nicaraguan Revolution,* 5, 14; Franco, "Dependency Theory and Literary History," 66; Galeano quoted in John Beverley and Marc Zimmerman, *Literature and Politics in the Central American Revolutions,* 97.

In Cardenal's poetry, the experience of the present is of time-without-hope: the seeming eternity of the dictatorship, the sense of a past that has been canceled, of the failed epic of a dominated and dependent Banana Republic. But there is at the same time a countermotion, which derives from Cardenal's representation of Nicaraguan and Central American history through the narrative frame of Christian eschatology. Despair is lit up from within by the promise of an imminent redemption from evil, a time when "the last shall be first," when human beings will attain a new community and a new body.[31]

It is this kind of backward glance, or repossession of history, that Franco emphasizes, a view of the past that foregrounds "the ideology of conquest and genocide implicit in the accounts of the discovery and exploration of America." Precisely for this reason did Cardenal go to Monimbó, the Indian district of Masaya, to establish the first poetry workshop in Nicaragua, "because of what Monimbó symbolizes in this Revolution." Here the ideology of European and Anglo-American imperialism has been resisted the longest. Here also "Nele," the Indian hero of *Homenaje a los indios americanos*, who exemplifies for Cardenal all the qualities of Nicaraguan national identity, organized the great anticolonial Indian revolt of the early 1920s. In this sense, *Homenaje a los indios americanos* is the first phase in the creation of what Glissant has termed "a prophetic vision of the past." This immersion in the "obsessively present" past, argues Glissant, is related "neither to a schematic chronology nor to a nostalgic lament. It leads to the identification of a painful notion of time and its full projection forward into the future, without the help of those plateaus in time from which the West has benefited, without the help of that collective destiny that is the primary value of an ancestral cultural heartland." Like Glissant, Franco encourages through the example of Cardenal's poetry the innovation of concepts that take into account the sudden emergence of new, epic forms of writing and that provide a framework that "foregrounds the technology of domination and the forms of resistance, thereby allowing us to separate the ideological facets of culture from its potentiality as a mode of cognition."[32]

In the second line of inquiry into questions of history and literature, the repossession of history, is, as Franco suggests, a mode of cognition. This

31. Beverley and Zimmerman, *Literature and Politics*, 68.

32. Franco, "Dependency Theory and Literary History," 79; Livingstone, trans., *Poets of the Nicaraguan Revolution*, 5; Glissant, *Caribbean Discourse*, 64; Franco, "Dependency Theory and Literary History," 79.

mode enables a reconceptualization of the relationship between history and literature. In the high period of decolonization, the great challenge posed to European and U.S. cultural hegemony by African, Asian, Latin American, Caribbean, and African American writers was their "assertion," in the words of Amílcar Cabral, "of the cultural personality of the dominated people by an act of denial of the culture of the oppressor." This involves liberatory cultural resistance, which meant for Cabral the simultaneous development of a "people's culture," a "national culture," a "scientific culture," and a "universal culture," unified by a new mode of cognition, which arises from the struggle for socialist national liberation. "The national liberation of a people," he wrote, "is the regaining of the historical personality of that people, it is their return to history through the destruction of the imperialist domination to which they have been subjected." Literature as a mode of cognition in socialist national liberation struggle is what Gramsci termed "counter-hegemonic ideological production." In *Resistance Literature*, Barbara Harlow has applied Gramsci's concept to a great variety of new writing from the decolonizing world. This writing, she argues, constitutes "their means of identifying themselves as a group, as a people, no less than as a nation, with a historicity of their own and a claim to an autonomous, self-determining role on the contemporary staging grounds of history." From Chinua Achebe's classic novel of decolonization in Africa, *Things Fall Apart*, to Rigoberta Menchú's *testimonio I . . . Rigoberta Menchú*, Harlow includes in this category of decolonizing writing the founding texts of anticolonial, liberatory cultural resistance. What they share is an awareness that they are "immediately and directly involved in a struggle against ascendant or dominant forms of ideological and cultural production."[33] In Franco's terms, the initial forms of resistance to colonialist oppression have become modes of cognition or ways of apprehending and politically confronting the new realities of neocolonial oppression, underdevelopment, and U.S. cultural imperialism. The collective repossession of the past has become a new popular ideology of anticolonial national liberation struggle.

In the third line of inquiry, the collective repossession of history refers directly to questions of aesthetics and politics. Kenyan writer Ngũgĩ wa Thiong'o has argued, for example, that "in literature there have been two opposing aesthetics: the aesthetic of oppression and exploitation and of acquiescence with imperialism; and that of human struggle for total liberation." In *Salman Rushdie and the Third World: Myths of the Nation*, Timo-

33. Cabral, "The Weapon of Theory," 134, 130; Harlow, *Resistance Literature*, 33, 29.

thy Brennan has defined, in general terms, the emphases of resistance aesthetics, which stand in defiance of the aesthetic shared by cosmopolitan writers such as Salman Rushdie, V. S. Naipaul, and Mario Vargas Llosa: "It is, of course, not possible to discuss this vision 'as a whole,' since it is not monolithic. But in general it focuses on a decisive valorization of 'the people' and an insistence on 'national culture'—in the sense that culture itself is meaningless if not considered 'in its national aspect.'" For Brennan, this vision has been effectively transformed by anticolonial nationalist writers into definite popular aesthetic preferences and modes of expression, a turn referred to by Gramsci as the emergence of "national aesthetics." Using Gramsci's concept, Brennan suggests that "the art of dialogue over that of 'irony,' and the art of ingenuousness and spontaneity," has produced new forms of writing in the decolonizing world and signaled the arrival of a revolutionary nationalist phase in the literatures of postcolonialism, based this time on the popular traditions of literature and culture.[34]

Imperialist Pressure

> Imperialist pressure hurt him more than once . . .
>
> —Nicolás Guillén, "Recuerdo de Langston Hughes"

In the aesthetics of postcolonial writing, Cuba's national poet, Nicolás Guillén, has written of exile from the standpoint of what José Martí called "our *mestizo* América." As a black writer in one of the "whitest" islands in the Caribbean, Guillén was well aware of the historical legacy of Spanish colonial rule in postindependence Cuba, still alive through the overhauled institutions of racial slavery, and of the greatly increased U.S. imperial presence ("la presión imperialista"). He approached the problem from the interstices of race, nation, and class. Guillén was never without country yet never fully with it, until the revolutionary triumph of 1959. His position within the Cuban struggle for national independence was enabled by his possession of all the qualities and attributes of *antillano* (Caribbean) identity. Guillén referred to these features of *antillano* as *mulatez* ("mulattoness")—an approach that was in bold contrast to any apotheosis of self-exile. It was in fact another kind of thought. To quote

---

34. Ngũgĩ wa Thiong'o, *Writers in Politics,* 38; Brennan, *Salman Rushdie and the Third World: Myths of the Nation,* 54, 49.

Jean Baudrillard, the approach was one in which there was now room to rethink "all the old solutions and help to hold the world in enigmatic tension."[35]

By the late 1920s, white Cubans had fully embraced "jes grew," as Ishmael Reed terms it in his masterpiece *Mumbo Jumbo:* a contagious "antiplague" of jazz culture and literary Négritude.[36] Blackness was "in vogue" not only in New York but throughout the Western European metropolises, as well as in the Caribbean literary and cultural centers of Haiti and Cuba. The Haitian review *La Revue Indigene* (1927–1928) and the Cuban publication *Revista de avance* (1927–1930) had led the way in articulating a Caribbean Africanist response to "the acquiescent, the static, the time-honored notions of grandeur" imposed on Caribbean history by European and Anglo-American colonialism.[37] In this period Guillén himself flirted with *negrismo,* or Afro-Antillean poetry, in particular the work of white Puerto Rican poet Luis Palés Matos. But Guillén and other Afro-Cuban writers and artists, such as Regino Pedroso and Marcelino Arozarena, were becoming critical of the turn among white hispanophone writers toward an exotic literary image of "blackness," a turn critic Josaphat B. Kubayanda has aptly termed "inventing the primitive African." According to Caribbean scholar Ian Isidore Smart, not until Guillén's first meeting with Langston Hughes in January 1930 was he able to discover a way out of the impasse.[38]

In his widely circulated newspaper article "Conversación con Langston Hughes," Guillén said that Hughes was the "black people's poet," in spite of looking "just like a Cuban '*mulatico.*'" What impressed Guillén most about Hughes was his nation-conscious longing for everything black in Cuba. He ended his article by recalling that Hughes requested that Guillén take him to places in Havana where black Cubans dwelled, where he could hear "real black music." "Blackness" for Hughes was a way of life— a politics of identification—not simply a way of looking, thinking, and

35. Martí, "Our America," 89; Guillén, "Recuerdo de Langston Hughes," 316; Baudrillard, *The Vital Illusion,* 57.

36. The term *jes grew* was familiar to Reed from James Weldon Johnson's use of it in the early 1900s to describe the emergent jazz aesthetic, as Reed notes in *Mumbo Jumbo,* 4.

37. These words are from the first issue of *Revista de avance* (March 15, 1972), a journal founded by Alejo Carpentier, Martín Casanovas, Francisco Ichaso, Jorge Mañach, and Juan Marinello.

38. Kubayanda, *The Poet's Africa: Africanness in the Poetry of Nicolás Guillén and Aimé Césaire,* 17; Smart, *Nicolás Guillén: Popular Poet of the Caribbean,* 34 (Smart provides a stellar overview of *negrismo* in his chapter "The Poet," 29–63).

feeling, or a method of writing poems. More, it was an approach to Afro-American culture that Guillén had not yet encountered in the cosmopolitan literary and cultural circles of Latin America and the Caribbean, in which blackness was perceived as a route away from the colonial nation-state rather than a path leading to its overthrow from below. For Guillén, Hughes revealed the vast possibilities inherent in the Négritude movement as a whole, which was in need of an antagonistic concept of blackness if it was to weather the storm let loose in the United States and Europe by the aggressive corporate appropriation of black jazz culture. Like Hughes, Guillén advanced a prescient critique of Négritude, looking past what had become an ideology of blackness toward what might be accomplished at the more concrete levels of national-popular culture. "Within three months of his meeting with Hughes," and in response to Hughes's specific insights on Afro-American popular art forms, as Smart notes, "Guillén set himself on the same course and discovered his own authentic voice, creating the *son* poem with the verbal rhythm of the Cuban people's best-known oral poetic form, the *son*."[39]

Guillén's concept of exile was based on the organic interconnections among social class, race, and nation. Since race and nation in Cuba are inseparable from social class, the experience of exile was felt most acutely by those who had been denied admittance to forms of social identity normal to the colonizing power, namely the black Cuban laboring classes. It is in this context that Guillén articulated his own vision of race, which was for him both an experience of exile—an act of living as an "outcast" in his own native land—and a liberating force of prophetic power. "I come to you as a black man," Guillén wrote, "but, paradoxically, I do not come with a discriminatory, exclusive racial concept of blackness. Rather, I am here to remind you that the Negro's position as outcast is his most powerful human driving force, a force which hurls him forward towards a wider horizon that is more universal, more just, towards a horizon for which all honorable men are struggling today." For Guillén, the collective repossession of history is a necessary stage in the nation-building process. In other words, "blackness" is a national strategic location, in the sense that it is through the political concept of race that social consciousness asserts itself. The *telos* is not a fully realized "racial" consciousness but instead a new national consciousness no longer based on race and thus no longer in the service of colonialism. Guillén's approach to blackness, in which national independence is linked to the eradication of racial op-

39. Guillén, "Conversación con Langston Hughes," 16; Smart, *Nicolás Guillén,* 32.

pression, is the same as that found in Fanon's *Wretched of Earth*—the beginning of a new phase of liberation involving the transformation of social consciousness beyond national consciousness. To arrive at this complex concept, Guillén needed to work out an aesthetics of cultural antagonism. This aesthetics rejected the existing methods of colonialist communication and replaced them with methods from below, through the national forms of the popular classes of Cuban society. For Guillén, the solution to *exilio* is *patria:* the class project of constructing a new national-popular culture from Cuba's interstices, the common points (or moments of *mulatez*) in which class, race, and nation clash and interchange, giving way to a new equalitarian social relationship.[40]

A synthesis of postcolonial writing by way of this concept of collective repossession is beyond the scope of this book and is also at odds with the spirit in which it is written. The immensity of postcolonial writing, in terms of language and geography alone, discourages generalizations. At the same time, a highly specialized approach is prone to overlooking the presence of multiple histories in the same place or of similar histories in multiple places. The main detour in approaching postcolonial discourse, then, involves method. What kind of analytical method is capable of appreciating this dialectic? Does one already exist? If so, where did it come from? And what are its specific powers of explanation? Finally, what is its relation with the dialectical method of the Marxist tradition—a tradition to which Guillén, Hughes, James, Lamming, Cardenal, Franco, Baraka, Ngũgĩ, Fanon, and Glissant each share vital points of contact?

For example, Franco's theory of dependency overturns the prevailing idealist and formalist methods of literary analysis by showing their inability to account for the transformation of oral narratives and poetry into new written forms of communication. Her discussion of Cardenal is especially suggestive because his work has been celebrated in Latin America yet ignored in "multicultural" American literary studies precisely because the neo-formalisms, including French theory, that prevail in the U.S. academy are indifferent to the turn to the history of colonial oppression that explains the emergence of new forms of writing. From the standpoint of the United States, this turn would amount to an indictment of U.S. imperialism in Latin America and the Caribbean, which is precisely the reason for Franco's use of Lenin's theory of imperialism in her essay. In or-

40. Guillén, *Prosa de Prisa,* 81 (my translation). On race, class, and nation in Cuba, see Nancy Morejón, "Race and Nation," and Rafael Duharte Jiménez, "The 19th Century Black Fear."

der to counter unhistorical literary analysis, Franco goes to the Marxist tradition's theory of history and society, for it is through this method that the relationship between imperial culture and anticolonial resistance is felt "contrapuntally," in Said's terms. Lenin's emphasis on "the indissoluble link between dependent economies and the industrial development of the metropolitan powers," Franco maintains, "means that it is no longer possible to treat the two terms as if they were separable. . . . And this concept of relationship allows us to turn back to Europe or North American culture and see it in a completely different way, marking what it negates and cancels out."[41]

Baraka's New Caliban

Fredric Jameson suggests that in the Marxist tradition the problems of history, culture, and society and their solutions "are numbered in advance." This approach to method is the premise of Franco's essay as she revisits Lenin's theory of imperialism to understand the current problems of colonial "dependency" for Latin American literature. Glissant's rejection of linear, undialectical conceptions of history in favor of a "prophetic vision of the past"—of missed political opportunities and revolutionary historical conjunctures—is also consonant, I believe, with the protocols of theoretical Marxism.

Likewise, Baraka's critique of the prevailing "white" methods of Anglo-American literary studies is a Marxist critique of bourgeois white racial ideology: an intervention in African American studies that argues for an ideological realignment of the African American tradition with that of theoretical Marxism. For Baraka, Du Bois is the path. "It is not possible to understand the history of ideas in the United States," he contends, "without reading DuBois. Not to know his work is to not have a whole a picture of Afro-American literature, sociology, history, and struggle and is to have a distorted view of American life in general."[42] In New World writing, the solutions to the problems of culture and empire are also "numbered in advance." Baraka's return to Du Bois seems routine if judged in unhistorical terms, for it requires great effort to avoid Du Bois's magisterial legacy. But in the context of the contradictory relations between white supremacy and U.S. imperialism—contradictory because poor

41. Franco, "Dependency Theory and Literary History," 67.
42. Baraka, "Revolutionary Tradition," 317.

whites do not benefit from U.S. conquest abroad—it takes on much greater significance.

Baraka's turn to the Marxist tradition in the 1970s was a direct response to the historic compromises in the late 1960s and early 1970s, at the end of the high period of decolonization, between black cultural nationalism and the neocolonialist regimes of Africa and the Caribbean, culminating in the destruction of the Black Liberation movement by the U.S. government. Through a reconstituted theory of pan-Africanism, the Black Liberation movement had asserted the historical continuity of the black freedom struggle on a world scale, linking itself ideologically with the national liberation movements in the Caribbean, Africa, Asia, and Latin America. Within the movement, black cultural nationalism emerged as a form of "non-Americanism" similar to that shared by many radical middle-class whites in the U.S. counterculture movement. As Baraka would later remark, it quickly became apparent to many African American activists and cultural workers that cultural nationalism was turning out to be "just a form of black bohemianism." Baraka wrote: "Take away the attention to Africa, and the 'weird' clothes, and 'communalism' can be found in any number of white hippie communities. Some of the cultural nationalists we began to recognize when we started to read the history of the Communist Party (Bolshevik). These old Russian hippies and cultural nationalists were called Nardoniks. When we read that, we recognized ourselves clearly." Baraka's savvy appropriation of Lenin's concept of the revolutionary party would enable the first programmatic response to this culturalist tendency within the movement, which had made itself vulnerable to the worst forms of individual opportunism and middle-class sectarianism. The question of the African American revolutionary party was not raised among the leadership of the movement until Baraka's resounding 1970 theses on Black Power forced to center stage the question of an independent African American working-class political party.[43]

Baraka himself has battled opportunists on virtually every level. For example, as a resident of Newark, New Jersey, where he founded in the late 1960s the Committee for Unified Newark (CFUN)—a united front of cultural and political organizations based in Newark—he helped bring Ken Gibson to power in 1968 only to see him sell out the independent black community movement a year later. As a founder of the Black Arts Repertory Theater/School in Harlem, Baraka witnessed the institution's takeover by middle-class opportunists and reactionaries, he says. And as a cre-

43. *The Autobiography of LeRoi Jones/Amiri Baraka*, 301.

ative artist and intellectual involved in developing Africana studies programs, he experienced the co-optation of many programs by bourgeois arts councils and educational institutes during the early days of affirmative action. In the wake of these experiences, Baraka argued that as a unifying principle of African American political struggle, racial nationalism made possible "self-knowledge, self-affirmation, and the move to liberation." But as an end in itself, he says, it quickly became reactionary and served to raise "a new bourgeoisie, the national bourgeoisie, to power." According to Baraka, "Senghor's Senegal is proof in living color of the reactionary nature of such cultural nationalism. The 'eternal mystical values' of black communalism, supposedly raised in a modern African socialism, are the excuse for the most shameless bootlicking of French imperialism, and for one of the most relentlessly class-stratified societies in West Africa today."[44]

As his critique of Négritude shows, Baraka's rejection of black cultural nationalism is also a critique of neocolonialism. This move returns African American literary and cultural theory and practice to the nexus of New World writing: to the point where the African-Caribbean-American connection is used politically in the struggle for new socialist party-building. It is in this sense that Baraka's reassessment of Aimé Césaire and the Négritude movement as a whole, as well as his renewal of the Marxist tradition, is a case of the backward glance. His historic intervention effected a break with the forms of cultural nationalism that had reduced the African American mass movement to an apocalyptic battle between Africa and Europe: to "white" versus "black" writ large and enduring. It also signaled a return to the question of anti-imperialist class struggle built into the civil rights movement itself. Indeed, as Ahmad has it, as a variant of "Three Worlds Theory" cultural nationalism's main limitation is its distorted definition of anti-imperialism:

> An ideological formation which redefined anti-imperialism not as a socialist project to be realized by the mass movements of the popular classes but as a developmentalist project to be realized by the weaker states of the national bourgeoisies in the course of their collaborative competition with the more powerful states of advanced capital served the interest both of making the mass movements subservient to the national bourgeois state and of strengthening the negotiating positions of that type of state in relation to the states and corporate entities of advanced capital. It was this sectoral competition between backward and ad-

44. Ibid., 215; Baraka, "Aimé Césaire," 329.

vanced capitals, realized differentially in the world, owing partly to colonial history itself, which was now advocated as the kernel of anti-imperialist struggles, while the national-bourgeois state was itself recognized as representing the masses.[45]

Hence, Baraka's backward glance is simultaneously a return to the antagonistic terms of working-class black struggle and an attempt to close the gap between avant-garde aesthetics and popular culture—a rich artistic field that had been left open to co-optation by the exponents of cultural nationalism.

Baraka's important interventions in the late 1970s and early 1980s created the conditions for a new aesthetics. To circumvent the civilizational opposition between Africa and Europe, he turned to the anticolonial revolutionary nationalism of Caliban. This alternative tradition of liberation struggle is based not on an ideology of already constituted bourgeois nation-states—as is the case with cultural nationalism—but on mass working-class political movements in opposition to bourgeois state power. As did the relationship between Guillén and Hughes, Baraka's redefinition of African American culture in relation to Caribbean and Latin American radical traditions has enabled a new concept of "America" and a direct engagement with the goals of liberatory cultural resistance in the hemisphere as a whole. If the ideology of cultural nationalism consolidates bourgeois state structures instead of rejecting them, thus keeping different yet overlapping New World cultural traditions hierarchically partitioned and isolated, a solution needs to be found that both surpasses cultural nationalism and makes use of its emphasis on self-affirmation. This solution has been most successfully proposed in the Caribbean and African American Marxist traditions. Lamming's essay on James's *Black Jacobins*, "Caliban Orders History," is a suggestive example of this.

In Lamming's view, "*The Black Jacobins* shows us Caliban as Prospero had never known him: a slave who was a great soldier in battle, an incomparable administrator in public affairs; full of paradox but never without compassion, a humane leader of men." James shatters Prospero's old myth of a speechless Caliban by making available to the world "the result of certain enterprises undertaken by men who are still regarded as the unfortunate descendants of languageless and deformed slaves." A Trinidadian writing the history of Toussaint L'Ouverture and the Haitian Revolution is for Lamming exactly what distinguishes the Caribbean

45. Ahmad, *In Theory*, 293.

"way of seeing" from that of the European colonialist and the white American immigrant. From the standpoint of European and U.S. imperialism, nationalism is a means of achieving military and economic "freedom"— that is, "free trade"—and its object is usually the consolidation of communal resources (labor-power and ecology) for the purpose of defending ideologically the costs of war, economic and territorial expansion, and the forms of ruling-class social control that keep U.S. capitalist society continuously functioning. As Brennan has argued persuasively, in Europe and the United States this view of nationalism is essentially Romantic.[46]

But for Lamming, *Black Jacobins* counters the romantic notion of nationalism by rejecting newly emergent state consolidation in favor of the national-popular tradition of working-class resistance, embodied for both Lamming and James by Toussaint himself. In James's epic narrative, Toussaint's heroism is the fulfillment of a whole working people's struggle for self-emancipation. Toussaint did not begin the Haitian Revolution nor did he complete it; rather, he brought the future to the present by making the romantic concept of self-emancipation into historical fact. "The future had found its architect in Toussaint L'Ouverture," Lamming wrote. In the appendix to the 1963 edition of *Black Jacobins*, James stated it tersely: "West Indians first became aware of themselves as a whole people in the Haitian Revolution."[47] Whereas European nationalism, represented by Napoleon, was invested in maintaining racial slavery in the French colonies, Haitian revolutionary nationalism, represented by Toussaint, was committed to its overthrow. Thus, by dislocating European imperialism in the Americas, the Haitian Revolution made possible, for the first time, the creation of an American socialist nationalism. No longer a "universal" means to a "national" end, the romantic idea of the nation was rejected and transformed in the Caribbean by the new national struggles for "universal" independence, which began with the overthrow of colonial slavery. No longer a conceptual projection of "common life," of what should or could be, nationalism in the Americas became the fulfillment of the common life that was already there: an untamed cross-cultural composite of peoples and histories.

Wordsworth's poem to Toussaint expresses this idea clearly, despite the nostalgic lament implicit in his famous elegy: "There's not a breathing of the common wind / That will forget thee." The turn toward "low and rustic life" announced by Wordsworth in his 1798 preface to *Lyrical Ballads*,

46. Lamming, *Pleasures of Exile*, 119; Brennan, "National Longing for Form," 44.
47. Lamming, *Pleasures of Exile*, 125; James, *The Black Jacobins*, 391.

in which "the essential passions of the heart find a better soil" and are "less under restraint," was brought into being as a historical subject by Toussaint and the antislavery revolutionaries in Haiti instead of existing merely as an inchoate object for the much aggrieved self-exiled poet. For Lamming, this is the premise of *Black Jacobins:* the rejection by the lowly and "languageless" of their status as objects in history and their embrace, as self-conscious subjects, of the ordering work that for the first time in history they no longer passively live through. Rather than being a flat negation of the romantic idea of the nation, which would simply reverse the flow of history from one pole (Europe) to its opposite (the decolonizing world), New World liberatory nationalism arrived explosively as a collective practice or epic form of popular struggle, involving the political fate of whole peoples as opposed to a self-styled "politics" of individual exiles.

Written during Mussolini's invasion and occupation of Ethiopia in the late 1930s, *Black Jacobins* was James's attempt to reassert this principle and to realign the project of nationalism with the anticolonial liberation struggle. As a way of seeing, then, New World nationalism is produced from below. Its sudden arrival is also its lasting point of departure. *Black Jacobins* is written from *within* the Western cultural tradition, as Said observes in *Culture and Imperialism,* but its mode of presentation, its style, and the standpoint from which it is written—black struggle in the Caribbean, the United States, and Africa—places the book in a different orbit. In Said's words, *Black Jacobins* "bridges an important cultural and political gap between Caribbean, specifically black, history on the one hand, and European history on the other. Yet it . . . is fed by more currents and flows in a wider stream than even its rich narrative may suggest." Lamming had alluded to this same quality of *Black Jacobins* in the opening sentence of his essay on the book: "The entire Caribbean is our horizon; for Caliban himself like the island he inherited is at once a landscape and a human situation."[48]

The logic is straightforward. Geographically, the Caribbean is the locus of three intersecting cultural traditions: the European, the African, and the Amerindian. No single history of the clashes and encounters that constitute the long and dense histories of these three storied peoples can account for the particular forms of cross-culturalism that have taken place in the New World. But the land on which they dwell carries these disparate histories just as they are both denied and sublimated by those who have

48. Said, *Culture and Imperialism,* 252; Lamming, *Pleasures of Exile,* 118.

ruled over them. What cannot be denied is the fact that the land itself has been transformed by those who were forcibly transferred, collectively exiled, and transplanted to the Americas but who now possess them: who have made this new world through their own labor and their own antagonistic forms of cultural resiliency, and whose identities are today inseparable from the history of this whole dynamic process. Caliban, the ultimate response to the bourgeois concept of exile, is more than a singular figure in this historic drama. He *is* the drama—the total expression of history's collective repossession.

Glissant has followed Lamming's argument closely by giving the idea of a Caribbean way of seeing exile a precise name, *cross-cultural poetics*. In his section on the Cuban landscape in *Caribbean Discourse,* Glissant places the dialectic of Caliban and Prospero in what he terms "the true Caribbean problematic, which extends well beyond the Caribbean sea":

> The theme of Caliban has touched Caribbean intellectuals in a surprising way: Fanon, Lamming, Césaire, Fernández Retamar. The fact is that Caliban, as the locus of encounters and conflicts, has become a symbol. Above and beyond Shakespeare's savage cannibal, a real dynamic is at play—not only in the Caribbean but in many places in the Third World—a dynamic constituted by encounters among these three necessities: the class struggle, the emergence or the construction of the nation, the quest for collective identity.[49]

Glissant's concept of Caliban as a complex web of anticolonial cultural resistance provides a useful point of contact with the diverse traditions of New World writing outlined thus far. Franco's analytical procedures rest on a simultaneous rejection of Prospero's vision of history and a call for anticolonial class struggle at the level of national literary theory and criticism. Lamming's revision of the figure of exile is, in this same way, a narrative of collective awareness and nation building from the perspective of Caliban. Baraka's attack on white Americanist theories of U.S. literature is based on Caliban's quest for an always class-conscious and cunningly antagonistic African American community. And Glissant's own interventions are intended to break the hold of linear and monocultural conceptions of history on the resistant cross-cultural imaginary in which class struggle, nation building, and the development of a collective identity are established all at once. These terms will be essential in the ensuing dis-

49. Glissant, *Caribbean Discourse,* 97.

cussions and constitute what I have been referring to as the backward glance, for one writer in particular helps animate the *class character* of it: Langston Hughes, whose historic example gives new shape and meaning to the cross-cultural aesthetic.

A "Functional Syncretism":
The Cross-cultural Aesthetics of Langston Hughes

> Yo Quisiera ser negro. Bien negro. ¡Negro de verdad!
>
> —Langston Hughes

This epigram from Langston Hughes, his expression of unreflecting love for black folk, was spoken, thought, and felt in the Spanish language. More, the statement was made in Cuba, where the "minority discourse" of race and ethnicity has signified quite differently for the writer of African origin than it has in the United States. For instance, in his renowned "Caliban" essay, Roberto Fernández Retamar describes Cuba as "a vast zone for which *mestizaje* ["racial" intermixing] is not an accident but rather the essence, the central line: ourselves, 'our mestizo America.'" In Cuba, blackness is not a sign of the Other, of what is problematic—of what is liminal, hybridic, exotic, marginal or "minor." Neither is it a separate ethnic spoke of that Anglo-American wheel known as "multicultural" or "pluralist" America. Rather, blackness in Cuba, argues Retamar, has been reclaimed as a mark of glory: "This is the dialectic of Caliban. To offend us they call us *mambí*, they call us *black;* but we reclaim as a mark of glory the honor of considering ourselves descendants of the *mambí*, descendants of the rebel, runaway, *independentista* black—*never* descendants of the slave holder."[50]

In this revolutionary national Cuban cultural context, Langston Hughes voiced one of his most impassioned declarations of racial belonging. That it was spoken in the presence of Cuba's national poet, Nicolás Guillén, is just as significant. As an Afro-Cuban, Guillén had achieved recognition as his country's most beloved and admired poet. By the time Guillén and Hughes met in Havana, Guillén's poetry had been canonized by Cuban critics and made into easily accessible recordings for Havana's working class. His column in Cuba's daily newspaper, *Diario de la Marina,* was read

50. Retamar, "Caliban: Notes toward a Discussion of Culture in Our America," 4.

throughout the country. Hughes had experienced the exact opposite in his native land. The largest African American daily newspapers had condemned his second volume of poetry, *Fine Clothes to the Jew,* and many of his peers, such as Countee Cullen, were irritated with the direction of his poetry, in particular with Hughes's personal immersion in the social life of Harlem's black working class.

The canonization of Hughes in American studies has conveniently omitted the fact that the "dean of black letters" was often rejected and disdained by both the Anglo-American and African American critical establishments. A classic case is noted by Arnold Rampersad in his biography of Hughes. Other than *Leaves of Grass,* he points out, "no other book of American poetry . . . had ever been greeted so contemptuously" in the United States as was *Fine Clothes to the Jew.* In most accounts of Hughes's reception nationally, his experience in front of the House Committee on Un-American Activities on March 26, 1953, is cited as emblematic of his political life as a writer. Yet the reactionary ideological rejection of his writing in his native country went much deeper. In contrast, critical work on his poetry was plentiful in Latin American and Caribbean literary studies, beginning in 1928 with the Cuban critic José Antonio Fernández's translation and discussion of Hughes's poem "I, Too." In a 1972 essay on Hughes published in the *Latin American Literary Review,* Carlos Pellicer observed that, while Hughes had enjoyed nearly four decades of critical attention in Latin America, "in North America he is a noble, forgotten poet." Similarly, Hughes scholar Edward Mullen argues in *Langston Hughes in the Hispanic World and Haiti* that, between 1931 and 1938, the five books of poetry Hughes published were met in the United States "with either mute silence or outright rejection." "At the time of his death," Mullen asserts, "Langston Hughes was more widely known in Latin America and the Caribbean than in the country of his birth."[51] In *Life of Langston Hughes,* Rampersad qualifies Mullen's statement, showing that the reception of Hughes's first five volumes of poetry in the United States was actually quite mixed. In Latin America and the Caribbean, however, Hughes's reception was anything but.

Neglected also in mainstream American studies has been Hughes's vital role in bringing to English-language audiences the poetry of Latin American and Caribbean writers, most notably Nicolás Guillén and Jacques Roumain. Hughes was the first to translate Guillén's poetry into

51. Rampersad, *Life of Langston Hughes,* 1:140–45; Mullen, *Langston Hughes in the Hispanic World and Haiti,* 15 (quoting Pellicer), 11.

English, in a volume published in 1948 as *Cuba Libre: Poems by Nicolás Guillén*, and he was also the first English-language translator of Roumain's classic novel *Gouverneurs de la rosée* (*Masters of the Dew*). Moreover, many of Hughes's earliest published articles and poems were written in Latin America and the Caribbean, including "The Negro Speaks of Rivers" (1921)—one of his most frequently anthologized poems—and his essays on Mexican culture, "Mexican Games" and "In a Mexican City" (both 1921), which have been translated into Spanish throughout Latin America. Also consistently published in translation in Latin America and the Caribbean has been his 1934 essay "People without Shoes," whose first appearance there was in the July 26 edition of *Haiti-Journal*. His first volume of poetry, *The Weary Blues*, includes three poems about the Caribbean and Latin America: "Caribbean Sunset," "Soledad: A Cuban Portrait," and "To the Dark Mercedes of 'El Palacio de Amor.'" These cross-cultural aesthetic themes would later become the driving force of Hughes's radical aesthetic innovations in *Ask Your Mama: Twelve Moods for Jazz* (1961)—a work that anticipated by a decade or so the coemergence of the Black Aesthetic cultural movement, jazz poetics, and the cross-fertilization of Afro-Caribbean popular cultures such as rumba and salsa with African Caribbean and African American popular forms such as dub, kaiso, bebop, and hip-hop.[52]

Despite these facts of Hughes's life and work, little—with the exception of the dynamic Hughes criticism during the 1970s and early 1980s, and several recent articles published in the *Langston Hughes Review*—has been written in the U.S. academy on his cross-cultural relations with Latin America and the Caribbean.[53] Especially in U.S. cultural studies has there been an odd silence. But even if the critic overlooks the geographic location of some of Hughes's poems and articles, as well as his extensive trav-

52. Hughes was assisted in his translation of Guillén's poems by Ben Frederic Carruthers and in his translation of Roumain's novel by Mercer Cook. For a discussion of "People without Shoes," see Carolyn Fowler, "The Shared Vision of Langston Hughes and Jacques Roumain," 85.

53. The articles published in the *Langston Hughes Review* are Berry and Lubin's "Langston Hughes and Haiti"; Jeannette S. White and Clement A. White's "Two Nations, One Vision: America's Langston Hughes and Cuba's Nicolás Guillén"; Dellita L. Martin-Ogunsola's "Langston Hughes and the Musico-Poetry of the African Diaspora"; Belén Rodríguez-Mourelo's "The Search for Identity in the Poetry of Langston Hughes and Nicolás Guillén": Ifeoma Nwankwo's "Langston Hughes and the Translation of Nicolás Guillén's Afro-Cuban Culture and Language"; and Paul Gardullo's "Heading Out for the Big Sea: Hughes, Haiti and Constructions of Diaspora in Cold War America."

els to Latin America and the Caribbean, as hard as this is to do, there remain Hughes's own statements about many of these biographical facts and details. For example, in his second autobiography, *I Wonder As I Wander*, Hughes recalled his initial immersion in the Spanish language and in Latin American literature, as well as his own experiences in the thriving cultural scene of Mexico City during the early thirties:

> For me it was a delightful winter [1934]. I have an affinity for Latin Americans, and the Spanish language I have always loved. One of the first things I did when I got to Mexico City was to get a tutor, a young woman friend of the Patiños, and began to read *Don Quixote* in the original, a great reading experience that possibly helped me to develop many years later in my own books a character called Simple. I also began to translate into English a number of Mexican short stories and poems by young writers for publication in the United States. I met a number of painters, the sad Orozco, the talkative Siqueiros, and the genteel Montenegro, whose studio was across the street from where I lived.[54]

Ironically, Hughes's politics of identification expressed in the statement "Yo Quisiera ser negro. Bien negro. ¡Negro de verdad!" (I want to be black, really black, truly black!) might strike the average Americanist as a bit peculiar. He is known in American studies as the poet laureate of black America, one of the founders of the New Negro movement and of the Harlem Renaissance, and the passionate author of the uncompromising Black Aesthetic manifesto "The Negro Artist and the Racial Mountain." For American studies, the phrase "I want to be black" is supposed to echo throughout the novels of Nella Larsen or in James Weldon Johnson's *Autobiography of an Ex-Coloured Man*, not come from the lips of Langston Hughes. In discernible ways, Hughes is for American literary studies the very sign of racial blackness: he sings of America *as a black man*, just as Whitman sang of America as the universal ("white") man. And so by the perverse racial logic ("white" or "black," nothing in between) of U.S. white supremacism, the blacker Hughes is said to be, the more universal does white racial ideology become. To put it differently, if Hughes's early poems to America were bracketed, a difficult contradiction would arise for the Americanist. The false distance between Hughes and such "nation-

---

54. Langston Hughes, *I Wonder As I Wander*, 14:285. Hereafter, all works by Langston Hughes included in *The Collected Works of Langston Hughes* will be cited in the text as *CW* with volume and page number.

centered" black poets as Nicolás Guillén and Claude McKay would vanish, essentially leaving the instructor of American literature without any poems to teach. African American poets such as June Jordan, Amiri Baraka, Sonia Sanchez, and Jayne Cortez have been denied admittance to the official American literary tradition arguably because there are no odes to the United States in their work. Some of Baraka's early poems, especially the poems in his 1964 volume *The Dead Lecturer*, have made their way into standard poetry anthologies, but almost nothing of his writing after 1975 has been anthologized in the United States or discussed in its academic literature. Sanchez and Cortez have met with complete marginalization. While Hughes is for American studies the total sign of blackness, Baraka, Sanchez, and Cortez are its irruption, its withdrawal, and its ultimate rejection.

But it was Hughes's genius to understand this kind of racial dialectic. Beginning with his insistence in "The Negro Artist and the Racial Mountain" on the African American writer's right to criticize African American society and white America equally, Hughes maintained a strategic relationship with black cultural nationalism, never fully endorsing it yet never rejecting it either. What he rejected was the ideology of white supremacy—a fact that has been registered by Americanists only selectively, usually when direct challenges to white racial ideology in the United States become difficult to repress. For example, the first major critical assessment in American literary studies of Hughes's intellectual legacy was published in 1971: Therman B. O'Daniel's critical anthology *Langston Hughes: Black Genius*. The book coincided exactly with the implementation of the Nixon administration's affirmative action programs, during the immediate aftermath of the African American popular revolts of the late 1960s. It is interesting to note in this context that the dissident U.S. educator and social critic Jonathan Kozol was fired from his first teaching post in 1964 for teaching a Langston Hughes poem to his class.[55]

On the occasion of this assertion of blackness, however, Hughes was in Cuba meeting with Nicolás Guillén. Not only was his reception there different, in terms of cultural awareness, popular respect, and appreciation, from his reception in the United States, but also the whole question of "race" was signified differently. Hughes had political choices as a black artist in Cuba that he lacked in his home country. The Jim Crow system of culture, which had forced African American and Euro-American writers alike to choose either "black" or "white" social identities for themselves

55. Kozol, *Savage Inequalities: Children in America's Schools*, 1–2.

as artists and as human beings, had been successfully challenged by José Martí and the Cuban creole class a generation earlier in the final stages of the struggle for Cuban national independence (1895–1898). In rejecting Spanish colonial rule, the Cuban *independentistas* also rejected the division of Cubans into "white" and "black." Martí's revolutionary nationalist ideology was based on the idea that complete independence for Cuba would be realized only when all Cubans were equal citizens, a belief that was powerfully expressed in his archetypal phrase "our *mestizo* America." The Cuban *independentistas* had argued—in the precise words of Eric Williams—that "the price of slavery for white colonials was eternal colonialism."[56] Thus, as a *"mulatico,"* Hughes in Cuba occupied much more of a mainstream social position, a location off-limits to himself and any other African American in the United States. In Cuba blackness was for Hughes a vital element of a broad class spectrum, not an official state ideology or a fixed sign of social identity, defined strictly according to "skin-color," as it was in the United States.

In *The Invention of the White Race,* historian Theodore Allen points to the salient difference between race in Cuba and race in the States during the period immediately following independence. "In the last Spanish census of Cuba, Mexican Indians and Chinese were classified as 'white,'" he documents, "but in 1907 the first United States census there classed these groups as colored." The difference was that in the United States white-skin privilege functioned as the main mechanism for keeping the American laboring classes internally segregated and disorganized and under tight ruling-class social control, whereas in Cuba white-skin privilege was useful only insofar as it helped legitimate a dying Spanish colonialism. Because the majority of Euro-Americans were, and still are, poor and propertyless, the U.S. situation required the social degradation of all not-whites, regardless of their education, skills, or property. To ensure the loyalty of working-class whites to their bosses, all not-whites were reduced to a social status beneath that of any white, no matter how base the particular white may be. In Cuba, however, the colonial ruling class faced different circumstances, which, according to Allen, were reflected in the change of racial classifications imposed by the United States after its overthrow of the Cuban independence movement in the early 1900s. Lacking a Spanish colonial population of sufficient size and capital, and because of the backwardness of the *penisulares,* Spain could ill afford to bar not-"white" Cubans, including mulattos, Mexican Indians, and the Chinese,

56. *From Columbus to Castro: The History of the Caribbean, 1492–1969,* 68.

from the status of full citizenship. In reversing this policy of Spanish colonialism, the United States was opting for its own tried and true method of socially controlling the laboring classes: the centuries-old system of English/Anglo-American white racial oppression that Guillén in the late 1920s was always referring to worriedly as "el camino de Harlem" (the "Harlemization of Havana").[57]

In the United States, Hughes had experienced directly the effects of white racial oppression. The critical reception with which his first two volumes were greeted had demonstrated the power of white racial ideology over the treatment of literature and culture. Ironically, some of the most favorable reviews of his early poetry came from white southern journals, while many of the most virulent were authored by African American reviewers in the North. The similarities here between Marcus Garvey's reception in the United States and the treatment of Hughes are striking. Opponents of Garvey among the African American intelligentsia were fond of citing the Ku Klux Klan's endorsement of Garvey's Back to Africa platform as ultimate proof of his ideological backwardness and as a reason to oppose his movement. Yet next to the mass support that both Garvey and Hughes were garnering from the African American working classes, these criticisms fell flat. With the crisis of U.S. capitalism in the 1930s and the simultaneous emergence of the Popular Front strategy in the South as the Communist Party's answer to white racial oppression, the question of nationalism for Hughes would take on a different character. But in the 1920s black nationalism in the United States was still, in the main, associated with separatism and self-defeat. There did exist, though, an in-between position, exemplified by the cosmopolitan Vachal Lindsay, who was the first U.S. critic to celebrate the cross-cultural possibilities in Hughes's poetry. Nonetheless, in the 1920s the assertion of literary blackness was viewed as either a direct challenge to the assimilationist strivings of the black bourgeoisie or a charming embrace of the ways of black folk. In both cases, Hughes's writing as well as the aesthetic innovations he was seeking to advance were relegated to a minor status.

If in the United States cross-culturality was the vocation mainly of cosmopolitans, in Cuba it was the "central line" of a national-popular culture. As Franco suggests, in the colonial and neocolonial Americas, any national-popular art form arose from the oral tradition: what Kamau Brathwaite has termed in his important essay "History of the Voice" "na-

57. Allen, *Invention of the White Race,* 27; Nicolás Guillén, "El Camino de Harlem," 3–6.

tion language"—a "submerged, surrealist experience and sensibility, which has always been there and which is now increasingly coming to the surface and influencing the perceptions of contemporary Caribbean people." Not to be confused with *national* languages, such as Spanish, French, English, Dutch, or Portuguese, which were organized at the level of empire building and came at the direct expense of local European colonial languages (Basque, Welsh, Gaelic), as well as all the indigenous languages of the colonial hinterlands in Asia, Africa, and the New World, "nation language" is an emergent, thoroughly modern language produced from below. It is premised on the political circumstances of its illegalization. Therefore, the site of the oppressed community's struggle for self-determination is always the current status of this underground language, its facts and possibilities, as well as the oppressed community's involvement in the production of the nation's popular culture. Anything less is quickly subsumed by the consolidating reach and total control of the oppressor's language, that is, its methods of communication and its own aesthetic preferences. These antagonisms are felt on many fronts, but the point at which they all converge is, for Brathwaite, nation language. He says: "Nation language is the language that is influenced very strongly by the African model, the African aspect of our New World/Caribbean heritage. English it may be in terms of its syntax. And English it may be in terms of its lexicon, but it is not English in terms of its syntax. And English it certainly is not in terms of its rhythm and timbre, its own sound explosion."[58]

"Sound explosion" is a crucial concept for the arrival of an antagonistic cross-cultural aesthetics. The nation language provides a specific method by which oral poetry, popular genres of dance and music, and the spread of information and knowledge—through everyday forms such as rumor and gossip, storytelling and humor—can flourish. In Glissant's conception, the success of any nation language lies in its determination "not to disappear from the world scene." Because he was writing in the late seventies from the standpoint of what he called "non-production" in the francophone Caribbean, and in the face of yet another decade of French colonial rule in Martinique, his position can be easily misread to imply a rejection of rejection—a "defiance of despair," as he phrases it. But there is much more to it. Understood in isolation from the rest of America, whether from the singular standpoint of either Martinique or New York, the language question can give rise to either self-inflated or

58. "History of the Voice," 267, 273.

self-negating ideologies. But conceived as a realm of creative activity, language becomes a means of universalizing the rebellious popular elements that are the basis of any collective national identity. In other words, the idea of language as *total expression* links together the "three necessities" identified by Glissant in his theory of cross-cultural poetics: the class struggle; the emergence or the construction of the nation; and the quest for collective identity. Nation language achieves this by staying close to the politics of everyday life. "Total expression comes about," Brathwaite writes, "because people live in the open air, because people live in conditions of poverty, because people come from a historical experience where they had to rely on their own breath patterns rather than on paraphernalia like books and museums. They had to depend on *immanence,* the power within themselves, rather than the technology outside themselves."[59]

My point about cross-cultural aesthetics and Hughes is related to this Caribbean concept of "total expression." Glissant's cross-cultural poetics depends on a people's lived experience in a shared geographic space—what he has termed "functional syncretism." "Our lands share three common spaces," he contends: "the heights of the Andes, where the Amerindian world passionately endures, the plains and plateaus in the middle, where the pace of creolization quickens, the Caribbean sea, where the islands loom!" When everyday life in these common spaces gives birth to the expression of a specific situation, as in jazz music, a process of universalization occurs: "Musical styles that emerge and become established are really the necessary creations of places where entire communities are struggling, not in a state of sustained oblivion, but in the face of a major, unrelenting threat: the slums of Kingston where reggae slowly takes shape, the ghettos of New York where salsa bursts into life."[60]

In the 1920s African American and white American scholars and critics did not, in general, see things this way. For example, in 1925 the white liberal scholar Melville Herskovits argued that "black America represents a case of complete acculturation," a contention upheld by African American writers such as Countee Culllen, George S. Schuyler, and William Stanley Braithwaite in their denunciation of the New Negro movement in general and black poetry in particular. Schuyler's contemptuous attitude toward the idea of black culture, expressed in his claim that the African American is "merely a lampblacked Anglo-Saxon," came from the white ethnic immigrant, melting-pot notion of U.S. society—an ideology that

59. Glissant, *Caribbean Discourse,* 115; Brathwaite, "History of the Voice," 273.
60. *Caribbean Discourse,* 115.

was serving then as a futile threat to the emergent jazz and blues aesthetic to which Hughes had devoted himself as a creative artist. The ideology of liberal American pluralism advanced by Herksovits, and accepted uncritically by Cullen, Schuyler, and Braithwaite, was vigorously opposed by Hughes.[61] In his famous response to Schulyer, "The Negro Artist and the Racial Mountain," Hughes argued that one of the black writer's greatest challenges was to transform into literature the specificity of African American everyday experience, with its "heritage of rhythm and warmth, [and] incongruous humor that so often, as in the Blues, becomes ironic laughter mixed with tears." This required, in the first place, a rejection of white American pluralism, an ideology that urged all laboring-class Americans toward "whiteness," resulting in self-denial and the disappearance of a whole people. "To my mind," affirmed Hughes, "it is the duty of the younger Negro artist, if he accepts any duties at all from outsiders, to change through the force of his art that old whispering, 'I want to be white,' hidden in the aspirations of his people, to 'Why should I want to be white? I am a Negro—and beautiful!'" (CW 9:33, 35).

Adoption of whiteness precluded the black poet from pursuing in his or her literature the sources of creativity that black musicians, painters, dramatists, and sculptors had already discovered in their own work, namely, the philosophy of African American everyday life. Hughes's rejoinder to Schuyler would become in late 1960s a rallying cry for the new Black Aesthetic writers, who considered his manifesto the touchstone text in helping lead young black artists away from sterile white values and back to the original nexus of African American cultural production: the interlocking traditions of black music and dance and black vernacular expression. In *Blues People*, Amiri Baraka calls this return "the blues impulse." In "Songs Called the Blues," Hughes defined the blues with his characteristic emphasis on everyday struggle:

> There are many kinds of Blues. There are the family Blues, when a man and a woman have quarreled, and the quarrel can't be patched up. There's the loveless Blues, when you haven't even got anybody to quarrel with. And there's the left-lonesome Blues, when the one you care for's gone away. Then there's also the broke-and-hungry Blues, a stranger in a strange town. And the desperate going-to-the-river Blues. (CW 9:213)

61. See Onwuchekwa Jemie's discussion of the views of Cullen, Schuyler, and Braithwaite in *Langston Hughes: An Introduction to the Poetry*, 3–9.

Implicit in "The Negro Artist and the Racial Mountain" is the concept of cross-cultural poetics. The blues was not, for Hughes, a "race music," as it would soon become for a new generation of white Americans in the immediate postwar period. But neither was the blues a standard "American music," as the hostile middle-class critics of *The Weary Blues* and *Fine Clothes to the Jew* were always quick to claim. Instead, as Hughes would state a decade later in "To Negro Writers"—a position paper delivered at the first session of the American Writer's Congress in 1935—the blues is a working-class ideology. For the African American writer, Hughes contended, a new kind of thought had been opened up by the failure of white racial ideology to conceal the bourgeois class structures of poverty and racial oppression. While the immiseration of the working classes continued, the U.S. capitalist elite had, by 1935, conceded almost nothing to white workers while to African Americans they offered charity and more Jim Crow. Consequently, the culture produced in this period was weak: more blackface minstrelsy, this time on Broadway and through Hollywood. Hughes put it sharply: "Hollywood insofar as Negroes are concerned, might as well be controlled by Hitler."[62]

For Hughes, the problem with white American writers was that they had elevated everything *except* the blues to the level of the national-popular, cutting off in the process the creative base of their art. The blues, like the Cuban *son*, could unify African American and white American artists in a common fight against "all the economic roots of race hatred and race fear," Hughes said in "To Negro Writers," precisely because the blues was closest to "the *solid* ground of the daily working-class struggle to wipe out, now and forever, all the old inequalities of the past" (*CW* 9:132). The blues could help direct the energies of black and white writers to the urgent task of raising to national recognition the foundational role of African Americans in making U.S. society better—of establishing, to paraphrase Guillén on the *son*, "the serious contribution of one culture to another, in an incessant and vital interchange."[63]

62. Donald Ogden Stewart, *Fighting Words*, 62.
63. Guillén quoted in Selwyn R. Cudjoe, *Resistance and Caribbean Literature*, 247.

2

Socialism, Nationalism, and Nation-Consciousness

The Antinomies of Langston Hughes

> If there is something in the African past that is of great importance to us to-day, we in the Western world will be able to find it and develop it when we have gotten rid of—and are free of—the domination of these imperialist countries. Then we will be able to find and decide what we really want. That is an idea that is to be put forward as a law and advocate. You cannot find something about Africa if French imperialists and other people are sitting on you. Your first business is to fight against them and get rid of that, and make yourself free. Then you can decide what you really want; what is your past and how much of it you really want to keep.
>
> —C. L. R. James, *Black World*

Claude McKay's poem "Outcast" can be read as a statement of nation-consciousness. He wrote: "But the great western world holds me in fee, and I may never hope for full release while to its alien gods I bend my knee. Something in me is lost, forever lost, some vital thing has gone out of my heart, and I must walk the way of life a ghost among the sons of earth, a thing apart." While European nationalism is commonly seen as having arisen in the early nineteenth century, when "a scene of individ-ual cultures chasing after nationhood" was ubiquitous,[1] McKay's poem

1. The phrase is from Simon During's "Literature—Nationalism's Other? The Case for Revision," 139.

offers a countermyth, a systemic alternative to European national politi-cal consciousness. This new myth of origins arises from the social relations between culture and nation building, where the past of a people has not yet been internalized. In it, the chase after nationhood is felt, fortuitously, as a missed opportunity rather than as the telos of history. The distinction between nation-consciousness and European bourgeois nationalism rests on the existence of an immediately available or already internalized an-cestral past. Jean Baudrillard has recognized the distinction lucidly. "France is just a country," he says; "America is a concept." Discussing the importation of European cultural theory by the U.S. academy, Baudrillard continues in the same vein: "That was a gift of the French. They gave Americans a language they did not need. It was like the Statue of Liber-ty."[2] It is in this spirit that my definition of nation-consciousness can be elaborated; for, absent a long ancestral past, nation-consciousness at-tempts to recover everything at once, refusing either to follow a linear path backward or to launch forward in the track of some consensually de-rived vision of the future. Instead "nation logic" requires only that the op-pressed community assert itself, its myths and imagination, by any means within its grasp.

In *Caribbean Discourse*, Edouard Glissant has argued that when an op-pressed nation-people cannot rely on a time-honored cultural hinterland, its members go underground and create a semiautonomous system of cultural production, drawing on everything that helps them endure as a people. Nation-consciousness is a logic an entire people produces. More, "nation-logic" is an *unreconstructed* community's drive for international recognition through national legitimacy. Its system of aesthetics is not part of the national community's consolidation but rather a struggle for new social relationships: relationships founded on the startling diversity of the new nation builders themselves.

One bridge between these two distinct nation drives—the bourgeois metropolitan one and that of the decolonizing proletarian world—was the art of Claude McKay. As a disillusioned Jamaican national, McKay brought to the United States a concept of nation-consciousness that was new to African American literature and culture. Aimé Césaire credited McKay's second novel, *Banjo* (1929), with initiating the Négritude move-ment in Latin America, Africa, the Caribbean, and the United States. Amiri Baraka, in his reconsideration of Négritude, supported Césaire's claim, arguing that McKay's lasting contribution was his call for a "move-

2. Jean Baudrillard, "Continental Drift: Questions for Jean Baudrillard."

ment of national self-consciousness, and then self-affirmation." Baraka argued that Leopold Senghor, Leon Damas, McKay, and Césaire "had declared themselves traitors to their class, openly breaking, at least on the surface, with the bourgeois assimilationist West Indian writers of the colonized mentality."[3]

But, according to Baraka, the break with European bourgeois racial ideologies was only partial. As a consequence, the Négritude movement advocated by McKay soon split into two opposing tendencies: black cultural nationalism and revolutionary black nationalism, with Senghor and Damas representing the former and Césaire the latter. In Baraka's terms, the cultural nationalist tendency "gave rise to an intensifying nationalism, a calling forth of a nationalist national bourgeoisie to replace the comprador assimilationist bourgeoisie, which helped to stabilize the earlier colonialism." In the revolutionary nationalist tendency, on the other hand, "there is self-knowledge, self-affirmation, and the move to liberation. Blackness is not a static, mystical, 'eternal' cultural quality; it is concrete consciousness and with that, concrete struggle."[4]

McKay's own insight was to have anticipated this ideological split within the Négritude movement by shifting the hitherto and limited critique of European "cultural values" to an openly antagonistic attack on European and Anglo-American colonialist ideology, which is presented powerfully in *Banjo*—the book that announced to the world the arrival of an international Black Arts movement. As Baraka has it:

> It was the openness, vitality, humanity, reality of black life and feelings, and the passionate embrace of black people and black life and the will to struggle to raise it to a higher level that attracted Senghor and others to the Harlem Renaissance. The emerging national consciousness of the Afro-American people was being taken up and turned to good account by a similar nationalist intelligentsia. The United States was the most advanced capitalist country, and the illusion called bourgeois democracy was being pushed to its furthest limits. Within the state the Afro-American people in their struggle for development exploded in self-consciousness and self-affirmation. Whether it was movement of the twenties or the bashing entrance of big-band jazz, the shots heard around the world.[5]

3. Glissant, *Caribbean Discourse*, 90–95; Baraka, "Aimé Césaire," 327.
4. Baraka, "Aimé Césaire," 324, 329.
5. Ibid., 327–28.

On the edge of this new nation-consciousness movement, McKay could imagine a black national identity without the old European nationalism: an ideology he equated rightly with reinvented forms of white supremacy. Yet he found it difficult to resolve the double-consciousness, or antinomy, of *Banjo*'s protagonist, the West Indian intellectual Ray. Attracted to Tolstoy and Rimbaud but completely untouched by their ideas, and equally ambivalent about the notion of a heroic African past, Ray identifies with the everyday struggle of black migrant workers in Marseilles. For Ray, "Close association with the Jakes and the Banjoes had been like participating in a common primitive birthright." The experience led him to oppose the Du Boisian concept of the veil:

> To Ray the Negro was one significant and challenging aspect of the human life of the world as a whole. A certain school of Negro intellectuals had contributed their best to the "problem" by presenting the race wearing a veil with sanctimonious Selahs. There was never any presentation more ludicrous. From his experience, it was white people who were the great wearers of veils, shadowing their lives and the lives of other peoples by them. Negroes were too fond of the sunny open ways of living, to hide behind any kind of veil. If the Negro had to be defined, there was every reason to define him as a challenge rather than a "problem" to Western civilization.[6]

In contrast to Du Bois, McKay is proud of not having any ancestral heartland on which to depend. "The sentiment of patriotism was not one of Ray's possessions," McKay wrote, "perhaps because he was a child of deracinated ancestry. To him it was a poisonous seed that had, of course, been planted in his child's mind, but happily, not having any traditional soil to nourish it, it had died out with other weeds of the curricula of education in the light of mature thought."[7] The turn McKay advocates in *Banjo* is toward the formation of nation-conscious artists and intellectuals. Ray is the prototype, and what he concludes at the end of his experiences with the black workers of Marseilles could be read as a main strand of the aesthetic manifesto running through his text:

> He was of course aware that whether the educated man be white or brown or black, he cannot, if he has more than animal desires, be irre-

6. McKay, *Banjo*, 321, 372–73.
7. Ibid., 137.

sponsibly happy like the ignorant man who lives simply by his instincts and appetites. Any man with an observant and contemplative mind must be aware of that. But a black man, even though educated, was in closer biological kinship to the swell of primitive earth life. And maybe his apparent failing under the organization of the modern world was the real strength that preserved him from becoming the thing that was the common white creature of it.[8]

McKay's use of reification to understand "whiteness" was his conceptual breakthrough, a move that would make him an intellectual hero to the poets and theorists of the 1960s Black Arts movement.[9] But unless one reads *biological kinship* as a political symbol for "race feeling," as the Harlem Renaissance writers often phrased it, there arises in his manifesto an antinomy: either the "white thing" is an ideological invention or it is biologically or civilizationally determined, *in advance*. The latter position would amount to a reconstitution of European racial ideology in inverted terms: blackness over whiteness in a timeless and permanent battle between warring "racial" civilizations. On the other hand, the former would require an ideological rejection of the "white race" on behalf of building a new anti-imperialist cultural front—what Houston Baker has termed "an ancestral matrix"—one that could involve nation-conscious writers, students, teachers, and workers directly in liberatory artistic activity.[10] McKay never finally resolves the contradiction between the two positions. But in *Banjo* one passage in the final pages moves beyond this antinomy and sets the stage for the emergence of Langston Hughes as the first American nation-conscious socialist writer of the twentieth century. Not surprisingly, the passage is about the language question:

> But [Ray] admired the black boy's unconscious artistic capacity for eliminating the rotten-dead stock words of the proletariat and replacing them with startling new ones. There was no dots and dashes in their conversations—nothing that could not be frankly said and therefore de-

8. Ibid., 323.

9. Addison Gayle's tribute to McKay, *Claude McKay: The Black Poet at War* (1974), is one of the best examples of the Black Arts movement's positive revaluation of McKay's legacy. Gayle suggests that McKay was the first "warrior-poet" of the African American tradition: "He performed this task well . . . so well, in fact, that here, during the latter part of the twentieth-century, when younger, more determined Black men carry on the war against cultural imperialism, his poetry serves as a living inspiration for those who refuse to bow down at the feet of alien gods" (18).

10. Houston A. Baker Jr., *Blues, Ideology, and Afro-American Literature,* 2.

cently—no act or fact of life for which they could not find a simple pass-able word. He gained from them the finer nuances of the necromancy of language and the wisdom that any word may be right and magical in its proper setting.[11]

McKay to Hughes:
Add on to the Cipher

Negroes were faced with a choice between racialism and radicalism.

—John Henrik Clarke, *Marcus Garvey and the Vision of Africa*

The folk were not the untutored; they were the teachers.

—Sterling Brown, "Arna Bontemps: Co-worker, Comrade"

In April 1921, McKay joined the staff of Max Eastman's magazine the *Liberator.* Two years earlier Langston Hughes had left Central High in Cleveland, Ohio, to spend the summer in Toluca, Mexico, with his father, James. The two events are linked by the fact that at Central, where red flags lined the hallways and John Reed's *Ten Days That Shook the World* was required reading, Hughes had read the *Liberator* religiously. Since April 1919, the *Liberator* had published McKay's poetry, which inspired Hughes to become a poet. "It was Claude McKay's example that started me on this track," said Hughes to those who asked about his embrace of the Bolshevik Revolution and his decision to write poetry from a black so-cialist perspective. McKay would become a trusted friend; although he and Hughes met only a few times, their correspondence was regular. Ac-cording to Arnold Rampersad, many of these exchanges were motivated explicitly by their shared antagonism toward and frustration with the pol-itics of the African American middle class.[12]

One of Hughes's confrontations with the African American middle class, which elicited promptly a letter of congratulations from McKay, happened in 1928 during his final year at Lincoln University. Disgusted at the "obvious incompetence" of the all-white Lincoln faculty and em-barrassed by the "horse play, lack of attention, bad manners and rude-ness" on the part of the all-black middle-class student body, Hughes set

11. McKay, *Banjo,* 321.
12. The correspondence of McKay and Hughes is quoted in Rampersad, *Life of Langston Hughes,* 1:30–31, 105–6.

out to "shatter the peace." In a comprehensive cultural studies project—an examination of Lincoln's history, its physical plant, the faculty, the student body, and especially the clubs and fraternities—he concluded that Lincoln must start a campaign to recruit African American scholars and teachers; begin offering cultural studies courses in English, philosophy, and history; improve the quality of food and services; do away with the existing black "bourgeois" fraternities; and overhaul the entire library system, which in his assessment was stocked with obsolete books. Hughes's survey caused an uproar at Lincoln and grabbed the attention of the African American intelligentsia in Boston, Washington, D.C., and New York, who registered mixed feelings about the survey's conclusions. McKay heard of Hughes's project in France and quickly sent Hughes an enthusiastic endorsement.[13]

Five years later in Moscow, Hughes would once again attack the African American middle class from a position closely aligned to McKay's. At a talk on the state of African American literature given at the Foreign Library, he called McKay "the outstanding living Negro writer," while referring ironically to Countee Cullen as "our Keats and Shelley" and to Walter White as "a white Negro." "What the class-conscious workers think of him [White]," said Hughes, "I will not repeat here. It would be too obscene." Nearly fifteen years had passed since he first read McKay's works, and by 1933 little had remained of the literary Harlem Renaissance. If the Harlem Renaissance was for Hughes a middle-class phenomenon, the writing of McKay represented an alternative black arts movement, what the elder statesman of African American literature, Sterling Brown, preferred to call the "New Negro movement." This movement had its social origins not in the black and white middle classes of New York, Boston, and Washington, D.C., but in the dispossessed rural proletariat of the black South and the Midwest. In his seminal *Negro Poetry and Drama* (1934), Brown argued that the five main contributions made by the New Negro movement to African American literature and culture were: (1) a rediscovery of Africa as a source for race pride; (2) the use of black heroes and heroic episodes from American history; (3) a propaganda of protest; (4) the treatment of black laborers (frequently of the rural proletariat, less often of the industrial workers) with more understanding and less apology; and (5) franker and deeper self-revelation.[14]

13. Ibid., 1:170–71.
14. Ibid.; Sterling Brown, "Arna Bontemps: Co-worker, Comrade," 95, and *Negro Poetry and Drama and The Negro in American Fiction*, 61.

To emphasize the class distinctions that obtained in the work of Alain Locke, James Weldon Johnson, Du Bois, and Jessie Fauset as compared to that of Hughes, himself, and Arna Bontemps, Brown routinely put quotation marks around the term *Harlem Renaissance*. Hughes, Bontemps, and Brown were not part of "that motley crew," he argued, because "any fool who thinks that Harlem could teach any elements of the high life to New Orleans and St. Louis at the turn of the century ought to have his head examined and stop writing books." Moreover, Brown's impatience with what he called in 1973 "those pundits on black literature," specifically David Littlejohn and Robert A. Bone—two white American scholars of the Harlem Renaissance who claimed that Bontemps's work was an outgrowth of what happened in the northern urban centers during the 1920s—stemmed from the exclusion of Bontemps and other southern and midwestern writers from the new wave of African American canon formation in the late 1960s and early 1970s, which the Black Liberation movement had stimulated. In his response to these developments, Brown spared no one. Under attack were not only the "white pontifical know-it-alls" but also the leading Black Aesthetic poets and theorists, as well as a host of African American critics and historians, all of whom "are cavalier to or ignorant of *Black Thunder,* Arna Bontemps's masterpiece." Of the Black Aesthetic writers, Brown wrote: "The experts on REVOLT, such as Amiri Baraka, Lawrence Neal, Louis Lomax, Eldridge Cleaver and Stokely Carmichael, write as if they had never heard of *Black Thunder,* but it was not so long ago that these cats had never heard of John Brown either, much less of Harriet Tubman, Sojourner Truth, Nat Turner, or Amistad."[15]

Evident in Brown's overview of the New Negro movement and in his critique of the Black Aesthetic writers, as well as of the white liberal critics of black literature, is a creative tension between nation-consciousness and black cultural nationalism. On the one hand, Brown rejects the turn to Africa on the part of the Black Aesthetic writers; on the other, he praises the "rediscovery of Africa as a source of race pride" in the poetry of the New Negro movement. He criticizes the Black Aesthetic poets for writing "Black" ("if there is such a monstrosity," Brown put it), but valorizes the writing of Bontemps in which "the live rural speech" of African American laborers is given supple expression. He chastises the advocates of Black Power for their fixation on promoting black revolt, yet in his considerations of the New Negro movement he endorses the use of literature for this same purpose—what he termed the "propaganda of protest."

15. Brown, "Arna Bontemps," 94.

What seemed to dismay Brown about the Black Aesthetic writers was their quickness to move forward without ever having looked back. The innovations in orthography, the use of African words, and the wearing of dashikis and "obsession with hair," in Brown's words, amounted to mere wish fulfillment, not an intellectual rediscovery of Africa.[16]

For Brown, the indifference toward Arna Bontemps's life and work among the new poets indicated that there had been no backward glance and was symptomatic of a much deeper crisis in African American literature and culture. The new black poets, some of whom had been students of Brown's at Howard University, were indeed operating with the logic of nation-consciousness, but at the same time they were self-destructively breaking ties with what many of them referred to derisively as "the Forties Negroes": the generation of African American writers such as Margaret Walker, Hughes, Brown, and Bontemps who had spent their lives creating the very cultural hinterland from which the new poets were now turning away with scorn and personal embarrassment. In his first autobiography, *The Big Sea* (1940), Hughes captured the essence of the so-called Forties Negro in an account of his break with the infamous white patron of black arts, the "Godmother" Charlotte Mason:

> She wanted me to be primitive and know and feel the intuitions of the primitive. But, unfortunately, I did not feel the rhythms of the primitive surging through me, and so I could not live and write as though I did. I was only an American Negro—who had loved the surface of Africa and the rhythms of Africa—but I was not Africa. I was Chicago and Kansas City and Broadway and Harlem. And I was not what she wanted me to be. So, in the end it all came back very near to the old impasse of white and Negro again, white and Negro—as do most relations in America. (*CW* 13:243)

In the 1960s, the idea that the fate of American civilization was a white problem, not the concern of African American artists, had been reconstituted by black cultural workers through the heroization of McKay and the forgetting of Brown, Bontemps, and Hughes. In this context, it is easy to see from Hughes's statement about Africa—"I was not Africa"—why such a radical break with the so-called Forties Negro was called for by the Black Aesthetic writers. If the United States was culturally and socially diseased, the last thing on the agenda was a rediscovery of the roots of

16. Ibid., 91, 95.

black culture *in* the United States—on poisoned soil. Such an approach would also have the highly undesirable effect of raising the United States's international stature in the face of massive upheavals in the de-colonizing world and, consequently, drawing into the orbit of U.S. cultural imperialism the newly independent nations of Africa and the Caribbean. It is in this sense that the emergence of black cultural nationalism in the late 1960s was neither the irruption of nation-consciousness (the re-creation of the folk) nor the assertion of anticolonial revolutionary black nationalism (McKay's and Garvey's popular notion of "the Negro challenge to Western civilization"). Instead, black nationalism marked a rejection of this impasse altogether, which had been attributed by the theorists of the Black Power movement to a long history of ideological vacillation and double-consciousness on the part of middle-class African American intellectuals.

Brown's admonition to the advocates of Black Power in their own journal, *Black World,* was meant to steer them back to the "ancestral matrix," to use Baker's term, of black struggle in the United States: to the black cultural hinterland on which their lives as artists and intellectuals ultimately depended. The final lines of Brown's essay express this point clearly: "I close this tribute with a blues line, and the question asked above by black critic Dudley Randall: *Who will replace these men?* Nobody will replace Arna (or me either, for I am the last remaining on the Montage). Nobody will replace Arna, I repeat. There are some men who are irreplaceable. The blues line runs: *Another good man done gone.*"[17] The references to Arna Bontemps and himself are, in this passage, signifiers of a whole cultural hinterland, not old intellectual authorities to whom the new generation must pay homage before going its own way. Failure to rediscover and then project forward the cultural hinterland would result in disaster, Brown warned: it would leave the new generation's progeny with African names, words, rituals, and fashions but not a trace of the living social heritage that is the only thing standing between African Americans and cultural annihilation.

As a generational critique, Brown's sharp criticism of the Black Aesthetic writers is straightforward enough, yet it misses what Houston Baker in *Blues, Ideology, and Afro-American Literature* has termed their attempt "to situate [the artistic word's] various manifestations within a continuum of verbal behavior in Afro-American culture." In Baker's view, the Black Aesthetic writers were seeking "to understand the continuum with-

17. Ibid., 97.

in the complex webs of interacting cultural systems that ultimately give meaning to such words." Baker's concept of "complex webs" will be helpful in understanding Hughes's approach to popular culture and avant-garde aesthetics.[18]

Looking back on Brown's tersely composed critique from the age of hip-hop culture, one can see its prescience; the feeling among today's black youth that they have been abandoned by the civil rights generation and left to struggle on their own is ubiquitous. In response, the task of rediscovering the black cultural hinterland has been taken on by the hip-hop generation often to the exclusion of all other goals and interests, including the "propaganda of protest" function of black art that so many critics of hip-hop have angrily denounced the music for lacking. But hip-hop's situation is this way for reasons Brown had already spelled out in his 1973 essay. Rather than laying blame on the doorsteps of those who refused to listen to Brown when it mattered most, it is better to identify and describe that cultural hinterland on which everything depends and to which hip-hop culture, for one, has single-mindedly devoted itself.

Hughes's poetry is compelling partly because it is one mode of cultural production among the more than a dozen he mastered during his lifetime. By the time of his passing in 1967, Hughes had written for radio, authored screenplays for Hollywood, mastered the libretto, and become a skilled sloganeer and a savvy journalist, in addition to being an accomplished artist in children's literature, an authority in folklore, a musicologist, a newspaper columnist, a humorist, a playwright, an essayist, an editor, an anthologist, a theater director, a translator, a writing teacher, a novelist, a short-story writer, and a popular lecturer. This eclecticism, in fact, is one of the main features of the New Negro movement as a whole: an approach to cultural work that sees culture itself as a many-fronted way of life and thus asserts black culture's central place in all aspects of American social and political development and change. Rediscovery of the black cultural hinterland required a full-scale immersion in every aspect of American social and intellectual life. Moreover, to choose one mode of cultural production to the exclusion of any other implied that African American culture was somehow incapable of expressing the totality of America and, worse, that African American culture might be merely a "minority discourse" and thus limited in what it has done, and continues to do, to profoundly shape U.S. history and society.

Hughes's legendary essay "The Negro Artist and the Racial Mountain"

18. Baker, *Blues, Ideology, and Literature,* 26.

posed a direct challenge to the rhetoric of "minority discourse"—which, inverted ironically, is much better suited to the white ethnic immigrant experience than to that of the native African American. Hughes argued for the usefulness of the African American writer's special, centuries-old location in U.S. society, and against the prevailing notion that blackness was a hindrance to artistic expression due to its connections to minority "race politics." The New Negro movement broke with the middle-class racial common sense of African American intellectuals such as Countee Cullen and George S. Schuyler, who had rejected the idea of a distinctly African American poetry. Hughes and the New Negro writers pushed this tension to its limits by rejecting blackness as a "minority discourse" and by advancing, simultaneously, the idea that black culture was actually the central line of all U.S. popular art and literature.

In his review of *The Weary Blues* for *Opportunity* magazine, Cullen found Hughes's poetry promising yet questioned whether his literary blues and jazz pieces should be considered poetry. But the real attack was Cullen's claim that "there is too much emphasis here on strictly Negro themes." Not surprisingly, this aspect of *The Weary Blues* was applauded by McKay, who found the poem "Cross"—Hughes's first "mulatto" poem—the best of the entire volume. He wrote to Hughes from France that the poem "shows that while others are vainly prating about artistic freedom among Negro writers, you have won out over all obstacles. You have opened up new vistas by touching a subject that thousands of Afro-Americans feel and yet would be afraid to touch."[19] The poem is about "racial" intermixing; as in Guillén's "Ballad of the Two Grandfathers," the fact of mulattoness (or *mestizaje*) is seen by Hughes as a distinct advantage rather than a dilution of blackness or a mark of either "racial" shame or danger. By voicing the everyday language of African Americans in speech forms such as the ballad, the ditty, and the blues, Hughes raised "racial" intermixing to a sign of honor and popular appreciation. There were special powers of insight and perspective specific to the African American racial experience in the United States, and radical aesthetic possibilities in its social location, that had yet to be fully acknowledged:

> My old man died in a fine big house.
> My ma died in a shack.
> I wonder where I'm gonna die,
> Being neither white nor black? (CW 1:37)

19. Countee Cullen, "Poet on Poet," 73–74; McKay quoted in Rampersad, *Life of Langston Hughes*, 1:129.

The dismissal by the leading intellectuals of the Harlem Renaissance of the mulatto theme as a subject worthy of literary expression is an important aspect of Hughes's relationship to the two conflicting nation logics. Writing from a nation-conscious standpoint, McKay praised the poem for its honesty and self-criticism. Cullen, on the other hand, found it inappropriate, suggesting that the use of "strictly Negro themes," such as the "mulatto" experience, made the Harlem Renaissance writers susceptible to a new round of charges from white American critics that the combination of "race feeling" and poetry produced inferior art. A year later Hughes would receive the harshest criticisms yet. His second volume of poetry, *Fine Clothes to the Jew* (1927), brought the wrath of white and black literary critics alike and mobilized a whole contingent of African American journalists and commentators against him. Under the headline "Sewer Dweller," William M. Kelley of the *New York Amsterdam News* called the book "100 pages of trash"; in its infamous review the *Chicago Whip* named Hughes "the poet 'low-rate' of Harlem." A year later Claude McKay would be attacked in much the same way and by the same opponents for his first novel, *Home to Harlem*. Du Bois, who had kept silent on the Hughes controversy, criticized *Home to Harlem* for glorifying black ghetto life. Saying that the novel gave him "the distinct feeling of taking a bath," Du Bois was ambivalent about this new turn in African American literary aesthetics.[20]

Du Bois's position on the uses of blackness in African American art and culture was in fact closely aligned to that of the New Negro writers from the Black Belt and the Midwest, such as Margaret Walker, Hughes, Brown, and Bontemps, who were stressing the need to develop an independent black national literary tradition before going on to the rediscovery of Africa as a source of race pride, and to develop and expand this tradition by looking to the African American working classes for artistic forms and aesthetic preferences. Du Bois had articulated this position in the opening chapter of *The Souls of Black Folk*, using the trope of the "American Negro," a revision of the older civilizational one of "the Negro." The latter term had been advanced as a universal category in the late nineteenth century by the founders of black nationalism: Bishop Henry McNeal Turner, Martin Delany, Dr. Edward Wilmot Blyden, and Alexander Crummell. Although Du Bois himself authored a modern version of the concept in *The*

---

20. Quoted in Rampersad, *Life of Langston Hughes,* 1:140; for Du Bois's comments on *Home to Harlem,* see his review, "Two Novels: Nella Larsen, *Quicksand,* and Claude McKay, *Home to Harlem.*"

Negro (1915), he hesitated to raise it to the status of a metaphysical category. In the chapter "Of Our Spiritual Strivings" in *Souls*, for example, where he formulated the concept of the veil, which McKay would later reject in *Banjo*, Du Bois asserted what would become the organizing principle of the New Negro movement:

> The history of the American Negro is the history of this strife—this longing to attain self-conscious manhood, to merge his double self into a better and truer self. In this merging, he wishes neither of the older selves to be lost. He would not Africanize America, for America has too much to teach the world and Africa. He would not bleach his soul in a flood of white Americanism, for he knows that Negro blood has a message for the world. He simply wishes to make it possible for a man to be both a Negro and an American, without being cursed and spit upon by his fellows, without having the doors of Opportunity closed in his face.[21]

By 1926, Du Bois's concept of the "American Negro" had been reappropriated by Hughes. Ten years later, it was revised through Hughes's experiment with a new archetype: the North American mestizo. It was a bold move, for as a positive valuation of mestizoness the new literary trope advanced Du Bois's concept of the "American Negro" precisely by providing it a more aesthetically supple and antagonistic form of expression. Du Bois's thesis in the first chapter of *Souls* is that the American Negro, as a distinct social type, has always been present in American society, making the struggle for black equality all the more urgent and fundamental. The task for Du Bois was, in part, to persuade white liberal bourgeois artists and intellectuals to raise the American Negro historical experience to the level of national-popular culture. As we will see, Hughes began from this Du Boisian departure point but chose to use a decidedly "non-American" set of terms to carry out the task.

First, Hughes had been inspired to write poetry by a combination of "non-American" influences and circumstances. According to Du Bois's presentation in *Souls*, Claude McKay and the communist *Liberator* magazine were on the periphery of American social life—were "non-American"—and each a different side of the same coin: the inorganic or cosmopolitan resolution of a distinctly American national problem—the color line. Du Bois had found McKay guilty of "Africanizing" America in *Home to Harlem* and devoted no more than a paragraph or two to criticism of the American Communist Party (CPUSA) throughout the decade of 1920s. In

21. Du Bois, *The Souls of Black Folk*, 45–46.

1924, Du Bois had in fact upheld the position of African American theologian J. W. C. Pennington: "The colored population of the United States has no destiny separate from that of the nation in which they form an integral part. Our destiny is bound up with that of America."[22] This remained Du Bois's thesis, although it was sharply revised in *Black Reconstruction* to mean the destiny of the U.S. working classes.

Du Bois saw nothing in the CPUSA of the 1920s to convince him that anything other than "white Americanism" was coming from the party's organizers and theoreticians. If the two opposing forces—black cultural nationalism and white American socialism—were ever brought together, he warned, powerful tensions would collide, explode, and wreak havoc for the socially fragile African American middle class. Du Bois was proved correct on this point, for the most vicious attacks on his leadership role in African American politics, and the black middle class more generally, came from the Afro-Caribbean communist Richard B. Moore. Moore repeatedly called Du Bois an "opportunist Negro bourgeois-nationalist" and accused him and the African American intelligentsia of "doing the dirty work of the bosses by attempting to stir up the Negro masses against the white workers."[23]

Second, Du Bois's opposition to Garvey turned on the mestizo question. For Hughes to raise that question to the level of a major social contradiction and then finesse it indicated that he sided with Garvey and McKay rather than with Du Bois. In his first critique of Garveyism, the essay "Back to Africa" (1923), Du Bois made the point that, historically, the more self-disciplined and self-conscious the African American middle class became, the less of a hold did white racial ideology have in U.S. society as a whole. It continues to be a provocative analysis, yet he registered it at the time to remind Harlem Garveyites of how different the racial situation they were facing was from that of blacks in the West Indies. To win the support of African Americans, Du Bois argued, the Garvey movement had to do away with the Caribbean ideology of "race" altogether:

> There were still obvious advantages to the negro American of lighter hue in passing for white or posing as Spanish or Portuguese, but the pressing demand for ability and efficiency and honesty within this fighting, advancing group continually drove the color line back before reason and necessity, and it came to be generally regarded as the poorest

22. Du Bois, "The Negro and Democracy," 78.
23. Quoted in Harold Cruse, *The Crisis of the Negro Intellectual: A Historical Analysis of the Failure of Black Leadership,* 145.

possible taste for a negro even to refer to differences of color. Colored folks as white as the whitest came to describe themselves as negroes. Imagine, then, the surprise and disgust of these Americans when Garvey launched his Jamaican color scheme.[24]

Du Bois was responding to a particular Caribbean way of seeing "race." Reflecting on his treatment by the mulatto middle class in Jamaica, Garvey had stated this concept of race lucidly:

Men and women as black as I and even more so, had believed themselves white under the West Indian order of society. I was simply an impossible man to use openly the term "negro"; yet every one beneath his breath was calling the black man a "nigger." I had to decide whether to please my friends and be one of the "black-whites" of Jamaica, and help improve and protect the integrity of the black millions, and suffer. I decided to do the latter.[25]

In *Marcus Garvey and the Vision of Africa,* John Henrik Clarke clarified the historical context of Garveyism's explosive arrival in the United States:

The Negro's disillusionment had mounted with the progress of the World War. Negro soldiers had suffered all forms of Jim Crow, humiliation, discrimination, slander, and even violence at the hands of the white civilian population. After the war there was a resurgence of Ku Klux Klan influence; and another decade of racial hatred and open lawlessness had set in, and Negroes again were prominent among the victims. Meantime, administration leaders quite pointedly tried to persuade Negroes that, in spite of their full participation in the war effort, they could expect no change in their status in America. . . . The liberal white citizens were disturbed by events, but took little action beyond viewing with alarm. . . . Negroes were ready for a Moses, and only a Black man could express the depth of their feelings. Intellectuals of the race tried to rationalize the situation, but not so the broad masses; their ideological leader, Du Bois, had gone overboard on the war effort and now found himself estranged from his people. Negroes were faced with a choice between racialism and radicalism. Marcus Garvey settled the question for thousands by forming the United States branch of the Universal Negro Improvement Association (UNIA) and preaching with

24. Du Bois, "Back to Africa," 109–10.
25. Quoted in John Henrik Clarke, ed., *Marcus Garvey and the Vision of Africa,* 8.

great zeal for a pilgrimage of Black men "back to Africa." He rallied men to the slogan, "Africa for Africans!"[26]

In Hughes's poem "Cross," this powerful tension between Du Boisian equalitarianism and Garvey's and McKay's nation-consciousness is felt at its most concrete level: a recognition of the *fact* of "racial" intermixing *despite the systemic and brutally enforced Jim Crow laws against it*. Yet the tension is not resolved or sublimated into an essential or normative (color caste) identity, which had been Du Bois's concern with Garveyism. Instead, the poem rides the edge of the two conflicting tendencies in search of the politically enabling tensions between them rather than the point in which they fuse together and crystallize. Sometimes called the anti-utopian logic of "the blues impulse," Hughes's gesture in the poem produces more of what Amiri Baraka termed in *Blues People* "the Negro as non-American."[27]

As the movement of U.S. imperialist power into the Caribbean and Latin America continued, the resocialization of the "white American citizen" became, in the interwar period especially, an immediate concern of the U.S. ruling class. The social type of the God-fearing, hard-working, patriotic, and law-abiding American required a new form of white democratization, since the old structures of the plantation colony had finally been broken and overhauled by the capitalist classes of both the North and the South, and with them the older forms of plantation social control. New forms were needed, and the rapidly expanding blues and jazz movement of the 1930s and 1940s provided ample ideological resources, as well as the aesthetic means, to help complete the task. But, as Baraka maintains:

> If the blues was a music that developed because of the Negro's adaptation to, and adoption of, America, it was also a music that developed because of the Negro's peculiar position in this country. Early blues, as it came to differ from the shout and the Afro-Christian religious music, was also perhaps the most impressive expression of the Negro's individuality within the superstructures of American society. Even though its birth and growth seems connected finally to the general movement of the mass of black Americans into the central culture of the country, blues still went back for its impetus and emotional meaning to the individual, to his completely personal life and death.[28]

26. Ibid., 9.
27. *Blues People: Black Music in White America*, 1.
28. Ibid., 67.

Here the stakes of Hughes's revision of the mulatto trope become much more evident, in terms of his relation to Du Boisian equalitarianism, black cultural nationalism, and liberatory socialism. Working as a "permanent persuader," in the Gramscian sense, Du Bois in the 1920s elaborated an ideology of black liberation struggle that reasserted the community's right to national self-determination, a primary role in the struggle for democracy and equality on U.S. soil, and thus the need for racial solidarity regardless of skin tone or class origin. His ideology rejected cultural nationalism just as it rejected ideologies of the "pure"—that is, white— American class struggle.

On the other side of Du Boisian equalitarianism was the CPUSA, which remained committed to the peculiarly white liberal notion of interracial (or "interethnic") solidarity within a white-only labor movement. It was Lenin's genius to sense this kind of contradiction, for everything changed in 1928 when his 1915 thesis on national self-determination was converted by the American party into a full-fledged organizational strategy. The party's successful defense of the Scottsboro Boys, as well as the impressive victories won by the Alabama communists during the Depression, was put in motion by this critical change in strategy. As Robin Kelley has observed, the Black Belt thesis asserted that, as an oppressed nation,

> African-Americans had the right to self-determination: political power, control over the economy, and the right to secede from the United States. In 1930 the resolution was altered to account for the differences between the North and the South. Northern blacks, the new resolution argued, sought integration and assimilation, and therefore the demand for self-determination was to be applied exclusively to the South.[29]

Mark Naison in *Black Communists in Harlem during the Depression* records systematically and analyzes perspicaciously the outcome of the 1930 resolution. As he shows, the resolution brought the CPUSA into direct competition with the mainstream of U.S. liberal bourgeois pluralism, white ethnic organized labor, the NAACP, black churches, and the growing black labor movement. The competition was for the loyalty and direct participation of new working-class constituencies: poor whites on the one hand and the new urban communities of migrant African American and Afro-Caribbean laborers on the other. The tension would ultimately force an organizational and hence political crisis within the Harlem party.[30]

29. Kelley, *Hammer and Hoe*, 13.
30. *Black Communists in Harlem during the Depression*, 52.

At the same time, this crisis point—crystallized in the October 1933 removal of one of the most popular black communists in Harlem, Cyril Briggs, as editor of the *Harlem Liberator*—produced a new opening for African American artists aligned with Du Boisian equalitarianism and the New Negro movement. For fear of squandering the formidable gains made during the first year of the Scottsboro case, the CPUSA quickly made overtures to Harlem artists, regardless of whether they accepted the party's policy on the "Negro Question," which had remained, self-servingly, an assimilationist one. Moreover, the party's reversal on black nationalism and its shift toward popular frontism had been prefigured by African American communists James Ford and Otto Hall when they argued, unsuccessfully, against Lenin's self-determination thesis at the Sixth Comintern in 1928. As Harry Haywood noted at the time, Ford and Hall's opposition to the Black Belt thesis "separated racism, the most salient external manifestation of black oppression, from its socio-economic roots, reducing the struggle for equality to a movement against prejudice. It was a theory which even liberal reformists could support."[31] The CPUSA had begun to see things Haywood's way.

The successful recruitment of Langston Hughes into the ranks of the CPUSA's Scottsboro Defense Organization—arguably one of the party's greatest victories on the cultural front—was an originary moment in U.S. labor history. For the first time, revolutionary black nationalism and Euro-American socialism found a dynamic point of contact that produced neither black nationalist nor communist ideology. Instead, as an examination of Hughes's popular chapbook *A New Day* will show, the point of contact made possible in the United States a politicization of the cross-cultural aesthetic through a compelling experiment with a new American structure of feeling. In Hughes's "Cross," where this new structure of feeling is first expressed, the interstice between black cultural nationalism, Du Boisian equalitarianism, and Euro-American socialism was the enigmatic mestizo experience itself, for this North American mestizo—unnameable prior to Hughes—was at home neither in black cultural nationalism nor in the internationalism of the CPUSA. This very personal sense of exile was for Hughes the source of a new kind of blues.

As Baraka stressed in *Blues People*, the blues impulse "to go back to the individual" came in response to the artificial homogenization, and eventual sterilization, of mainstream American culture. Hughes sensed the danger of any such white democratization of the American citizen, since

31. Haywood, *Black Bolshevik: Autobiography of an Afro-American Communist*, 254.

under racial democracy—the mass allocation of anomalous white-skin privileges to laboring-class Euro-Americans, on the condition they keep blacks down and out—the dissemination and reproduction of white supremacist ideology would necessarily accompany this larger project of social and cultural democratization. That is, the result would be a new and more powerful form of white racial democracy, not black equality. The "white race" card needed to be removed from the deck. In this aspect, the title of Hughes's poem can be read in a double sense: as a defiant crossing of "blood"-lines and as a subtle and cunning revision of the black nationalist trope of the black Christ, which is implicit in the title itself. The first two stanzas of "Cross" speak directly to this antinomy:

> My old man's a white old man
> And my old mother's black.
> If I cursed my white old man
> I take my curses back.
>
> If ever I cursed my black old mother
> And wished she were in hell,
> I'm sorry for that evil wish
> And now I wish her well. (CW 1:36)

Recognition of the historical fact of American mestizoness took the burden off the individual—off the "cross" of white racial ideology. The individual no longer had to worry about what he was going to be, but instead could focus on what he already was. But this new moment of nation-conscious self-recognition also meant that no space existed in which the North American mestizo could find aesthetic expression. A new archetype was required, for the dominant structure of feeling—"white" or not-"white"—denied the U.S. mestizo figure just as it denied in practice black equality. Hence, rather than being a discernible, official social type as in the Caribbean and Latin America, the mestizo in North America was more of a symbol and a direct ideological challenge to the biological category of "race" itself, referring neither to "white" nor "black" but rather to the suffering and enduring deprivations of the individual American in a white supremacist society.

As Du Bois's critique of Garveyism made manifest, the political costs of grafting the Caribbean racial experience, or "color scheme," onto the U.S. situation were significant. The African American intelligentsia would be the first casualty, since its ranks were filled with those of a lighter hue. The second casualty would be the African American working classes, as the uselessness of skin-color distinctions was no more apparent in the vastly mixed phenotypic composition of organized black labor. As McKay pointed out in *Banjo,* racialism was an invention of the English and Anglo-American ruling classes; its internalization by not-white workers only made European and American colonialism stronger. If the African American working classes started seeing themselves in terms of skin color, not race and class, the job of socially controlling the laboring classes as a whole would be made much easier. The masses of poor and propertyless European Americans could then be resocialized into the "white race," leaving the emergent proletarian organizations without a constituency, and black labor with instant enemies instead of allies. For Du Bois, each of these factors had to be thoroughly considered before translating the mulatto theme into cultural form or, worse, into a full-blown ideology, which was where Garveyism seemed headed.

As Walter Rodney demonstrated, by 1830 free blacks and mulattos of the Anglo-Caribbean had been promoted to equal status with whites. Following emancipation in 1838, they had been used by the British as a means of keeping local whites in power.[32] This mulatto social-control stratum in Jamaica had been Garvey's most immediate enemy, and McKay had been politically radicalized by the forms of personal discrimination he experienced as a dark-skinned Jamaican. As black intellectuals, both Garvey and McKay would spend their lives waging war against this Caribbean intermediate social-control group—the petit bourgeois mulatto class—by drawing attention to the system of national oppression that British colonialism had opted for in the early nineteenth century, a system that took racial oppression and completely overhauled it to suit the needs of British colonialism in the new conjuncture—that is, the period of post-Haitian independence. The revised color-caste system in the British Caribbean was therefore conscious and deliberate, not an unspoken, monolithic, and often insidious aspect of everyday life as it was in the United States, where a system of white racial oppression remained firmly in place. Consequently, the attempt to politically radicalize African Americans on the basis of what Du Bois referred to dismissively as "the Jamaican color scheme" would serve only to further divide light-skinned African Americans from their darker-skinned fellows.

Not surprisingly, the "mulatto" issue was a tension at the heart of the African American intelligentsia's opposition to the Garvey movement, to McKay, and to Hughes's early poetry. Publication of *The Weary Blues* and

32. Rodney, *The Groundings with My Brothers,* 25.

Fine Clothes to the Jew came in the midst of an intense battle over the ascendancy of Garveyism in African American politics. By the end of 1923 African American labor leaders Chandler Owen and Asa Randolph had organized a "Garvey Must Go!" campaign in Harlem, Du Bois had published several stinging critiques of the Garvey movement, and the black communists W. A. Domingo, Cyril Briggs, and Richard B. Moore—all three from the British Caribbean—were using their influence within the CPUSA to launch an even fiercer attack on Garvey, warning party leaders in New York that Garvey was nothing less than a fifth column in U.S. labor battles. The U.S. government had been seeking deportation orders for Garvey since he arrived in Harlem—a strategy that would find fertile soul among the white American left and the African American intelligentsia. This environment provided the go-ahead for Garvey's successful prosecution in federal courts.

In *The Crisis of the Negro Intellectual,* Harold Cruse argued, in his controversial assessment of the West Indian role in African American politics during the 1920s and 1930s, that Domingo, Briggs, and Moore played the part of cheap opportunists in the left opposition front against Garvey. According to Cruse, the three West Indian radicals sought acceptance and legitimacy among the white left and saw in Garvey a perfect opportunity to distance themselves from black revolutionary nationalism, thus proving to white party leaders that their loyalties as black radicals to international communism were undivided. It is interesting in this context that George Lamming strongly endorsed Cruse's analysis when his book first appeared, while C. L. R. James dismissed it as reactionary. Like Garvey himself, whom Cruse had attacked just as severely as he did the West Indian intellectuals in opposition to Garveyism, Cruse hit the central nerve of African American–Afro-Caribbean political relations. His analysis forced a taking of sides on the question of black nationalism and on the role of Afro-Caribbeans in African American politics and culture. For intellectuals such as Lamming, the Africa-America-Caribbean nexus was a vital element of black struggle in the English-speaking diaspora. His first novel *In the Castle of My Skin* (1953), for instance, ends with the return to Barbados of the black youth Trumper, who had been politically radicalized during his stay in Harlem. Trumper returns to spread the ideas and slogans of black revolutionary nationalism to his peers in Barbados. The moment is a liberating one, as Lamming's protagonist, G, is now forced to rethink radically his relationship to the British. For James, on the other hand, Cruse's reading of West Indian intellectuals was filled with useless hates against Caribbean peoples and served only to fracture any political alliance in the United States between African Americans and Afro-Caribbeans.[33]

What Cruse failed to mention in his analysis was the mestizo question—or, better, the "not-'white'" issue. Without it as a factor in the equation, Cruse was certainly right to criticize those who preyed on the structural weaknesses of African American political groups and organizations from the standpoint of skin color. But the omission of the mestizo question led him to draw the wrong conclusions about Moore, who, along with Domingo, received the brunt of Cruse's invective. In Cruse's reading, Moore simply pandered to white party officials, which was exemplified for Cruse in Moore's successful defense of Finnish American communist August Yokinen. Yokinen had been put on trial by the CPUSA for practicing white supremacism at the Finnish Workers Club in Harlem, where he had refused to admit African American workers to a dance the club had sponsored. Moore took up Yokinen's defense at the trial, arguing passionately against the party's decision to expel him. Moore encouraged the party instead to carry out an extensive educational campaign in the white ethnic communities of Harlem, to root out white supremacist attitudes and practices. Moore's defense was a success, and Yokinen was spared the disgrace of a public expulsion. Seeing the wisdom of Moore's counsel and the strong support he received at the trial from African Americans and white Americans alike, the party ordered Yokinen to correct his behavior toward African Americans by working cooperatively in black neighborhoods and by educating his fellow Finnish American workers on how white racial oppression worked against the class interests of the proletariat.[34]

Cruse read Moore's speech at the trial as a capitulation to white racial maneuvering within the CPUSA—a take on the situation somewhat at odds with the facts. As Mark Naison points out in *Black Communists in Harlem during the Depression,* Moore's handling of the situation marked a great turning point in the party's organizing efforts in Harlem. Following the trial, Naison explained,

> Finnish, Polish, Hungarian, Irish, Italian, and Slavic Communists became passionate exponents of the Party's position on the Negro ques-

33. Cruse, *Crisis of the Negro Intellectual,* 115–46. For Lamming's comments on Cruse's book, see Wilson Harris's *Kas-Kas: Interviews with Three Caribbean Writers in Texas,* 19; for James's, see *Kas-Kas,* 39.

34. For a summary of the Yokinen trial, see Naison, *Black Communists in Harlem,* 47–49.

tion. . . . [T]he Party had begun to generate an interethnic encounter within its ranks of great force and complexity, linking groups that shared a strong consciousness of oppression, but possessed vastly different histories, cultures, and economic profiles. Disguised, for the movement, within the massive Party mobilization against "white chauvinism," this encounter would serve both as an important source of Party energy, and a sign of its marginality and vulnerability within the larger American culture.[35]

For Cruse, in contrast, all "interethnic encounters" within the party spelled doom for African American group autonomy. But his reading of the trial's long-term implications is close to Naison's assessment:

Communist policy, remember, was aimed at the eradication of ethnic group units within the membership structure—in the pursuit of working-class unity—even when it was detrimental to the interests of the workers involved. So fantastic was the Communist Party on this subject, that its leaders could almost be accused of willful sabotage of the Party's self-elected role in society, if their ambivalent motivations were not understood. In "defending" Yokinen, Richard B. Moore's words reveal the Negro Marxist-integrationist, Party-line defender of the 1930s at his impassioned best.[36]

Although Cruse's renegade critique of the Communist Party's relationship to black nationalism still lends itself to shallow forms of red-baiting, the issues he raised are essential for understanding Hughes's relationship to socialism, for it was to Hughes that the CPUSA looked when the international class struggle reached a decisive stage, in roughly 1929–1934. Without having resolved the "Negro Question," in the last six months of 1934 the CPUSA reformulated the entire basis on which communists throughout the United States organized in black communities. In less than five years, the party had come full circle on black nationalism. For example, by December 1934 Harlem communists had formed their first "united front" with the Garvey movement, organized around the defense of Ethiopian independence. It was Hughes who prefigured this shift in the party's position on black revolutionary nationalism, and Hughes who had already articulated the reasons for it in his poetry and drama. While it was the rise of fascism in Europe that forced the change in party policy,

35. Ibid., 49.
36. Cruse, *Crisis of the Negro Intellectual*, 134.

the change for Hughes had more to do with the emergence of liberatory anticolonial resistance movements in Latin America and the Caribbean. From *The Weary Blues* on, Hughes had been searching for an archetype that could express the organic links between African Americans and the colonially oppressed nation-peoples of the modern world. And through the blues mode came the mestizo trope. Coming as it did from the vantage point of the United States, rather than the Caribbean and Latin America, his vision of the mestizo broke free of the obsession with skin color altogether and signified instead a fresh utopian moment of American national identity, a mestizo North America—a concept startlingly new in the U.S. context yet already present in the everyday social life of the laboring classes.

Red, White, and Black: Hughes's New American Archetype

This is my land, America. Naturally, I love it—it is home—and I am vitally concerned about its *mores,* its democracy, and its well-being. I try now to look at it with clear, unprejudiced eyes. My ancestry goes back at least four generations on American soil and, through Indian blood, many centuries more. My background and training are purely American—the schools of Kansas, Ohio, and the East. I am old stock as opposed to recent immigrant blood. . . . They may repeat the Oath of Allegiance with its ringing phrase of "liberty and justice for all," with a deep faith in its truth. . . . I repeat the oath, too, but I know that the phrase about "liberty and justice" does not apply fully to me. I am an American—*but I am a colored American.*

—Langston Hughes, "My America"

By the mid-1930s the formation of a multiclass bloc was advanced by the American Communist Party as the main political strategy against the U.S. ruling class. This endeavor produced two works of classical Marxist historiography and an outpouring of revolutionary socialist poetry, drama, journalism, and fiction. Du Bois's *Black Reconstruction* and James's *The Black Jacobins* both were written during the same period in which Langston Hughes, Margaret Walker, Richard Wright, and Paul Robeson tried out their most ambitious experiments with avant-garde socialist art. An antinomy had surfaced between the new social-movement trajectory of the CPUSA (the 1935 United Front strategy and also the 1937 Popular Front) and the new flourishing of revolutionary African American forms of working-class consciousness. Naison explains the situation: "The united-front policy opened the way for a significant expansion of Party activities among Harlem's creative intelligentsia—writers, artists, musicians, and theater people. For the first time, enough of these individuals began to join the Party and its affiliated groups to generate a black cultural movement explicitly identified with the left—aesthetically as well as politically." As he says,

> it involved support for black theater, WPA-sponsored and independent; efforts to encourage the teaching of black history in college and schools; the sponsorship of concerts and musical theater aimed at winning recognition for black musicians; and campaigns to end discrimination in amateur and professional sports. Through Party organizing on the WPA arts projects and in the Harlem schools, and through the cultural activities of its own organizations, it touched the lives of hundreds of black artists and thousands of "ordinary" Harlem citizens.[37]

The first major project of the CPUSA following its change of policy on black nationalism was the creation in 1935 of the Negro People's Theater. Composed of more than twenty African American and Euro-American actors and actresses, the theater's first presentation was a signifyin' revision of the most popular protest drama of the era, Clifford Odet's *Waiting for Lefty*. The Negro People's Theater riffed on the play's story about a New York City taxi strike by adapting it to the particular conditions of Harlem and replacing Odet's Jewish taxi drivers with African Americans. Staged at the Rockland Palace Ballroom in Harlem, the play drew more than five thousand people. A year later, Naison notes, "the left's image as a center of initiative in Afro-American life" was fully confirmed. Convened under the leadership of the Popular Front, the Second Convention of the National Negro Congress, held in Philadelphia in October 1937, attracted thousands of participants and dozens of prominent African American writers and artists. Adam Clayton Powell Jr. said of the congress that it was "the only nationalism that, in the long run will be effective, a nationalism that aims toward solidifying our race into a militant oneness and to cooperate with other groups in the fight for social justice." "In the Popular Front," Naison explains, "the Party diverged sharply from the perspectives on black culture which it had espoused in the early thirties—when critics demanded a black music free from 'commercial influences' and a literature totally dominated by a social protest message." Even more

37. Naison, *Black Communists in Harlem*, 151.

important, for the first time white communists began using the same argument that had been advanced by Du Bois: that African American working-class self-emancipation was the fulcrum on which all working-class equalitarian social change in U.S. society hinged. As Naison puts it,

> In the Popular Front era, writers close to the Party spoke of the attraction whites historically displayed to black music, dance, and theater—or even black language and the black sense of style—as the affirmation of a democratic impulse rather than a journey to the heart of darkness. In so doing, they helped give the struggle for racial equality the aura of a movement of cultural regeneration. . . . It was this vision of cultural interdependence, deeply American in its symbolism and psychology, that helped inspire white Communist teachers to approach black education as a mission of special importance, YCL organizers to fight baseball Jim Crow, and Young Communist scholars like Herbert Aptheker and Philip Foner to investigate slave revolts and black abolitionism.[38]

If it took the emergence of the Popular Front to reformulate more than ten years of delays and errant judgments on the "Negro Question" by the CPUSA, in 1938 the Anglo-American ruling class's system of white racial oppression remained securely in place. The 1928 resolution—the Black Belt thesis—was the party's greatest theoretical breakthrough, yet the black self-determination thesis was limited by party theoreticians to the South; with a new wave of African American migrant workers to the North, and the proletarianization of white American laborers in southern textile mills, the strategy in its current form could no longer hold. Poor and propertyless white Americans in the South were also without national self-determination, which further complicated the Black Belt thesis by making party organizers more prone to Klan violence. In response, the Popular Front's focus was turned to black and white unity, which translated for Euro-American communists into dedicated revisionary work on African American history and culture and rigorous attention to the specificity of African American experience. At the same time, the popular leftism of the CPUSA left untouched the overarching question of American colonialism and its relation to white racial oppression.

The question of American class struggle turns on the fact that the historical origins of white racial oppression are colonial—the premise of James's *Black Jacobins*—and that the first imposition of this system was against the Catholic Irish, whose skin color was no different from that of their oppres-

38. Ibid., 153, 202, 217.

sors, the English plantation owners. In other words, racial oppression, as a system of capitalist social control, was dispersed under the Popular Front, thereby reducing it in theory to a deep-seated set of reflexes, attitudes, and behaviors that were said to be the root cause of the enduring racial inequalities, partitions, and ruptures between white workers and African Americans. As a form of "American nationalism"—as Adam Clayton Powell aptly termed it—the Popular Front actually stabilized white supremacism by equating it with European fascism, a link that fundamentally misread the bourgeoisie's control of the American working classes.

The rise of fascism in Spain, Germany, and Italy was a consequence of national bourgeoisies that were weak in relation to the state. There the problem of controlling the working classes had caused an international crisis for the European imperialist ruling classes and prepared the way for fascist rule, which the European bourgeoisies much preferred over the prospect of any kind of equalitarian socialist nationalism. In the United States, on the other hand, the bourgeoisie had white racial oppression as a means for controlling the working classes. Thus, the precondition for fascism's rise in the United States would be, logically, the end of white racial oppression: an absurdity Hughes was always fond of pointing out in his popular column for the *Chicago Defender.* "One of the things that always worries me about race," he wrote in one column,

> is that when the Allies invade Europe, the American forces might take with them onto the Continent more race prejudice than Hitler and Mussolini together have been able to manufacture in the last decade. Unless many of our army officers, troops, and Red Cross workers have changed since they left home, our conquering armies will carry along Jim Crow units, separate clubs for service men, and Jim Crow cans of blood.[39]

Hughes's consistent stress on "Hitlerism at home" seems to be intended to remind U.S. leftists that the international fight against fascism was structurally linked to the endurance of white racial oppression. Further, the particular system of keeping working people under the boot of the U.S. ruling class—the system of white racial oppression—was a much older and more reactionary form of exploitation and social control than that mobilized in Europe by Franco, Hitler, and Mussolini. In his "Simple" stories, for instance, Hughes had Simple saying that Hitler was a "thorn in the side of our white folks," suggesting that the emergence of

39. "If Dixie Invades Europe," 146.

European fascism was nothing less than an epic case of the chickens coming home to roost. The perspicuity of Hughes's analysis in his *Chicago Defender* columns can be measured by the way it has been recast by Caribbean poets and critics such as Aimé Césaire and Roberto Fernández Retamar. Retamar makes the same point in his famous essay "Caliban":

> The white population of the United States exterminated the aboriginal population and thrust the black population aside, thereby affording itself homogeneity in spite of its diversity and offering a coherent model that its Nazi disciples attempted to apply even to other European conglomerates—an unforgivable sin that led some members of the bourgeoisie to stigmatize in Hitler what they applauded as a healthy Sunday diversion in Westerns and Tarzan films. Those movies proposed to the world—and even to those of us who are kin to the communities under attack and who rejoiced in the evocation of our own extermination—the monstrous racial criteria that have accompanied the United States from its beginnings to the genocide in Indochina.[40]

As a strategy of working-class struggle, the Popular Front was premised on the emergence of fascist rule in Europe, a correlation that led white American communists to identify politically with oppressed minorities. This is evidenced by the revitalization of left-wing support for the production and dissemination of black culture. Yet, in terms of political theory, the Popular Front provided a vision of national unity and consensus indistinct from that of bourgeois ideology, that is, white democratic pluralism. What the Popular Front occluded was the basic feature of white racial oppression: the principle of class collaboration and social control. As Theodore Allen has pointed out with respect to Irish-American workers:

> It was in the interest of the slave-labor system to maintain the white-skin privilege differential in favor of the European-American workers. At the same time, however, it was equally in the interest of the employers of wage-labor, as well as of bond-labor, that the differential be kept to no more than a minimum necessary for the purpose of keeping the European-American workers in the "white race" corral. . . . The chains that bound the African-American thus also held down the living standards of the Irish-American slum-dweller and canal-digger as well.[41]

40. Retamar, "Caliban," 4.
41. Allen, *Invention of the White Race*, 192.

In other words, the dilution of white racial oppression into merely another form of fascist power returned the party to the much older and self-servingly liberal white pluralist notion of racial slavery and racial oppression as aberrations or flaws rather than as the form of social oppression chosen again and again by U.S. ruling elites, from the early 1700s, in the immediate aftermath of Bacon's Rebellion—the greatest multiethnic labor uprising in the history of the nation—down to the present. Once more, white racial oppression was seen in the useless terms of American exceptionalism, which meant that its solution was to be found not in a ceaseless attack on white supremacy and the Klan but in a new form of national unification and interracial cooperation or "social equality." Consequently, the enduring effects of white racial oppression on all American workers were pushed aside, as was this system's poorly understood relation to the rapidly rising U.S. empire.

Not until the 1960s would the question of U.S. imperialism be addressed in the context of white racial oppression, as a direct result of the U.S. war of aggression in Indochina and through the vexed concept of the "Third World." The key point is that, while the historical uniqueness of the black freedom struggle received the full attention of the American Communist Party during the Popular Front period, the critique of U.S. imperialism and white supremacy, which had been strong in the early 1920s under the influence of Claude McKay and Marcus Garvey, faded into the background. The organic interconnections between class oppression and white racial oppression in their colonial origins remained unrecognized, deferring the question of how to properly overthrow white supremacism in U.S. society.

Following Allen's thesis about the deleterious effects of white racial oppression on Irish-American workers, it can be argued that the Popular Front strategy worked to the indirect advantage of the U.S. ruling class precisely by allowing the exploiting classes to readjust wages to a new minimum. As the 1935 Harlem Riots demonstrated, the differentials in housing, health care, education, and employment between white Americans and African Americans had been so vast that African Americans were ready to take up violent action against the state. As Naison shows, it was the Harlem riots and Italian colonialism in Ethiopia that triggered, more than any other set of events and social conditions, this shift in the CPUSA's organizational strategy in regard to the black struggle. The obvious interconnections were there. Yet, rather than understanding clearly and consciously the links between American working-class political weakness and the maintenance of white-skin privilege, the Popular Front strategy dispersed them into a kind of metaphysical project intended to settle the major social conflicts in U.S. society as a whole. It was done on behalf of "the nation," which served to stabilize white supremacy and U.S. capitalism and at the same time let Anglo-American colonialism off the hook. The missing terms—which Du Bois had produced meticulously in *Black Reconstruction*—were white racial oppression and social control. As Du Bois stated it:

> The race element was emphasized in order that property-holders could get the support of the majority of white laborers and make it more possible to exploit Negro labor. But the race philosophy came as a new and terrible thing to make labor unity or labor class-consciousness impossible. So long as the Southern white laborers could be induced to prefer poverty to equality with the Negro, just so long was a labor movement in the South made impossible.[42]

Under the Popular Front, the Communist Party turned its attention to correcting "white prejudice" and "white attitudes" toward African Americans rather than attacking white-skin privileges within the labor movement, which it had done brilliantly for a brief period in the early 1930s. Ironically, it was just as Du Bois was showing in *Black Reconstruction* that white racial oppression has no bearing on attitudes and behaviors—that it is about maintaining capitalist social control over the American laboring classes as a whole, through poor-white class collaborationism—that the American party abandoned this crucial Du Boisian departure point. Allen has referred to this political abandonment as "White Reconstruction": "the re-establishment of the social control system of racial oppression, based on racial privileges for laboring-class 'whites' with regard to 'free' land, immigration, and industrial employment."[43] Without getting a significant section of the Euro-American working class to defect from the "white race," so that they could perceive themselves finally as American workers instead of as "whites," the attempt to unify African Americans with poor European Americans, and other oppressed groups around the world, ended up consolidating the power of the exploiting class, as the African American civil rights struggle was marginalized and Euro-American workers resocialized into a new "white race"—this time under a reinvented ideology of American ethnic pluralism and social equality.

42. Du Bois, *Black Reconstruction: An Essay toward a History of the Part which Black Folk Played in the Attempt to Reconstruct Democracy in America, 1860–1880*, 680.
43. Allen, *Invention of the White Race*, 144.

Hughes's approach to the continental, colonial roots of white racial oppression, and his literary figuration of the North American mestizo, is best expressed in two works. The first, *Scottsboro Limited* (1932), is a play and four poems structured around the Communist Party's defense of the Scottsboro Boys. The second, *A New Song* (1938), is an elaboration of a myth of a race-free, as opposed to a raceless, American nation. While the main innovation of the latter work is the creation of a North American mestizo archetype, the former's contribution is this archetype's transformation into a U.S. working-class political ideology. Hughes's efforts in these two important and underread works reveal that the process depicted in the former is impossible without the full, prior development of that articulated in the latter. Without the creation of a mestizo archetype, Hughes suggests, the liberatory dialectics of the North American mestizo will remain submerged beneath the weight of the "white race," or what Du Bois referred to in *Black Reconstruction* as "the Blindspot." Because the white identity prevents class consciousness among Euro-Americans, the "white race" has to be overthrown before the North American mestizo can come into its own.

In her perceptive and original essay on Alice Walker's novel *Meridian*, Melba Joyce Boyd presents a powerful thesis on the mestizo question in the United States.

> The strength of the Mestizo is the magnetism of the parts. Our continental selves are related by blood and culture to every race. Despite denial, the evidence of essence contributes to a transcendent perspective, interweaving the primal of the human race. The spiritual offerings living in the soul of music and poetry express the pain of our ancestral strivings, but only through activist resistance against repressive arrogance and destructive, complicit ignorance, can a healing of our infected humanity and our dissipating Earth be affected.[44]

Hughes's making of archetypes in *A New Song* was intended, openly, to stimulate this kind of "activist resistance" in working-class American communities. Hughes's chapbook came not from the dominant interethnic or social-equality line of the CPUSA or from the "national consensus" ideology of American liberal pluralism. Rather, his symbol of the North American mestizo came from "outside": it was an original application of Lenin's concept of black America as an oppressed nation to the

44. Boyd, "The Politics of Cherokee Spirituality in Alice Walker's *Meridian*," 126.

situation facing *all* U.S. workers. In this sense, it sought explicitly what Boyd calls "interweaving the primal of the human race." What Hughes proposes in both works is simple yet profound: What if all the American workers were mestizo and all the capitalists were white?

Hughes's work during these years circumvented the new Popular Front-ist strictures placed on the black self-determination thesis by following to its logical conclusion Lenin's basic argument, which had been put on the shelf in 1930 when organizers in the North stepped up their efforts to "as-similate" African Americans into the party's rank and file. Hughes took Lenin's thesis that African American self-determination—that is, the cre-ation of a new language, new working-class concepts, and a new vision of America—was a necessary step in the formation of a new U.S. working-class mass political movement and converted it into a new way of feeling and knowing the "natural elements," to use José Martí's terminology, of U.S. society. In the terms of nation-consciousness, Hughes's new arche-type of the North American mestizo was an attempt to direct the Com-munist Party back to the three bases, or nation-peoples, of America: the African, the Amerindian, and the European—the red, white, and black. But rather than seeing the three elements in terms of "race" or nationali-ty, which implies a continuous lineage, Hughes understood them as cul-turally intercrossed and in urgent need of "re-integration," as he would later put it in a "Simple" column. Further, his use of the pamphlet form (the chapbook) for this project reveals the political immediacy with which he apprehended the dialectics of "Our Mestizo North America."

Published by the International Workers Order in 1938, *A New Song* be-gins and ends with a new vision of social relations in American society. The first poem, "Let America Be America Again," puts into effect what Henry Louis Gates Jr. has called the "double-voicedness" of the African American literary text.[45] Hughes wrote not only in response to the dis-cursive debasement and appropriation of blackness by white America but also to counter the prevailing white bourgeois ideology of the self-made, democracy-loving, freedom-seeking American immigrant pioneer from which this racialized African American "other" derives. The second voice is, in fact, that of the subaltern African American, but the occasion for speaking is precisely to signify on the futility of answering back from the standpoint of a long-standing "racial" minority. Rather than being a mi-nority discourse, Hughes's signifyin' gestures in the first poem are a dec-laration of North America's socialist character, expressed through the

45. Gates, *Signifying Monkey,* xxv.

mestizo. For Hughes, it is not enough to assert the ethnic plurality of U.S. society; to fully grasp what we mean by "multicultural America," he suggests, it is first necessary to link diversity with its own objective. Thus, his strategy in *A New Song* is to have the mestizo express itself through the self-emancipation of labor—its objective—and by entering on America's behalf a prompt and formal bid to join the ranks of international socialism, where the method for realizing this objective was, for Hughes and many others, readily at hand.

The International Workers Order chose Hughes as its first author in a series of "literary pamphlets for the people" and put this slogan into practice by printing ten thousand copies of the first edition. "The lament of every modern poet," wrote communist publisher and critic Michael Gold in the introduction, "is that he has no audience in America. If the International Workers Order with its 140,000 members can create a great people's audience for poetry here, it will have contributed to the rise of that democratic culture of which Walt Whitman prayed and dreamed."[46] The cross-cultural politics of the IWO made Hughes an easy selection, as many of his poems in *The Weary Blues* and *Fine Clothes to the Jew* had, like "Cross," evoked proudly the mestizo heritage of U.S. society. In "Let America Be America Again" the organic interconnections between oppressed American nation-peoples are advanced as a popular aesthetic preference, for the seer is not the self-exiled and marginalized poet but the class-conscious North American mestizo worker.

Arranged into eleven stanzas, the poem is a call-and-response with five different voices, each representing a different social constituency: the dominant ruling-class Anglo-American minority; the American Indian; the African American; the poor white; and the American communist. As in the opening stanza, the poem follows throughout a popular song sequence, in which the founding white myths of American democracy are reiterated one by one and then calmly debunked by the African American worker, whose words are voiced parenthetically and in the blues mode:

> Let America be America again.
> Let it be the dream it used to be.
> Let it be the pioneer on the plain
> Seeking a home where he himself is free.
>
> (America never was America to me.)

46. Michael Gold, "Introduction," 8.

The second stanza follows the rhyme pattern of the first, continues the same theme, and is counterpoised with the same response, only slightly altered this time to indicate the blues mode in which it is written:

> Let America be the dream the dreamers dreamed—
> Let it be that great strong land of love
> Where never kings connive nor tyrants scheme
> That any man be crushed by one above.
>
> (It never was America to me.)

In the third stanza, the Jeffersonian platitudes reach their loftiest pitch, just as the blues form itself concludes, but this time as the ultimate riposte:

> O, let my land be a land where Liberty
> Is crowned with no false patriotic wreath,
> But opportunity is real, and life is free,
> Equality is in the air we breathe.
>
> (There's never been equality for me,
> Nor freedom in this "homeland of the free.")

This third stanza signals the end of both the Jeffersonian platitudes and the blues mode, which is expressed through the next two italicized lines, voiced by the American communist: *"Say who are you that mumbles in the dark? / And who are you that draws your veil across the stars?"* The sympathetic interloper is then answered by the North American mestizo worker, who speaks in bold rhythms and a straightforward language:

> I am the poor white, fooled and pushed apart,
> I am the Negro bearing slavery's scars.
> I am the red man driven from the land,
> I am the immigrant clutching the hope I seek—
> And finding only the same old stupid plan.
> Of dog eat dog, of mighty crush the weak. (*CW* 1:131)

As do the Jeffersonian platitudes, the next three stanzas climb upward, beginning to sound airy and abstract, as if the new mestizo forgot with whom he was speaking. It is at this point in the poem that the blues mode once again intervenes, to bring the mestizo back to the ground of African American working-class struggle. The last two lines of the seventh stanza —"And torn from black Africa's strand I came / To build a 'homeland of the free'"—are countered with a short blues line—"The Free?"—that begins a new movement in the poem. The final five stanzas stay in the blues mode but shift back and forth among the four voices that in the first six stanzas—the American Indian; the African American; the poor white; and the American communist—directly followed the initial voice of the U.S. bourgeois. The poetic effect is lyrically hybrid, as each voice remains in tension with the other three by refusing to fuse or integrate into an easy plurality. In the eighth and ninth stanzas, the four countervoices crystallize into an antagonistic mestizoness and are intonated with dashes and words in italics to express the mestizo worker's defiant turn in the face of the dominant voice of the bourgeois:

> O, let America be America again—
> The land that never has been yet—
> And yet must be—the land where *every* man is free.
> The land that's mine—the poor man's, Indian's, Negro's, ME—
> Who made America,
> Whose sweat and blood, whose faith and pain,
> Whose hand at the foundry, whose plow in the rain,
> Must bring back our mighty dream again.
>
> Sure, call me any ugly name you choose—
> The steel of freedom does not stain.
> From those who live like leeches on the people's lives,
> We must take back our land again,
> America! (*CW* 1:133)

Here Hughes's vision of America breaks new ground. While Gold sees Hughes's verse as a radical continuation of Whitman's vision, the more vital connection is with the vision of the Cuban *independentista* and national hero José Martí. In Martí's famous essay "Our America," published in 1891, he argued that the problem of anticolonial national liberation does not lie merely in a change of socioeconomic forms "but in a change of spirit." Faith in the people's ability to make a new society is Hughes's main concern in "Let America Be America Again," just as Martí's aim in "Our America" was to persuade the Cuban popular classes that "faith in the best of men" should be the new revolutionary beginning and a conscious counter to the notion that the oppressed seek only to do to their oppressors what has been done to them. Hughes's challenge to the leaders of the popular classes is meant to direct them back to the natural components of their own society, so that they may have direct knowledge of them.

"Knowing is what counts," Martí wrote. "To know one's country and govern it with that knowledge is the only way to free it from tyranny."[47] Likewise, an emphasis on the mestizo is Hughes's main innovation in "Let America Be America Again," as the organic elements of U.S. society are understood on their own terms, not as "minorities" requiring assimilation into a larger pluralistic "white" whole but as already "magnetized" parts, to paraphrase Boyd, of an already "racially" intermixed and transculturated American working class. The American Indian, the African American, and the poor white are not "racial" Americans but rather mestizo builders of the American working-class nation.

Hughes's insistence on the presence of the North American mestizo in U.S. history and society—the use of "again" in conjunction with the making of this new America—is a riffing on the utopian vision of American democracy, carried out through the blues mode. In Hughes's terms, because the dream of equality and justice for all has been turned into a manipulative, meaningless populism, where parodic claims to white Americanness on the part of the nation's downtrodden have made the promise of American equalitarianism all the easier to repress and postpone, it is necessary to create a new language in which these same claims can be reasserted from the standpoint of "not-white" organized labor. Thus, popular images of the daring conquistador, the politically besieged Protestant rebel, the European famine immigrant, the native-born toiler, the rugged pioneer, and the transplanted African captive are rearticulated in the seventh stanza, without any irony. Also repeated, but this time with a growing sense of self-irony, is the belief that the creed in which they are all invested is "to build a 'homeland of the free,'" the stanza's concluding line. Yet the mestizo worker's response is deeply ironic (as the quotation marks around "homeland of the free" indicate) and voiced in the present tense, which sets the stage for the poem's third movement, beginning with the opening lines of the eighth stanza, now back in the blues mode:

> Who said the free? Not me?
> Surely not me? The millions on relief today?
> The millions shot down when we strike?
> The millions who have nothing for our pay?
> For all the dreams we've dreamed
> And all the songs we've sung
> And all the hopes we've held
> And all the flags we've hung,

47. "Our America," 90.

The millions who have nothing for our pay—
Except the dream that's almost dead today. (*CW* 1:132)

The blues line that's repeated—"The millions who have nothing for our pay"—is altered in the final two lines through the blues technique of ironic restatement, with a corresponding change in content and tone. For Hughes, the blues impulse is the most revolutionary element of the new and mestizo American nation precisely because the blues is the most ironic and self-knowing form of class consciousness. Whereas the other nation-peoples continue to see the United States from the standpoint of the founding myths of bourgeois democracy rather than from their own, the mestizo worker speaks about America in the blues mode, where the deeper myth of America is the one that has to be re-created, this time from the standpoint of the working classes. It is in this way that the final stanza reveals the occasion for Hughes's new archetype: a paralyzing sense of hopelessness and despair shared by the American laboring classes as a whole:

Out of the rack and ruin of our gangster death,
The rape and rot of graft, stealth, and lies,
We, the people, must redeem
The land, the mines, the plants, the rivers,
The mountains and the endless plain—
All, all the stretch of these great green states—
And make America again! (*CW* 1:133)

Thus, while the third movement of the poem returns to the blues mode to break apart the white bourgeois mythification of American democracy, the final movement is a restatement of this myth from the point of view of a newly self-conscious, self-ironic, and antiracist working class, and a reappropriation of America's founding slogans on behalf of this new mestizo archetype. This movement in the poem represents a savvy attempt at bricolage. As such—as Robin D. G. Kelley has shown powerfully in his historiography of African American culture and communism—it contradicts the notion of African American culture as some undifferentiated whole:

While the Party's essentializing of black culture created more space for cultural expressions which otherwise would be in conflict with Communist ideology, it also obscured the degree to which "folk" culture was actually bricolage, a cutting and pasting, and incorporating of various cultural forms which then become categorized in a racially/ethnically coded aesthetic hierarchy. . . . What [African American communists] produced was hardly "folk" music; it was a bricolage drawn from the Party's ideology, black cultural traditions and collective memories, and a constellation of lived experiences.[48]

Kelley's insight can be appreciated in Hughes's own form of bricolage in *A New Song*. But what makes Hughes's work advanced aesthetically, and convincing politically, is that the mode of cultural production is poetry, a place of ideological tension in which aesthetic hierarchies are rigidly class-based compared to the popular-democratic song, where social class is often announced loudly and proudly. The impersonal nature of the ballad, for instance, allows for the expression of a public voice, where aesthetic hierarchies are open for counterattack and reappropriation. Free-verse lyricism, on the other hand, tends toward the celebration of bricolage and an aesthetics of indeterminacy, serving to sublimate historical experience to the level of private expression. Thus, the key for Hughes is the chapbook form itself, as the promptness of his free verse finds a corresponding form of dissemination in the volume's rapid production and distribution. It is the historical necessity of the verse that makes this method possible, and the method that is able to turn necessity into will or human agency. Not until the 1960s Black Arts movement would this insight be used systematically in the production of poetry, when the distribution of poetry in chapbooks form became, for the first time in U.S. history, the most popular method of literary communication. Dudley Randall's Broadside Press is the best example, as his Detroit operation published hundreds of thousands of chapbooks between 1967 and 1977, including original work by Nikki Giovanni, Gwendolyn Brooks, Henry Dumas, Margaret Walker, Sonia Sanchez, Don L. Lee, and Etheridge Knight, among many others.[49]

Antonio Gramsci wrote on a similar aspect of nation building in regard to the working classes of modern Italy: "[When] Man knows himself, he knows the value of his individual will and how it can become powerful by obeying and disciplining itself to necessity such that he ends up dominating that same necessity by identifying it with his own ends. Who knows himself? Not man in general, but only he who suffers the yoke of necessity."[50] Gramsci's insight is the premise of Hughes's creative method in *A New Song*. Like Martí's rhetorical strategy in "Our America," it is a

48. Kelley, *Race Rebels: Culture, Politics, and the Black Working Class*, 117–18.

49. See Melba Joyce Boyd's excellent biography of Dudley Randall, *Wrestling with the Muse: Dudley Randall and the Broadside Press*.

50. Gramsci, *History, Philosophy and Culture in the Young Gramsci*, 10–11.

return to the real historical individual—the one "who suffers the yoke of necessity." This comes through clearly in the sixteen poems that follow "Let America Be America Again": "Justice," "Park Bench" is in the words of a homeless man; "Chant for Tom Mooney" is written for Mooney on behalf of all political prisoners in the United States, Africa, China, India, Germany, and Argentina; "Chant for May Day" is in the form of a people's chorus; "Pride" sees physical hunger as the spark of revolution; "Ballad of Ozie Powell" is a popular anti-Klan anthem; and "Kids Who Die" is for young communists who risk their lives organizing sharecroppers in the South and factory workers in the North. "History" is a four-line poem that explicitly invokes this "yoke of necessity"; in it Hughes wrote, "The past has been a mint of blood and sorrow—that must not be true of tomorrow" (*CW* 1:140).

The other poems in *A New Song* follow this same nation logic: "Ballads of Lenin" is voiced from the standpoint of the victorious laboring classes of Russia to the colonially oppressed of the Caribbean and Asia; "Song of Spain" calls on U.S. workers to support the Spanish Republicans; "A New Song" continues the mode of "Let America Be America Again"; "Sister Johnson Marches" speaks in the name of African American women workers; "Open Letter to the South" urges white workers of the South to abandon the "white race" and join the communist movement; "Negro Ghetto" is a brief sketch of slum conditions, written in the voice of a communist organizer; "Lynching Song" is a play on white racial ideology, where the ideologeme of "whiteness" being conditional on keeping African Americans oppressed is ironically inverted; and the final poem, "Union," calls forth "all the whole oppressed poor world" to end "the rule of greed" and replace it with a political party of the American working classes. In each of the poems, "only he who suffers the yoke of necessity" finally knows himself or herself, but the knower does not arrive at self-knowledge through an imputation of class-consciousness. Rather, self-knowledge is achieved through class struggle, which is signified by Hughes through the discontinuously arranged set of "nation-conscious voices," each fully aware of the other only at the level of the U.S. labor movement and in the active process of overthrowing the "bourgeois yoke," to use Lenin's conceptualization.[51]

A good example of this form of nation-consciousness is "Open Letter to the South." In the poem, Hughes carries out an ingenious revision of Booker T. Washington's ideology of black nationalism in order to per-

51. V. I. Lenin, "Preliminary Draft of Theses on the National and Colonial Questions," 21.

suade Euro-American workers to defect from the "white race." Echoing Washington, but on a register that white workers knew firsthand, Hughes recognizes the labor crisis that the heroic Great Migration had massively determined:

> For me, no more, the great migration to the North.
> Instead: migration into force and power—
> Tuskegee with a new flag on the tower!
> On every lynching tree, a poster crying FREE
> Because, O poor white workers,
> You have linked your hands with me. (*CW* 1:148)

This last line riffs on Washington's statement that blacks and whites must be "as separate as the fingers." The reference to Tuskegee "with a new flag on the tower" sets up cleverly this revision. In the same way that he presented the bourgeois ideology of the melting pot in "Let America Be America Again," Hughes sees Washington's ideology of black separatism and political accommodation with the U.S. ruling class as a conjunctural problem: that is, he reappropriates Washington's concept of black self-help for all American workers, rather than just taking it literally. The juxtaposition of images is striking: the Great Migration and Tuskegee; white mob violence and the black freedom struggle; white separatism and American working-class solidarity.

Consistent with Hughes's revisionary tropes of U.S. labor history in the first section of *A New Song,* there emerges in the volume's final four poems an argument for the building of an American socialist party. The call for a new party is voiced by the black worker and addressed to all white workers:

> I am the black worker,
>   Listen:
> That the land might be ours,
> And the mines and the factories and the office towers
> At Harlan, Richmond, Gastonia, Atlanta, New Orleans;
> That the plants and the roads and the tools of power
> Be ours. (*CW* 1:147)

There is also an understanding of history in these last poems that breaks free of what Hughes calls "the old dead dogmas of the past":

Let us new lessons learn,
All workers,
New life-ways make,
One union form:
Until the future burns out
Every past mistake
Let us together, say:
"You are my brother, black or white,
You are my sister—now—today!" (*CW* 1:148)

Leading the new party are African American workers and radical European American defectors from the "white race." This is Hughes's message in *A New Song* from beginning to end.

His intervention, then, operates at three different levels: First, it reminds the American Communist Party that the argument for "interracial" unity must first gain acceptance among African American workers—that working-class unity cannot be imputed to black workers, especially not under white racial oppression. Second, it locates the struggle for a new revolutionary party at the point where the ideology of the "white race" is most vulnerable—organized labor. Third, it imagines working-class solidarity from the standpoint of women workers. Hughes writes as a feminist in *A New Song* by including poems devoted to women workers and women organizers. In "Open Letter to the South," for example, white women factory workers are called into existence, and in "Sister Johnson Marches" a black woman organizer explains to her fellow black women workers why she is marching in a May Day celebration:

Here I go with my banner in my hand!
What's the matter, chile?
Why we owns de land!
It's de first of May!

Who are all them people
Marching in a mass?
Lawd! Don't you know?
That's the working class!

It's de first of May! (*CW* 1:146)

As "Sister Johnson Marches" shows, Hughes's vision of the "new life-way" for the U.S. working classes is premised on the equal participation and leadership of women organizers. Not only does he call women workers into existence, as in a kind of "shout-out," but his lyricism itself is woman-centered. In "Negro Ghetto," for instance, the voice of the labor organizer is moved by political analysis *and* sentimentality:

> I looked at their black faces
> And this is what I saw:
> The wind imprisoned in the flesh,
> The sun bound down by law.
> I watched them moving, moving,
> Like water down the street,
> And this is what moved my heart:
> Their far-too-humble feet. (*CW* 1:149)

Kate Baldwin has argued in *Beyond the Color Line and the Iron Curtain* that Hughes's feminism in this period was inspired by his immersion in Uzbek society during his fourteen-month sojourn in the Soviet Union:

> The influence of Hughes's experiences in Soviet Central Asia shape not only the unanthologized pieces of his work but also some of his better-known and canonized writings. . . . The proscriptive delineation of the color line as mediated through double consciousness and a life of the veil, the woman's role in racial liberation, the ways in which otherness becomes denigrated as feminine, and the generative potential of disruptive boundary crossings with a summoning of matter out of place, are all ideas that carry over from Central Asia to figure prominently in the stories about U.S. society.[52]

While Baldwin's thesis is suggestive insofar as it shows persuasively the worldliness of Hughes's literary imagination, it risks tendentiousness by implying that, before experiencing firsthand the ups and downs of women's self-emancipation struggle in Soviet Central Asia, Hughes had no recourse to any African American concept of "woman's role in racial emancipation." Given the long and famous tradition of African American women's writing on self-emancipation, from Harriet Jacobs down to Francis Harper and Ida B. Wells, Baldwin's thesis teeters on a shaky premise: that Hughes needed to witness women's liberation struggle in Soviet

---

52. Kate Baldwin, *Beyond the Color Line and the Iron Curtain: Reading Encounters between Black and Red, 1922–1963*, 126–27.

Central Asia to arrive at a male feminist approach to women's equality in the United States.

Hughes's experiences with international communism, including his travels in the Soviet Union, Latin America, and the Caribbean, enabled him to advance successfully the case that the struggle for black equality in the United States was not only as important, in principle, as the anti-fascist class struggles in Europe but was also the most enduring problem of the U.S. class struggle itself. Working from a Du Boisian beginning, Hughes argued that until white supremacy is defeated in the United States, every class struggle is vulnerable to Anglo-American bourgeois counterrevolutionary sabotage. Hughes did not consider himself a "minority" writer in search of other "minority" cultures and societies. Rather, in the context of socialist internationalism, Hughes always considered himself, and the African American tradition whence he came, to be solidly mainstream, in spite of being under the boot of white racial oppression. To cite just one example, in his 1925 poem "Rising Waters" Hughes argued that the white American oppressing class should be regarded not as the U.S. mainstream but, rather, as "foam on the sea" (CW 1:164).

In "Open Letter to the South," this same structure of feeling is present: the utopian idea of American multiethnic working-class unity is visualized in the holding of hands. Yet Hughes's revision is striking, since his hand-holding is not in the form of a barricade or in the context of an "integrated" protest march but instead as a gesture of African American love and nurturing. It is here that Hughes's revision of Booker T. Washington's trope of "separate as the fingers" is most cunning. He builds on Washington's self-help program rather than attacking it, for Hughes's impulse comes from the universality of the blues, not from a party directive or the ideology of American pluralism. For Hughes, self-help is based on the love of laboring humanity. This is what for Hughes makes the African American worker's self-emancipation struggle the foundation of all U.S. working-class struggle. That is, it is from the African American revolutionary tradition that his proposals are made—not from the perspective of racelessness or "black and white, unite and fight," although this is A New Song's most dominant theme. His argument is that only through the African American tradition can a "race-free" American working-class struggle even be imagined.

Hughes grounds the American working-class struggle in a structure of feeling that has produced its own concept of self-emancipation and its own methods of communicating itself to the world—Washington's black self-help program being one of them. It is in this way that A New Song is an expression of nation-consciousness, for the grounding is made within the interstices of black cultural nationalism, Du Boisian equalitarianism, and the internationalism of the American Communist Party. In the U.S. context, these interstices are fruitful for revolutionary class struggle, since each ideology is based on a great moment of possibility—a utopian moment yet to come but already ever-present. And the impulse itself is based on the blues: the most lucid and systematic articulation of labor consciousness to be advanced in U.S. society.

Hughes and Lenin

Lenin's self-determination thesis, which first appeared in his "Preliminary Draft Theses on the National and Colonial Question" in 1920 at the Second Congress of the Comintern, posits that the national question registers on two levels. In the advanced capitalist nation-states, he argued, the struggle is against petit bourgeois "pacifist distortions" of the concept of the equality of nations, while in the more backward nations, "in which patriarchal-peasant relations predominate," the goal is the people-nation itself. The task here, Lenin wrote, is to "assist the bourgeois-democratic movement in these countries" by convincing "the workers of the country upon which the backward nation is dependent colonially or financially" to fight for national self-determination in the colonially oppressed countries. Cautious about the self-serving middle-class invocations of anti-imperialism in the European and U.S. metropolises, Lenin urged communists to critique the ideological trends that combined "the liberation movement against European and American imperialism with an attempt to strengthen the positions of the khans, landlords, mullahs, etc." Rather than joining these middle-class anti-imperialist movements, communists must instead support them "only on condition that, in all backward countries, the elements of future proletarian parties, parties communist not only in name, shall be grouped together and educated to appreciate their special tasks, viz., to fight bourgeois-democratic movements within their own nations."[53]

In *A New Song*, Hughes's intention is to give a precise name to the "future proletarian party" of the United States by reconceptualizing the social relations between the American laboring classes and the U.S. bourgeoisie. The right to national self-determination is *A New Song*'s point of departure, as each "nation-element" of the U.S. working class he visual-

53. Lenin, "Draft of Theses," 21.

izes has been cheated out of U.S. "democratic development," including white American workers. For the "White Blindspot" has always confused, or rather conflated, democracy with white supremacy—this has been the baited hook. This democratization of whiteness is reflected through one of the volume's unifying themes: the bamboozlement of white workers by the U.S. ruling class.

In a white racial democracy, democratic rights for poor and property-less Euro-Americans are conditional on keeping African Americans racially oppressed, which is the subject of Hughes's "Lynching Song," in which he links thematically a line from "Let America Be America Again"—"the rape and rot of graft, and stealth, and lies"—with "white-ness" and, by implication, with the overthrow of the popular-democratic African American revolution during Reconstruction. In "Lynching Song," African American resistance to the Klan is directly linked to the death of "whiteness," an image that Hughes places at the center of "Let America Be America Again." In "Lynching Song," however, the image is expressed more concretely through the mass participation of poor whites in the lynching of a black youth:

> Pull at the rope! Oh!
> Pull it high!
> Let the white folks live and the black boy die,
> Pull it boys,
>
> With a bloody cry
> As the black boy spins
> And the white folks die. (*CW* 1:149)

This setting up of a seemingly enigmatic question—how can it be said that white workers are making themselves victims of class oppression right along with the innocent African Americans they are racially persecut-ing?—is consistent with Hughes's main themes throughout *A New Song*, as the next stanzas assert, startlingly:

> *The white folks die?*
> *What do you mean—*
> *The white folks die?*
>
> That black boy's
> Still body
> Says:
> NOT I! (*CW* 1:149–50)

For Hughes, the political backwardness of U.S. society is both a cause and a consequence of white racial oppression. The question is how can the white working classes have been fooled, through something as transparently base and antidemocratic as white supremacism, by the transparently self-serving bourgeois promises of democracy and progress for all. The liberal bourgeois—what Dr. King called "the white moderate"—is the key. Portrayed in *A New Song* as an opportunist seeking a "lousy peace" between the former slave-owning class in the South and the northern capitalist classes, the liberal bourgeois can always be counted on to leave workers to die at the hands of the state. In "Kids Who Die," the progressive bourgeoisie

> Who pen editorials in the papers,
> And the gentlemen with Dr. in front of their names,
> White and black,
> Who make surveys and write books,
> Weave words to smother the kids who die. (*CW* 1:139)

Lenin's self-determination thesis seems to be built into these lines, for the premise of Lenin's breakthrough argument for seeing the "Negro Question" in the context of colonialism was that the bourgeois-democratic revolution in the United States had been left unfinished. Hughes reads this premise into the situation facing the American laboring classes by heroizing young communist organizers who struggle to build organic working-class institutions, independent of the liberal bourgeoisie, fully conscious of the backward social conditions of the South. These conditions are then traced by the poet to the pacification of the white working classes in New York, Chicago, and the farmlands of the West, including the situation facing new Asian American and Chicano workers.

It is this aspect of *A New Song*, I think—the rich literary application of Lenin's insight on self-determination to the U.S. class struggle—that makes it such a startling, nation-conscious text. Hughes links the fragment with the whole and the general with the particular. Black struggle is understood dialectically, as the oldest, most steadfast and resilient form of U.S. class struggle and thereby the most universal. Thus, the more familiar Euro-American socialists are with the history and politics of the African American resistance to white supremacy and the system of racial oppression's integral role in preventing U.S. labor consciousness, the greater are the possibilities for American working-class self-emancipation. The projection of this dialectic is Hughes's most urgent task as each poem speaks in a different "nation voice," yet each voice is one in which black equality is the occasion for the speaking.

The title poem is the fullest and most open-ended expression of this idea and the only poem to claim to represent the African American working classes. The opening lines announce the poet's true intention: to let those who have suffered the yoke of necessity speak clearly, and without interruption, about the new society in which they now want to live.

> I speak in the name of the black millions
> Awakening to action.
> Let all others keep silent a moment.

As the stage is set and the momentum of the poem begins to build behind the black worker's singular voice, the rest follows in a steady rush of declarative sentences:

> I have this word to bring,
> This thing to say,
> This song to sing:
>
> > Bitter was the day
> > When I bowed my back
> > Beneath the slaver's whip.
>
> That day is past.
>
> > Bitter was the day
> > When I saw my children unschooled,
> > My young men without a voice in the world,
> > My women taken as body-toys
> > Of a thieving people.
>
> That day is past. (CW 1:144–45)

Here the forms of white racial oppression imposed on African Americans—the illegalization of literacy, the deprivation of civil rights, and the displacement of family rights and authorities—are perceived by Hughes as the main instruments of ruling-class social control and the fulcrum on which every other form of oppression in U.S. society turns. The new song is itself one of America's oldest songs: the struggle for black equality. But its rejection of the past is an act of nation-consciousness, for no long and unbroken tradition of national democracy is referenced in the poem—in fact that tradition is explicitly demystified. On the contrary, the re-creation of "Americanness" is premised on the overthrow of enduring white racial oppression, which Hughes shows to be an immediate possibility and new in its potential scale.

The song's "newness" is that it is being sung for the first time by all oppressed Americans, who see their own destinies reflected in the forward struggle for black equality. Yet Hughes is quick to refuse any claim that equality and democracy are "American" ideals: the ironic blues restatement of these ideals in "Let America Be America Again" counters this fantasy from the outset. His argument instead is that democratic traditions are created historically. They need not rehabilitate bourgeois ideologies of American democracy precisely because the new song begins where they leave off: at the moment when "lousy peace" is once again made among the poor whites, the liberal bourgeoisie, and the southern landowners. It is in this sense that Hughes goes outside the tradition of American democracy for his symbols, tropes, and images, while at the same time remaining firmly within the real historical situation for which *A New Song* was written.

In *Blues, Ideology, and Afro-American Literature*, Baker has put the matter eloquently: "Rather than a rigidly personalized form, the blues offer a phylogenetic recapitulation—a nonlinear, freely associative, nonsequential meditation—of species experience." For Hughes, in this same light, the present is all that matters, and the spontaneous expression of its verbal possibilities is what makes the predictable bourgeois myth of freedom so completed, limited, and ultimately irrelevant. It is for this reason, perhaps, that the volume has been so poorly treated by literary scholars and critics, especially by those who seek a linear development in Hughes's career, or by those interested only in finding thematic patterns and formal continuities in his poetry.[54]

Neither of these approaches can appreciate the deliberate discontinuity of *A New Song* and the challenges it poses to simplistic reductions of Hughes's poetry into progressive phases, from "Afrocentrism" to "Proletarian" to "populism." As we will see, Hughes's transition from poet to journalist also cannot be explained by idealist or evolutionary models or through pragmatic or formalist approaches. Hughes did not write newspaper columns for monetary reasons or for art's sake: the income earned from his journalism could barely pay his heat bill let alone sustain him as

54. Baker, *Blues, Ideology, and Literature*, 5. See in particular Sundiata Keita Cha-Jua's "'Lest Harlem See Red': Race and Class Themes in the Poetry of Langston Hughes, 1920–1942," in which he fails to mention *A New Song*.

a writer. His decision to write for the popular press was encouraged by his readers, rather than arising as a flash of brilliance inside his own head, however brilliant many of his columns are.

As Naison has shown in his study of the Harlem Communist Party, the shift in the language and imagery of U.S. communists that Hughes helped originate in *A New Song* would take hold for only a brief moment. And just when this paradigm shift took place, a reactionary counter to it was hurriedly advanced in the form of a new psychocultural argument: that, using today's liberal rhetoric, "racial differences" between African Americans and whites were the problem, not the persistence of white racial oppression as a system of ruling-class social control. Conjuncturally, then, Hughes's new archetype in *A New Song*—the North American mestizo—as well as his complex inversions and radical revisions of the concept of interracial solidarity, can be read as an original moment in U.S. literature and popular culture and appreciated as a bold aesthetic experiment with nation-consciousness that continues to serve as an excellent argument for making "old" ideas new again.

3

The Poet as Journalist

Aesthetics of Black Equality

We use the word radical and use it descriptively to say radical journalism.
Well, a lot of people get afraid when they hear that: "Ooh, radical!" Radical
just means, "from roots," and that means we should be in touch with the
roots of our people, to speak their truths, to reflect their realities and to give
their voice to the world.

—Mumia Abu-Jamal, *Live from Death Row*

That Langston Hughes could imagine America in terms of the mestizo
rather than through the prevailing ideology of American pluralism reveals the presence of a different way of thinking about race in the United
States. In assessing Hughes's legacy as the Dean of Black Letters, literary
critics have often focused on his passionate love of the blues aesthetic and
the artistic labors he devoted to making the blues into a nationally popular literature. But this love of the blues explains only one side of Hughes's
creative activity. Such a one-sided focus has the tendency to racialize a
multivalent body of writing that is known outside the United States for
precisely the opposite reasons, namely, as a rejection of "race provincial-
ism" (as Du Bois referred to conservative kinds of black nationalism), as
an embrace of intellectual worldliness, and as a search for new aesthetic

forms through which workers, teachers, artists, students, and intellectuals could carry on the American struggle for socialist equalitarianism.[1]

While the formalist criticism on Hughes has served a valuable function by showing the beauty and complexity of his verse forms, and in turn reaffirming the blues and the tradition of African American rhetoric and oratory as major achievements in world literature and culture, it has failed to consider his poetry in direct relation to his drama, his writings for young people, his musicological research and folklore studies, and especially his journalism. In this respect, Hughes is the prosecution's star witness against American formalism and New Criticism. His novel *Not without Laughter*, which the white formalist critic Robert Bone dismissed as ill conceived, has no underlying plot and draws on the epistolary tale, the blues poem, the memoir, and the bildungsroman for its complex structure. In design and intention, Hughes's plays are operatic, not dramatic. His writings on folklore and popular culture and their interrelations were intended for young people, not an academic audience. And his acclaimed Simple stories are revised newspaper columns that were originally conceived as a radio soap. If by "mulatto literature" Cuba's Nicolás Guillén meant the kind of writing that celebrates a nation's diversity by claiming a right to *all* its artistic forms, Hughes belongs among this literature's avantgarde.[2] At the same time, by no means is this an argument for reappropriating his poetry and prose on behalf of American multiculturalism or ethnic pluralism. What I propose is much more modest and straightforward.

Hughes's aesthetic preferences and his conscious decisions as a writer and intellectual followed from his commitment to making equalitarian ideas popular in the United States. In the Gramscian sense, he was one of the country's greatest "permanent persuaders." But here arise certain false expectations and the inevitable charge of tendentiousness. After all, Hughes began distancing himself from the Communist Party in the 1940s. In the 1950s he publicly renounced his "political poetry" of the 1920s and 1930s to appease the anticommunist right, excising all his verse that contained such words as *capitalism, socialism, Lenin, proletariat,* and *revolution*

1. Two important books on Hughes's reception outside the United States, which provide evidence that Hughes's international reputation as a socialist writer actually grew during the 1940s and 1950s, are Deming Brown's *Soviet Attitudes toward American Writing* and Mullen's *Hughes and Haiti.*

2. Robert Bone, *The Negro Novel in America,* 75–77. For Guillén's concept of "mulatto literature," see Morejón's "Race and Nation."

when preparing the first edition of his *Selected Poems* (1959). Indeed, the idea that he "moved away" from socialism has been treated as a given, by liberal bourgeois and Marxist critics alike.[3] It is claimed that as Hughes's attitude toward the American Communist Party changed, so too did his creative interests in a socialist alternative. As I will show, the claim rests on a concept of aesthetics in which the writer's political tendency is seen to determine his or her literary or cultural tendency. In the case of Hughes's newspaper writing of the 1940s and 1950s, the uselessness of this conception is clear, for in his work for the *Chicago Defender* it was his advanced literary tendency that included his political tendency. And that political tendency, rather than turning centrist as some critics have claimed, actually became more radical, more advanced aesthetically, and closer theoretically to the Marxist tradition.

Following the insights of Walter Benjamin in his essay "The Author as Producer," I want to shift the question of Hughes and socialism, and the problems of literature and politics that it raises, back to the starting point of dialectical criticism where, as Benjamin has it, there is "absolutely no use for such rigid, isolated things as work, novel, book. It has to insert them into the living social context." He proposed the paradigm shift in straightforward terms. "Rather than ask, 'What is the *attitude* of a work to the relations of production of its time?' I should like to ask, 'What is its *position* in them?'" Moreover,

> This question directly concerns the function the work has within the literary relations of production of its time. It is concerned, in other words, directly with the literary *technique* of works. . . . [T]he concept of technique provides the dialectical starting point from which the unfruitful antithesis of form and content can be surpassed. And furthermore, this concept of technique contains an indication of the correct determination of the relations between tendency and quality. . . . If, therefore, I stated earlier that the correct political tendency of a work includes its literary quality, because it includes its literary tendency, I can now formulate this more precisely by saying that this literary tendency can consist either in progress or in regression in literary technique.[4]

Benjamin's classic example of the dialectical tensions between literary form and content, as opposed to the abstract and formalist *unity* of form

---

3. Cha-Jua argues in "'Lest Harlem See Red'" that Hughes left the Marxist tradition after 1938.

4. "The Author as Producer," 222.

and content, is the Soviet Russian newspapers of the early 1920s. The mission of the Soviet journalists was "not to report but to struggle; not to play the spectator but to intervene actively." Their slogan was "Writers to the *Kolkhoz!*" (the collective farm), and their principal tasks were the following: to call mass meetings; to collect funds to pay for tractors; to persuade independent peasants to join the collective farm; to inspect the reading rooms; to create wall newspapers and to edit the *kolkhoz* newspaper; to report for Moscow newspapers; and to introduce radio and mobile movie houses. For Soviet newspaper writers had found in the bourgeois press an insoluble antinomy between science and literature, criticism and production, and education and politics. At the same time that the productive forces in capitalist society were creating more readers, with far broader interests and concerns, the social organization of literature was rapidly falling apart, as the social relations of production remained essentially unchanged from their preindustrial forms. Benjamin refers to this dialectical moment as "the decline of writing in the bourgeois press," an insight that could be easily applied to radio and television journalism today, in particular to the current dominance of the talk-show format, the daily opinion poll, and reality television:

> The fact that nothing binds the reader more tightly to his paper than his impatient longing for daily nourishment has long been exploited by publishers, who are constantly opening new columns to his questions, opinions, protests. Hand in hand, therefore, with the indiscriminate assimilation of facts goes the equally indiscriminate assimilation of readers who are instantly elevated to collaborators. In this, however, a dialectic moment is concealed: the decline of writing in the bourgeois press proves to be the formula for its revival in that of Soviet Russia. For as writing gains in breadth what it loses in depth, the conventional distinction between author and public, which is upheld by the bourgeois press, begins in the Soviet press to disappear. For the reader is at all times ready to become a writer, that is, a describer, but also a prescriber. As an expert— even if not on a subject but only on the post he occupies—he gains access to authorship. Work itself has its turn to speak. And the account it gives of itself is part of the competence needed to perform it. Literary qualification is founded no longer on specialized but, rather, on polytechnic education, and is thus public property. It is, in a word, the literarization of the conditions of living that masters the otherwise insoluble antinomies, and it is in the theater of the unbridled debasement of the word—the newspaper—that its salvation is being prepared.[5]

5. Ibid., 225.

The Blues Critique of Everyday Life

I don't see why white folks don't have no blues—they got all cash money and brownskin women, too.

—T. C. Johnson, *Blues and the Poetic Spirit*

To understand black is to understand work—and the denial of work.

—Lerone Bennett Jr., *The Shaping of Black America*

With *Blues People*, Amiri Baraka was the first scholar to argue that the blues irrupted as African American labor's cultural response to the right-wing overthrow of Reconstruction in the 1870s and 1880s—what Du Bois termed in *Black Reconstruction* "the counter-revolution of property."[6] In Baraka's originary account, it was during this high period of white political reaction—"the white backlash," in today's language—that the early blues artists introduced to American culture a new structure of feeling. The early blues singers raised work—and the denial of work—to the category of the aesthetic, a grounding of the blues that Hughes would spend a lifetime popularizing through sound recordings, writings for the stage, and extensive national and international lecture tours, as well as in poetry, prose, and journalism. "The leisure and movement allowed to Negroes after the Civil War," Baraka argued,

> helped to standardize the new blues form as well as spread the best verses that were made up. . . . But the thousands of black blues shouters and ballit singers who wandered throughout the South around the turn of the century moved from place to place not only because Negroes were allowed to travel after the Civil War, but because for a great many Negroes, emancipation meant a constant desperate search for employment. . . . The Negro had to have wages to live: for the first time he needed money and had to enter the fierce struggle for economic security like any other poor man in this country. Again, even the economic status of the Negro after his freedom proposed new changes for his music. "I never had to have no money befo' / And now they want it everywhere I go." The content of blues verse had become much changed from the strictly extemporized lyrics of the shouts and hollers.[7]

In his magnum opus, Du Bois described the post-Reconstruction period thus:

6. Du Bois, *Black Reconstruction*, 580.
7. Baraka, *Blues People*, 64–65.

The Negro's access to the land was hindered and limited; his right to work was curtailed; his right of self-defense was taken away, when his right to bear arms was stopped; and his employment was virtually reduced to contract labor with penal servitude as a punishment for leaving his job. And in all cases, the judges of the Negro's guilt or innocence, rights and obligations were men who believed firmly, for the most part, that he had "no rights which a white man was bound to respect."[8]

Baraka's theory of the blues asserts the primacy of the dialectics of work and leisure by establishing a new beginning for modern aesthetic theory, since the prevailing notion that aesthetics and everyday life belong to separate spheres of existence never obtained with the blues. "*Blues* means a Negro experience," Baraka claimed,

> it is the one music the Negro made that could not be transferred into a more general significance than the one the Negro gave it initially. Classic blues differs a great deal from older blues forms in the content of its lyrics, its musical accompaniment, and in the fact that it was a music that moved into its most beautiful form as a *public entertainment*, but it is still a form of blues, and it is still a music that relates directly to the Negro experience. Bessie Smith was not an American, though the experience she relates could hardly have existed outside of America; she was a Negro. Her music still remained outside the mainstream of American thought, but is was much closer than any Negro music before it.[9]

These two passages from *Blues People*, seen in the context of Du Bois's summation of the post-Reconstruction period, present two essential concepts.

First, class-consciousness is not imputed to African American workers but rather produced out of their constant struggle for wage-labor. African Americans know themselves as workers not because the laws of capitalism confront them "as invisible forces that generate their own power," to use Georg Lukács's classic terminology,[10] but rather because these state laws are imposed by *visible* forces generated by an *alien* power—alien because the power is inhuman and brutally antidemocratic. The forces are those of whites-only labor unions, racist foremen, lynch mobs, reactionary state legislators, KKK-affiliated judges and sheriffs, local landowners and

---

8. Du Bois, *Black Reconstruction*, 167.
9. Baraka, *Blues People*, 94.
10. Lukács, "Reification and the Consciousness of the Proletariat," 87.

storekeepers, overseers, prison guards, supervisors, and police. Historian William H. Harris provides an excellent overview of the postbellum situation in *The Harder We Run: Black Workers since the Civil War:*

> Through a series of vagrancy, apprenticeship, enticement, and other restrictive measures, southern whites practically bound blacks to their previous slave status. Most heinous were the laws of vagrancy, a concept southern whites defined broadly when applied to blacks. Afro-Americans found that moving about, even when looking for work, could cause them to be arrested and hired out to the highest bidder, provided the previous owner had first preference. Moreover, minor children of black parents deemed unable to provide for them could be "apprenticed" to their former owners until they reached adulthood. Such apprenticeship amounted to peonage. In desperate efforts to find work, blacks signed agreements that committed not only the head of the family, but other members as well, to labor from sunup to sundown in the fields and to accept numerous other tasks that made them responsible for the crops and the surrounding property. In addition, they had to suffer the indignity of calling their employers "master."[11]

To put it differently, for African Americans the process of working-class consciousness is radically discontinuous with what Georg Lukács has described as labor's progressive rationalization and mechanization under capitalism—a process by which the worker's "lack of will is reinforced by the way in which his activity becomes less and less active and more and more *contemplative.*"[12]

Recognizing this great turning point in U.S. history and society, when African American labor confronted new forms of white racial oppression and a reorganized capitalist ruling class on whose behalf these new racist measures were imposed, is vital for understanding the specific forms and concepts of African American working-class consciousness. African American labor did not arrive at self-consciousness merely through the subordination of man to the machine but rather through the circumstances of a new phase of white racial oppression in which its members' subordination was to other poor people—the poor whites. As we will see, for Hughes this meant that African American aesthetics also adhered to a different logic and developed according to a different historical process. Consider Lukács's next sentence:

---

11. *The Harder We Run: Black Workers since the Civil War,* 9–10.
12. Lukács, "Reification and the Consciousness of the Proletariat," 89.

The contemplative stance adopted towards a process mechanically con-
forming to fixed laws and enacted independently of man's consciousness and impervious to human intervention, i.e., a perfectly closed system, must likewise transform the basic categories of man's immediate
attitude to the world: it reduces space and time to a common denomi-
nator and degrades time to the dimension of space.[13]

Baraka's argument is that the contemplative stance favored by the bourgeois aesthetic, which has been resisted, revised, or reappropriated by the
popular classes in U.S. society at different historical conjunctures, never
was accepted as an option by African American working-class artists and
intellectuals. The dialectic in Baraka's conception of the blues aesthetic
explains the historical dilemma of "black music in white America," the
phrase used for the subtitle of *Blues People.* Writing in the midst of major
changes in jazz music and culture—in particular, the emergence of the
hard-bop movement led by Ornette Coleman, Sonny Rollins, Cecil Taylor,
and John Coltrane, to whom Baraka gave the name "the new generation's
private assassins"—he sought an aesthetic theory that could explain these
jazz artists' noble and defiant return, in the face of unprecedented commercial success and legitimacy, to the nonchordal screams, rants, and
hollers of the early blues. "The implications of this music," Baraka wrote
in the final pages of *Blues People,* "are extraordinarily profound, and the
music itself, deeply and wildly exciting. Music and musician have been
brought, in a manner of speaking, face to face, without the strict and often grim hindrances of overused Western musical concepts; it is only the
overall musical intelligence of the musician which is responsible for shaping the music. It is, for many musicians, a terrifying freedom."[14]
    What is essential is the stress Baraka places on tonality, gesture, and the
"total area" of the blues in explaining the hard-boppers's return to the
roots of African American music. He shows that, given the logic of cultural production under late capitalism—the democratization of the commodity in which a corresponding standardization of personal expression
is ongoing, and an eventual co-optation of even the most resistant and
idiosyncratic forms of art and literature is inevitable—the staying power
of the blues is due to its historically determined social relation to white
America. This relation Baraka gives the name "non-American," as a political symbol of the persistence of white racial oppression—his point

13. Ibid.
14. Baraka, *Blues People,* 227.

about the life of Bessie Smith, who died bleeding outside a whites-only hospital—and a call for African American artists to renew the blues as a systemic alternative to white bourgeois aesthetics.

Although it remains a controversial point, Baraka says that what distinguishes U.S. capitalist society from other capitalist societies is "the socio-economic psychological disposition" of the white American. When not a sin against nature, leisure for whites is merely a debased, anomalous reward for racially privileged work and wages. Thus, for Baraka the ideology that binds the white worker to his poor and propertyless status in America is not only Christian, national, patriarchal, and racial, it is also transparently capitalist. For the African American, he argues, the opposite is true: leisure is labor's dialectical counterpart. When not a socially vital pleasure and community resource, leisure assumes the form of an attack on capitalist work discipline. In other words, when leisure is reified and debased, as under white racism, it becomes alienated in the same manner it was in a system of wage labor. Hence, for Baraka the African American work songs are the nation's first religious songs. Their offspring are the nation's blues people, the bearers of its first working-class ideology. "The diverse labors of the African," he explains, "which were the sources of this [the transplanted African American work song], had been funneled quite suddenly into one kind of labor, the cultivation of the white man's fields. The fishing songs, the weaving songs, the hunting songs, all had lost their pertinence. But these changes were not immediate. They became the realized circumstances of a man's life after he had been exposed sufficiently to their source and catalyst—his enslavement."[15]

The second concept advanced by Baraka in *Blues People* is that, in the blues, leisure is always an essential element of labor, in the sense that leisure for the African American worker is not an anomalous social privilege as it is for the white American. In the blues, leisure is a struggle for work and work is a struggle for leisure. As a turning point in U.S. labor history, the blues response from African American freedmen and freedwomen to the overthrow of Reconstruction and the horrors of the postbellum period created a space within which the particularities of African American struggle could be firmly established. For in the blues, wrote Hughes, "behind the sadness, there is almost always laughter and strength" (CW 11:291). In the terms of *Blues People*, this tension within the blues comes from the historical experience of being at one and the same

15. Ibid., 6, 20.

time "free" (no longer a racially enslaved lifetime bond-laborer) and un-free (still racially oppressed). For this reason, *the struggle for work,* as op-posed to the classless notion of *the experience of work,* is the blues singer's principal passion and concern.

In the main, jazz scholars have argued that the experience of work is the basis of the blues' universal appeal. But in few scholarly investigations of the blues is there an awareness of the dialectics involved, namely the blues aesthetic's relation to historical movement and change. From the begin-ning, scholars have made claims for the blues that rest on formalist crite-ria and that privilege "timeless" features, such as the blues singer's "self-pity," over the overall blues aesthetic preference and conscious method of making art. This kind of blues scholarship got its start with Howard W. Odum and Guy B. Johnson's classic collection of African American folk songs, *Negro Workaday Songs* (1926), in which they devoted a chapter to the blues. They argue that the blues is the ultimate form of rationalization, "by which process the singer not only excuses his shortcoming, but at-tracts the attentions and sympathy of others . . . to his hard lot."[16] The for-malist limits on the blues are also evident in Samuel Charters's *The Coun-try Blues* (1959) and in its sequel, *The Poetry of the Blues* (1963). Charters argues that in the blues can be found all the poetic devices of great En-glish poetry: imagery, symbolism, versification, form, personification, simile, metonymy, and more.

In his introduction to *The Country Blues Songbook* (1973), Stephen Calt takes Charters's argument one step further by arguing that, because the blues draws on Bible verses, English ballad forms, and folk couplets, it discredits itself as poetry. Predictably, Calt mentions only those blues in which "traditional" poetic forms are used. The idea is that only "original" verse forms constitute poetry; all else is merely "tradition-based" and therefore nonpoetry by definition. In Charles Keil's *Urban Blues* (1966), the absurdity of seeing the blues as an assimilative cultural form comes through in his odd application of the Bales Interaction Scale to various blues lyrics. Keil maintains that, in listening to big-beat radio stations, he can no longer distinguish between white and black blues singers. In his effort to gain the blues formal approval by the Anglo-American academy, Peter Guralnick claims in *Feel Like Going Home* (1971) that the blues can-not be considered protest music because the lyrics "do not even deal with the subject." For Guralnick, the blues are a typical American music in that they speak to the artist's precarious relation to commerce and exchange.

16. Odum and Johnson, *Negro Workaday Songs,* 20–21.

In his brilliant *Langston Hughes and the Blues*, Steven Tracy contradicts sharply these formalist approaches: "Since blues performances are both communal and individual expressions, dynamic and varied, based on factors such as time, location, dominant local performers and traditions, availability of phonograph recordings, and individual skills and creativity, the depth and breadth of the term 'blues' can indeed overwhelm anyone trying to reduce it to a pithy phrase."[17]

Yet the African American laborer's struggle for work is but one side of the blues dialectic: the other side is the worker's *rejection* of wage labor as the fate of humanity and a simultaneous political critique of the supposed "natural" (or "progressive") transition from bond-labor servitude to "free labor." Herein lies the radical discontinuity between the blues as a mainstream American music and the blues as a "non-American" aesthetics of antagonism. Unfortunately for blues criticism, Hughes's concept of the blues has never been acknowledged by academic musicologists, much less taken seriously, for Hughes sensed new aesthetic possibilities in the blues for understanding the complex social relations between work and leisure. He also located the interstices of this larger blues narrative of revolt, against white capitalist assimilationism, decades prior to the blues impulse's full projection by the Black Power movement in the 1960s and 1970s. By understanding the blues as a way of seeing and knowing—as an antagonistic counter to "integrated" interpolation by bourgeois ideology—rather than as a mere antidote to depersonalization and new forms of capitalist work discipline, Hughes diagnosed a major problem in aesthetic theory. Henri Lefebvre has shown in *Critique of Everyday Life* that the modern discourses of sociology, specifically industrial sociology and the sociology of leisure, have conceived of labor and leisure as external to one another. "The notion of free leisure is valid up to a certain point," Lefebvre argued. "Beyond that point it is inadequate. If we push it too far we run the risk of forgetting that there can be *alienation in leisure as in work* (and alienation precisely in so far as the worker is trying to 'disalienate' himself!")[18] The key terms are *reification, disalienation, leisure,* and *work,* for they each provide departure points for Hughes's sundry aesthetic experiments with the literary blues mode.

Hughes's intervention in *The Weary Blues* is to argue that the blues is an aesthetics of liberation or, better, disalienation, because in the blues leisure is never considered apart from work. The blues artist is for Hughes a

17. Keil, *Urban Blues,* 47; Guralnick, *Feel Like Going Home,* 39; Tracy, *Langston Hughes and the Blues,* 60.
18. Lefebvre, *Critique of Everyday Life,* 39.

working-class hero in that the language of work can also be the language of love and social relationships. He recognized the blues singer's actual social relations with the African American working classes, in which he or she is loved precisely because of the alternative kinds of pleasure the blues offers: alternative in the sense of not determined by the market. For this reason, a lot of Hughes's blues poetry takes place in the blues club. In this environment "alienation in leisure as in work" is usually the main issue at hand. In the title poem of *The Weary Blues,* for instance, the nuances of the blues singer's style are directly related to the ecstasy offered by the sheer excess of his labors onstage. No one knows when he will finish for the night, since everything in his playing style indicates ease and effortlessness:

> Swaying to and fro on his rickety stool
> He played that sad raggy tune like a musical fool. (*CW* 1:23)

Here the dialectics of work and leisure are compressed into a single line: the drowsy swaying gesture is the external appearance of the blues, while its inner pace is at the highest level of physical exertion and stamina. In African American aesthetics, to play, sing, write, or dance "like a fool" signifies a tireless work ethic, where a certain level of desire and intensity has been attained by the creative laborer in his or her own social activity. Within this concept is an admiration for physical stamina, intelligence, and resiliency. Additionally, there is the recognition that only in *disalienated* labor is this type of ecstasy through work possible—so much so that Hughes's blues singer in "Weary Blues" never finally stops playing the blues, or punches out for the night, even after going home to sleep:

> And far into the night he crooned that tune.
> The stars went out and so did the moon.
> The singer stopped playing and went to bed
> While the Weary Blues echoed through his head.
> He slept like a rock or a man that's dead. (*CW* 1:24)

The labor of the blues singer is disalienated because *he* decides when to quit for the night, not a club owner, a record company promoter, or a business manager. His labor is disalienated because his work discipline is on his own terms and because it depends on the particular needs of his current audience, who are in the process of disalienating themselves right along with the blues singer. Hughes uses a call-and-response format throughout the poem to emphasize this aspect, through the collective expressions "O Blues!" and "Sweet Blues!" When the calls and responses end so, too, does the blues singer's performance. Hence, Lefebvre's powerful insight about the problem under capitalism of being alienated while seeking relief from alienation is answered by the blues singer through the blues form itself: the blues is done only when the process of collective dis-alienation is done, at least for the night. It is in this sense that Hughes's concept of the blues singer as a working-class hero corresponds closely with Hegel's description of the "higher language" of tragedy. "The hero," argues Hegel,

> is himself the spokesman, and the representation given brings before the audience . . . *self-conscious* human beings, who know their own rights and purposes, the power and the will belonging to their specific nature, and who know how to state them. They are the artists who do not express with unconscious naiveté and naturalness the merely external aspect of what they begin and what they decide on, as in the case in the language accompanying ordinary action in actual life; they make the very inner being external, they prove the righteousness of their action, and the "pathos" controlling them is soberly asserted and definitely expressed in its universal individuality.[19]

The blues are antagonistic because they understand the struggle for work in its social reality and thus include in the category of labor the work of women and children as well as the wage-labor of men. For example, in Hughes's blues opera *Don't You Want to Be Free?* (1938), where he employs a twelve-bar blues stanza consisting of two lines followed by a refrain—a rare blues variation made famous by Ma Rainey in the early 1920s—he shows the range of the blues singer's heroic character by giving voice to African American women's struggle for work and pleasure—a new concept that would serve as the basis for his volumes of blues poetry *Shakespeare in Harlem* (1942) and *Montage of a Dream Deferred* (1951). In his blues opera, Hughes introduces a structure of feeling that would become dominant in the 1960s through the efforts of the creative artists and intellectuals of the Black Arts movement: a heightened awareness of the assault on the African American family that is one of the hallmarks of white racial oppression.

> Cook them white folks dinner
> Wash them white folks clothes,

19. Hegel, *On Tragedy*, 291–92.

Be them white folks slave-gal,
That is all she knows
Be them white folks slave-gal,
That is all she knows.

. . . .

Whip done broke his spirit,
Plow done broke his back.
All they wants a slave, that's all,
When a man is black.
Nothin' but a slave, that's all,
If a man is black. (*CW* 5:543, 544)

Tracy makes a profound point about these blues stanzas in *Langston Hughes and the Blues:*

> The stanzas also represent an inversion of the standard twelve-bar blues pattern in the repetition of the third and fourth as opposed to the first and second. It was a peculiarly effective way of emphasizing the social message of the stanzas by repeating that point, not what led to it. It was as if the echo of that line is the echo that is heard throughout the lives of African Americans, or the one that should be heard, expressing the bitterness that might urge them into action.[20]

Raising the work of African American women domestics to the category of national labor should be seen in both a political and an aesthetic light. Historian Carter G. Woodson claimed in 1930 that black washerwomen were responsible for all the progress made by African Americans since the civil war; Hughes's inclusion of their working-class labor power in his blues opera reaches even further. For example, the U.S. Congress's passing of the National Industrial Recovery Act (NIRA) in 1933 had established a minimum wage, but the legislation exempted virtually every field of work in which African American women were employed: domestic work, agricultural labor, and "yard" work at various southern textile mills. Because NIRA exempted these jobs from minimum wage coverage, the immediate, as well as the future, effects on African American women workers and their families were brutal, as the newly formed Social Security agency also exempted this work from coverage. Compounding this bad situation was the complete immiseration of African American farm workers during the depression, especially sharecroppers.

20. Tracy, *Hughes and the Blues*, 72–73. For Hughes and Ma Rainey, see 150–51.

African Americans suffered declines in employment in all classes of agricultural work during the depression, while the number of white farm owners actually increased. "Conditions were so tight," notes William Harris, "that black women seeking housework in New York would go to a subway station in Harlem and stand along the platform as white housewives who needed a maid for the day came along and casually surveyed them. The conditions closely resembled those of the domestic slave markets of the antebellum South."[21]

In this context, the dialectics of work and leisure in the passage from Hughes's blues opera can be understood on two levels. In qualitative terms, work after emancipation was no different for African Americans than it was under slavery. In addition, this qualitative *sameness* was felt by African American workers as a sudden change in consciousness of themselves as black national workers. For if the reason for suffering under racial slavery was felt to be "racial" in character, in postemancipation U.S. society that reason could no longer hold. The power of labor became consciously and collectively understood, in the sense that wage labor became the primary site of the African American freedom struggle. Further, what comes through in Hughes's stanzas above is that the African American worker sensed this transformation of labor—from racialized to reracialized—through a backward glance to slavery: an art of analogy that provided African Americans with a unique perspective on work under U.S. capitalism and that made possible the formation of a new kind of working-class consciousness, precisely because labor was under the same system of white racial oppression. In other words, just as white American workers were putting their faith in such factors as the industrialization of the South as marking the beginnings of a healthy labor movement, African American workers saw in the process of industrial transformation the beginnings of another stage of white racial oppression. In industrialization, what black workers were perceiving was nothing more than a transparent means "to reestablish as quickly as possible," in the words of D. A. Tompkins, a prominent white cotton mill entrepreneur, "respectability for white labor." In 1940, southern historian W. J. Cash had stated the strategy of white cotton mill owners plainly: "we shall create a sanctuary for the falling common whites and place thousands of them in employment which by common agreement shall be closed to the Negro."[22]

21. Woodson, "The Negro Washerwomen: A Vanishing Figure"; Harris, *The Harder We Run*, 101–7.
22. Tompkins and Cash quoted in Allen, *Invention of the White Race*, 154, 156–57.

It is in this context that the bluesman J. C. Johnson's ironic query about "why white folks don't have no blues" receives a provisional answer: white workers don't have the blues because they neither think nor act like workers. As Lukács argued convincingly in "Reification and the Consciousness of the Proletariat," groups in capitalist society "which have both the appearance of stability (the routine of duty, pensions, etc.) and also the—abstract—possibility of an *individual's* elevating himself into the ruling class" are "the constitutive type of capitalist socialisation." In this way Lukács's thesis that the transformation of all objects into commodities means that workers can "become conscious of the social character of labour"—that class consciousness is thereby imputed to the working classes—is qualified strongly by the blues. The missing term is class struggle, for in the blues it is African American labor's struggle for the right to exist as a laboring class that produces class consciousness, not the increased rationalization, mechanization, and quantification of the world confronting Arican American workers.[23] As such, the blues artist's insistence on seeing gender relations, current events, play, religion, erotic pleasure, laughter, violence, rest, food, travel, alcohol and drugs, the landscape, technology, night, and animals as each having a definite social character has to do with the circumstantial politicization of everyday life under white racial oppression.

In this way, too, the blues proves Lukács's theory of reification, but with the same qualification. Take his explanation of the reification of everyday life:

> It appears in the first instance as the pure *object* of societal events. In every aspect of daily life in which the individual worker imagines himself to be the subject of his own life he finds this to be an illusion that is destroyed by the immediacy of his existence. . . . The quantification of objects, their subordination to abstract mental categories makes its appearance in the life of the worker immediately as a process of abstraction of which he is the victim, and which cuts him off from his labour-power, forcing him to sell it on the market as a commodity, belonging to him. And by selling this, his only commodity, he integrates it (and himself: for his commodity is inseparable from his physical existence) into a specialised process that has been rationalised and mechanised, a process that he discovers already existing, complete and able to function without him and in which he is no more than a cipher reduced to an abstract quantity, a mechanised and rationalised tool.

23. Lukács, "Reification and the Consciousness of the Proletariat," 172.

According to Lukács, whereas the bourgeois is able to persuade himself that the reification of everyday life has not wrecked his personality as it has the worker's, the worker, "who is denied the scope for such illusory activity," sees the split in his being "preserved in the brutal form of what is in its whole tendency a slavery without limits. He is therefore forced into becoming the object of the process by which he is turned into a commodity and reduced to a mere quantity."[24]

The blues qualification is thus that the scope for illusory activity is not denied to the African American worker; instead, the worker's undoing lies precisely in the bourgeois worlds of illusion that constantly interpolate him. Moreover, contemplative activity itself does not have to be illusory. It can be used to heroize the lives of workers who resist reification and thus create a political critique of bourgeois ideology itself. To quote Lonnie Johnson's blues "contemplation" on the Depression, "Hard Times Ain't Gone Nowhere,"

> Peoples raving 'bout hard times, tell me what it's all about.
> Hard times don't worry me, I was broke when they first started out.
> Friends, it could be worser, you don't seem to understand.
> Some is crying with a sack of gold under each arm and a loaf of bread
>   in each hand.
> Peoples raving 'bout hard times, I don't know why they should.
> If some people was like me, they didn't have no money when times
>   was good.[25]

Hughes and His Simple Strategy

[M]y best poems were all written when I felt the worst. When I was happy, I didn't write anything.

—Langston Hughes, *The Big Sea*

The way one speaks indicates not only the way one thinks and feels, but also the way one expresses oneself, the way one makes others understand and feel.

—Antonio Gramsci, *Selections from Cultural Writings*

The blues is a feeling and when it hits you, it's the real news.

—Leadbelly, *Negro Folk Songs as Sung by Leadbelly*

24. Ibid., 171.
25. Quoted in Paul Garon, *Blues and the Poetic Spirit*, 80.

The blues critique of everyday life, as Ralph Ellison explained eloquently in *Shadow and Act*, is "an impulse to keep the painful details and episodes of brutal experience alive in one's aching consciousness, to finger its jagged grain."[26] This impulse is where Hughes's interventions as a journalist and his conception of the blues make contact. A year prior to beginning work at the *Chicago Defender*, Hughes published an essay in the *Crisis* that called attention to the growing distance he felt between African American literary artists and the blues as a way of making literature. Entitled "The Need for Heroes," the essay expressed his concern that the blues impulse had been abandoned by African American writers in favor of bourgeois aesthetics, specifically a preoccupation with death, tragedy, defeat, madness, and impotence. The heroic elements of the blues were in need of a literary revival:

> The written word is the only record we will have of this our present, or our past, to leave behind for future generations. It would be a shame if that written word in its creative form were to consist largely of defeat and death. Suppose *Native Son*'s Bigger Thomas (excellently drawn as he is) was the sole survivor on the bookshelves of tomorrow? Or my own play, *Mulatto*, whose ending consists of murder, madness, and suicide? If the best of our writers continue to pour their talent into the tragedies of frustration and weakness, tomorrow will probably say, on the basis of available literary evidence, "No wonder the Negroes never amounted to anything. There were no heroes among them." (*CW* 10:223)

As if announcing a year in advance his decision to start writing regularly for the African American press, Hughes went on to praise the black press in general and the *Defender* in particular for accomplishing what in his view many African American literary artists had failed to do: recording the narratives of everyday African American heroes. "Don't look for [heroism] today in books," he wrote, "because our few writers haven't gotten around to putting it down yet—but look in the back files of the Negro press: *The Chicago Defender* in the riot days of 1919 in that tough and amazing city" (*CW* 10:225–26).

In the context of Hughes's statement that he wrote poetry only when sad and depressed, his turn toward newspaper writing in the early 1940s appears to be one answer to the lack of heroes in African American literature that he had, with a heavy heart, diagnosed in his essay. Although there are heroes in his blues poetry, they arise from a deeper blues feeling or lyricism and are not, in the main, heroic characters per se. In discover-

26. *Shadow and Act*, 78.

ing in the black press stories of heroic African American women and men, Hughes also discovered a new form in which everyday heroism could be expressed, and for the next twenty years he explored its many possibilities. In Hughes's newspaper writing, the dialectics of work and leisure not only animate the presentation of ideas but also make possible the treatment of African American working-class heroism through a blues *technique*, as distinct from a blues form or a blues content. In this technique of antagonism is included the socialist political tendency that he is said to have abandoned at the end of the 1930s.

On February 13, 1943, Hughes introduced "Simple" in his column for the *Defender*, which he had given the name "Here to Yonder." Hughes's Simple columns would become his most popular literary innovation since his blues poems of the 1920s and 1930s, generating a musical play, *Simply Heavenly*, and five books of stories: *Simple Speaks His Mind, Simple Takes a Wife, Simple Stakes a Claim, The Best of Simple*, and *Simple's Uncle Sam*. As the compiler of Hughes's *Defender* columns, Christopher C. De Santis, has nicely put it, "For Hughes, Simple became a voice—sometimes happy, sometimes disgusted, always irreverently humorous—through which he could comment on international race relations and current events to a wide audience. It was also through Simple that Hughes's desire to bring the concerns of the black working class to the forefront of African American consciousness was most successfully manifested."[27]

Simple became a feature of the "Here to Yonder" column immediately, and within a few years fans were sending Hughes hundreds of letters a month. In her study of the Simple stories, *Not So Simple*, Donna Akiba Sullivan Harper has shown that many letter writers were under the assumption that Simple might just be a passing phase in Hughes's work as a columnist, since his appearance during the first year of the column was irregular and always unannounced. One fan wrote: "For two whole weeks, now, we have looked for word of Mr. Simple in your weekly column, but to no avail. . . . Mr. Simple has become a pleasant habit to us; a habit we wouldn't like to break." As Harper documents, many fans stressed the intellectual nourishment that Simple provided African American workers, as well as the pride they took in Simple's stance against the elitism and pretentiousness of the middle classes. "The majority of my friends are simple minded also," read one letter to Hughes, "and we just love to see our thoughts in print where some of our more *complicated*

27. De Santis, ed., *Langston Hughes and the "Chicago Defender": Essays on Race, Politics, and Culture, 1942–62*, 14–15.

minded brothers and sisters, both *white* and *black,* might see them and *stop* and *think a moment* about what we are thinking about." Harper notes that some of the letters included suggestions for future Simple columns, while others were accompanied by more practical offerings, including the Holford inhaler for hangovers that Hughes received in 1946.[28] Harper provides plenty of evidence to support the claim that it was these letters that inspired Hughes to envision the dialogues between Simple and himself as material for a book. But in the early stages, the fans simply wanted more Simple columns, which Hughes gave them. He increased their number from ten in 1943 to seventeen in 1946. In 1949 the Simple column ran twenty-three times.

This dialogical relationship between Hughes and his *Defender* readership both produced and was a product of African American working-class culture. The *Defender* itself has a legendary reputation in African American popular culture. For instance, in a recently reissued sound recording from 1946, *Blues in the Mississippi Night,* bluesmen Big Bill Broonzy, Memphis Slim, and Sonny Boy Williamson recall that in many places down South a lookout man was needed if black folk planned on reading the *Defender* in public or even behind closed doors. As Big Bill talks about the difference between a "bad nigger" and a "crazy nigger"—a "bad nigger" will kill another black man but not his white oppressor, whereas a "crazy nigger" will fight his white oppressor and "open the eyes of a lot of Negroes, tell 'em things that they didn't know"—he proceeds to tell a story about an African American sharecropper who used to read the *Defender* to his fellow workers. When the white overseer found out, he ran the sharecropper out of town. Memphis Slim, who doesn't agree with Big Bill's definition of a "bad nigger," adds to Big Bill's story with one of his own:

> I were in a place called Marigold, Mississippi. And you know, they had a restaurant in there and in the back they had a peephole. And I thought they were gambling back there or something, and I went back there to see was they gambling. In fact, I was kinda stranded. I wanted to go back there and shoot a little crap and make me a little stake. And you can imagine what they were doing back there. They were reading the *Chicago Defender,* and they had a man on the door, a lookout man on the door wid a peephole. And if a white man or something come into the restaurant, they'd stick the *Defender* in the stove, burn it up and start playing checkers. That's the way they had to smuggle the *Defender* down there.

28. Harper, *Not So Simple: The "Simple" Stories by Langston Hughes,* 92–93.

That's what they really call a bad Negro, a Negro that had nerve enough to smuggle the *Chicago Defender* down in the state of Mississippi where they didn't allow them to put 'em off there.[29]

Hughes's "Here to Yonder" column was itself based on a conversation between himself and an African American worker in Harlem—a "Conversation at Midnight," as he titled the draft of his first Simple piece. It was clear from the beginning of the column that the art of conversation was for Hughes no "simple" release mechanism or means of compensation after a long day of work. The conversational mode itself was "a place to set and think in," as Simple would soon put it. Harper calls this aspect of the stories a case of "heteroglossia," where "the dialogic technique of the Simple stories immediately places into an artistic order the voices of Simple and the foil. . . . We as readers do not witness . . . events from the standpoint of an objective third-person narrator; we witness Simple's recounting of them."[30]

Harper's analysis is important, for the tendency in the Simple criticism has been to see Hughes's innovation either as a specifically African American phenomenon—an authentic black narrative style, coming from the boasts and the toasts, the blues, the work songs, the animal stories, and so on—or as a formal literary device, in the tradition of Whitman, Finley Peter Dunne (the creator of "Mr. Dooley"), James Thurber, and H. L. Mencken.[31] Comparing Hughes to Whitman, Donald Gibson argued, "Both adopt personae, preferring to speak in voices other than their own." Harper cites the theories of M. M. Bakhtin to break up the stolidity of these twin approaches to Simple, pointing directly to Hughes's *technique*. As Harper asserts astutely, "Whereas Mencken laughed at people, Hughes laughed with them." For this, much more than a mere literary device was required.[32]

To get a sense of Hughes's technique, it is best to quote from the very first Simple column. After Hughes is invited over to Simple's table at a

29. *Blues in the Mississippi Night;* my transcription.
30. Rampersad, *Life of Langston Hughes,* 2:62. Harper, *Not So Simple,* 46.
31. The position that Simple belongs in the African American oral tradition is advanced by two critics in particular, Roger Whitlow and Richard Barksdale. See Witlow's *Black American Literature: A Critical History* and Barksdale's "Langston Hughes: His Times and His Humanistic Technique." The corollary—that Simple is a "universal" archetype—is held by Donald Gibson in "The Good Black Poet and the Good Gray Poet: The Poetry of Hughes and Whitman" and by Arthur Power Dudden in "The Record of Political Humor."
32. Gibson, "Good Black Poet and Good Gray Poet," 66. Harper, *Not So Simple,* 64.

neighborhood bar in Harlem, they break the ice by discussing the virtues of nighttime, a popular theme of the blues, which leads them into a lively debate over the relations between fascism in Europe and white racial oppression in the United States. The topic was raised by Simple as a matter of "current events," since Harlemites had been informed by New York City officials, several weeks earlier, that a new curfew was in effect. Simple hates curfews, which gives Hughes the idea that he can persuade Simple to join the racially segregated U.S. Army on the grounds that the Nazis would impose even stricter curfews on Harlem residents if they prevailed in the war. This kind of dialectical turn from the specific to the general and back again would come to characterize every Simple column:

> My Simple Minded Friend said, "Day time sure is a drag. I like night time a lot better."
>
> "I do too," I said. "Day time hurts my eyes. I was born at midnight but my mama told me I didn't start crying until morning. After that, I hollered and cried every morning straight for two years."
>
> "I could holler and cry every morning now when I have to get up and go to work."
>
> "That's why you don't get ahead in the world," I said. "The people who get ahead in the world are the ones who get up early."
>
> "I get up early," said my Simple Minded Friend. "But I don't get ahead. Besides, what you say is not necessarily right. Joe Louis likes to sleep—and he got ahead."
>
> "I'll bet he doesn't sleep in the army, though."
>
> "I'll bet he does," said my Simple Minded Friend, "'cause he's always on furlough. How come Joe Louis is always on furlough?"

These opening lines provided an enticing introduction to Simple's rhetorical style and indicated the kind of discourse readers could expect in future columns. In addition, they established that the great poet Hughes was someone readers of the column might bump into themselves while conducting their everyday affairs in Harlem. As one of the most famous Harlemites of the time, Hughes went a long way in this introductory Simple column, with just a few suggestive formulations, toward distinguishing himself from other literary celebrities of the age—black, white, or otherwise. This particular celebrity could be found not at cocktail parties on Park Avenue or in the trendy literary salons of Greenwich Village, but relaxing with a cold beer with fellow Harlemites at the corner lounge, discoursing on current events in a cutting-edge, laid-back, unpretentious manner. Also, the conversation between Hughes and his new friend indicated that all chitchat would, thankfully, be left out of the discussion. In this way Hughes was showing his readers high respect by elevating the standards of their discourse.

In the column, the Hughes character admits that he can't answer Simple's loaded question, which enables Simple to show off more of his rhetorical skills:

> "I can't answer you that," I said, "but I guess it's because he's doing Special Services."
> "Naw! It's because Joe said, 'We're on God's side.' White folks like religious Negroes."
> "Well, we are on God's side, aren't we? Naturally, God's against the Nazis."
> "Who made the Nazis?"
> "Are you trying to blame Hitler on God?"
> "Who made Hitler?"
> "Well, who made him?" I asked.
> "God," said my Simple Minded Friend.
> "Then He must have made him for some purpose."
> "Sure, He did," declared my Simple Minded Friend. "God made Hitler to be a thorn in the side of our white folks."
> "Aw, you're crazy!" I said. "Hitler would stick a bigger thorn in your side, if he could get hold of you."
> "HE AIN'T going to get hold of me," said my Simple Minded Friend. "I'm gonna fight him. I been reclassified in 1-A."
> "Good! When you hear that bugle blow in the mornings . . . you'll feel swell. The army will make you like rising early."
> "Nothing can make me like rising early," said my Simple Minded Friend. "Nothing."
> "Then why don't you go to bed at some decent hour at night?" I asked.
> "Why don't you?" demanded my Simple Minded Friend in return.
> "I'm a writer," I said, "and I don't have to get up until noon."[33]

Blues scholar Jeff Todd Titon has argued astutely in his anthology *Downhome Blues Lyrics* that this kind of storytelling structure rejects the pattern of European American balladry in which a linear, progressive, and final resolution is standard. In this respect, Hughes's blues technique in the "Here to Yonder" column is Simple's refusal to accept reform as the ultimate solution to white racial oppression. Titon shows that resigned acceptance and attempts at reform resolve only a minority of blues songs.

33. Quoted in Rampersad, *Life of Langston Hughes*, 2:62–63.

In his words: "Most often, the victim, declaring his independence, steps out of his role with an ironic parting shot and leaves."[34] In Hughes's "Conversation at Midnight," the blues aesthetic is modulated self-ironically, as he turns the parting shot against himself.

This is just one aspect of the complexity of the Simple columns, one that many critics have passed over by seeing the Hughes character's function in the columns in strictly formalist terms, that is, as a "foil," or as a case of "consubstantiality," as critic Harry L. Jones has termed it. Jones argues that Hughes the writer is the "foil" in the column—he "is the more moderate, less militant, Simple." Yet Hughes's role as Simple's favorite drinking partner cannot be reduced to a literary device, since the "foil" argument implies that Simple needed such a foil to improve his standing with readers, to have someone in contrast to whom he could appear "better." Some critics seem to have forgotten that the *Defender* was not only a black-owned publication but also the third largest African American newspaper in the country, with an editorial stance much closer to the communist press than to the mainstream black periodicals of the period. Thus, there was never a need to raise Simple's stature through the use of a "moderate" foil. If anything, the opposite was true: there was a need to raise the stature of Simple's reclusive, college-educated drinking partner, who knows less than Simple about the community and even less about the ways of white folks, a point that Simple always returns to when his interlocutor accuses him of being "obsessed with race."[35]

In this sense, in Hughes's construction of the complex Simple-narrator dualism can be seen lucidly what Houston Baker has called the shaping of "a *profitable*, expressive identity . . . to play on possibilities—to divide one's self . . . into 'public' and 'private' personalities."[36] Still, the idea that Simple is provincial and even racist has been taken as a truism in the Simple criticism. For example, Arthur P. Davis suggested:

Insofar as an author may be his own creations, Langston Hughes is the earthy, prejudiced, and race-conscious Simple as well as the urbane, tol-

34. Titon, *Downhome Blues Lyrics: An Anthology from the Post–World War II Era*, 3.

35. Jones, "Rhetorical Embellishment in Hughes' Simple Stories," 138–29. See Harper's informative introduction to *Not So Simple* (1–19) for a discussion of the *Defender*'s editorial stance and circulation numbers. For an interesting account of the *Defender*'s relationship to the communist movement, see Ben Burns, *Nitty Gritty: A White Editor in Black Journalism*. Von Eschen, *Race against Empire*, also features a discussion of the *Defender*.

36. Baker, *Blues, Ideology, and Literature*, 59.

erant, and sophisticated "straight man" in the sketches. The two characters are opposite sides of the same coin, and from their observations
and insights, interacting one upon the other we get the twofold vision
found in much of Mr. Hughes' best work, whether prose or poetry.[37]

A more accurate characterization of Hughes's Simple strategy is to say
that Simple is single-minded or "provincial" about one thing only: the rejection of second-class citizenship. In "Black Power," C. L. R. James described H. Rap Brown in these same terms—as an African American artist
and political leader who shared Simple's command of signifyin' and other African American rhetorical tropes and strategies.

> What Brown is doing is this, he is taking care that the total rejection of
> second-class citizenship, the single-mindedness, the determination to
> fight to the death if need be, which now permeates the Negro move-
> ment, will not be corrupted, modified, or in any way twisted from its
> all-embracing purpose by white do-gooders and well-wishers of whom
> the United States is full. . . . It is not racism, it is politics, and the rapid-
> ity with which [African Americans] are learning politics is proved by the
> masterly solution of this problem that they have arrived at. They say to
> whites who want to fight, "We welcome the addition of your forces to
> the struggle. But there up in the North, in your own town, there are ar-
> eas where a Negro is not allowed to own a house or even to rent. There
> is an opportunity to fight American race prejudice. You want to fight?
> Go *there* and fight *there*. We can manage down here without you."[38]

In all the criticism on Hughes's Simple saga, it is hard to find a characterization of Simple as all-embracing as the political analysis James devoted
to H. Rap Brown. To take this analogy further, I will focus on two key aspects of Hughes's newspaper writing: his treatment of the fragment and
the whole—the movement from "here to yonder" and back again—and
the dialectics of literary style and political tendency, or what I have been
referring to as the relations between the African American civil rights
struggle and the aesthetics of black equality.

The Fragment and the Whole

> And if we complain of the general inability to perfect a language of the peo-
> ple in creative expression, that should not prevent us from insisting on

37. Davis, "Langston Hughes: Cool Poet," 19.
38. James, "Black Power," 369.

speaking for them until the moment arrives when literature can celebrate its great wedding, when the private voice and the public voice become one.

—Mahmoud Darwish, *Memory for Forgetfulness*

Hughes began his work for the *Defender* in June 1942 when he was asked by the editor-in-chief, Metz Lochard, to write an article on Negro writers and the war for a special Victory Edition of the paper. Hughes's contribution, "Negro Writers and the War," appeared on September 26, 1942, alongside articles by W. E. B. Du Bois, Franklin and Eleanor Roosevelt, Wendell Willkie, Supreme Court Justice Hugo L. Black, A. Philip Randolph, Alain Locke, H. G. Wells, Pearl Buck, and Walter White. In his piece, Hughes proposed three tasks for African American journalists and literary artists, each a component of the Communist Party's organizing strategy during the Popular Front period. First, they should refrain from seeing fascist rule in Germany, Italy, and Japan as a catalyst for African American advancement in the U.S.; second, they should urge African Americans to see World War II in its international context, not solely in terms of "race"; and third, they should

> reveal the international aspects of our problem at home, to show how these problems are merely a part of the great problem of world freedom everywhere, to show how our local fascists are blood brothers of the Japanese fascists . . . to show how on the great battle front of the world we must join hands with the common people of Europe, the Soviet Union, the Chinese, and unite our efforts—else we who are American Negroes will have not only the Klan on our necks in intensified fashion, but the Gestapo as well. (*CW* 9:217)

One illuminating aspect of Hughes's program for black journalism during the war was his cautionary advice to African American journalists about the appeal of Hitler, Mussolini, and Hirohito, for many members of the African American working classes depended on black newspaper writers (editors, reporters, correspondents, and columnists) as sources of information and opinion. Hughes drew a clear distinction between African American literary artists and African American print journalists. For African American creative writers with access to the mainstream press and to corporate publishing, his advice was completely unnecessary. Du Bois had set the precedent during the Harlem Renaissance when he criticized Claude McKay for valorizing racial uplift ideology in *Home to Harlem,* and the consensus among African American literary artists fifteen years later, during a period of major changes for African American labor, maintained Du Bois's stance against using literature to express the values and sentiments of racial nationalism. But reporters in African American communities across the country would hear daily the combat-style attitudes toward the war, like the idea that Hughes cited in his first *Defender* article—whoever hurts my enemy is my friend. Several subsequent columns and Simple pieces indicate that Hughes sensed a new form of political militancy among African American workers. Rather than moderating it, he chose to understand its logic in order to present a laboring-class alternative for African Americans, based on their social position in the racial order. In fact, his attentiveness to the appeal that racial nationalism held for black workers during the war seemed to be a Leninist strategy. In his *Theses on the National and Colonial Questions* (1920), Lenin posed the problem this way:

> It is ... the duty of the class-conscious Communist proletariat of all countries to treat with particular caution and attention the survivals of national sentiments among the countries and nationalities which have been longest oppressed, and it is equally necessary to make certain concessions with a view to hastening the extinction of the aforementioned distrust and prejudices. Unless the proletariat, and, following it, all the toiling masses, of all countries and nations all over the world voluntarily strive for alliance and unity, the victory over capitalism cannot be successfully accomplished.[39]

Another illuminating aspect of Hughes's program for black journalism was that his stress on using the war to better inform African American workers about alternatives to U.S. imperialism deviated from the position taken by many African American literary artists and intellectuals. Du Bois's position, for example, was "we close ranks again"—an explicit reference to his resolution on World War I in which he urged African Americans to "close our ranks shoulder to shoulder with our own white fellow citizens and the Allied nations that are fighting for democracy."[40] Whereas Du Bois made no mention in his support of the war of a socialist alternative in the Russian Revolution, Hughes made that alternative the centerpiece of his argument. In this he was also attentive to the African American workers' racially segregated social status and, more important, adamant that the "question of Negro patriotism to the United States," as Du Bois had framed it, be considered from the standpoint of African

39. V. I. Lenin, "Preliminary Draft of Theses on the National and Colonial Questions," 28–29.
40. Du Bois, "Closing Ranks Again," 739.

American workers first and foremost. In contrast, Du Bois viewed the question as a matter of two "extreme attitudes" in African American communities that required reconciliation: total acquiescence "in whatever the white nation says," and open rebellion against taking up arms for the United States. For Du Bois, the task was to find and then advocate the middle ground between these two extremes.[41] For Hughes the task was much more complex, since the former extreme—"total acquiescence"—did not obtain with the African American working class. Therefore, it was not necessary to pose the question in this way—as a matter of two extremes—for to do so missed the point that the second "extreme attitude" was extreme only in the extent of its white racist determination. For instance, noting that white mob violence would serve to silence African Americans in the South who questioned black participation in the war, Hughes asserted, "It is the duty of our writers to express what these voiceless people cannot say, and to relate their longings for decency and fairness to the world aims of the President's Four Freedoms for everybody" (CW 9:219). This dialectical movement in Hughes's thinking on the war is important for understanding his newspaper writing in general and his Simple columns in particular, for through Simple these two kinds of writing—journalism and literature—would generate a new aesthetic: the art of "listening fluently," as Simple was always fond of stating it.[42]

Hughes's first regular column for the *Defender* was published on November 21, 1942. Under the heading "Here to Yonder," he used the column to state his intentions as a journalist and commentator. He repeated the point he had made in "Negro Writers and the War" that "An offensive against Hitler abroad demands for its success the intensification of the attack upon Hitler at home." He then clarified the meaning of "Here to Yonder." Politically, it had to do with linking the fight against fascism in Europe to the fight against white racial oppression in the United States, but aesthetically it also signified Hughes's own love of travel. He would spend his columns writing about worldly places and people because, "for the last twenty years, half writer and half vagabond, I have traveled from here to yonder around the world and back again." But Hughes's emphasis was that his column would keep African American workers eager to read, since "Your folks and mine—as colored as me—scattered all over

41. W. E. B. Du Bois, "Negro Editors on Communism: A Symposium of the American Negro Press," 17.
42. "Listen fluently" is what Simple tells Boyd before he recites his own poetry. See Hughes, "Wooing the Muse."

the world from here to yonder . . . shall be the subjects of this column." Nonetheless, the focus of this first column was not so much his aims as a columnist but rather on a conversation with an African American truck driver who had just been drafted. The conversation took place at a government clinic in Manhattan where Hughes and the truck driver were in line for their first physicals. Hughes had been wired a card from the draft board on November 2, 1942. While in line at the clinic, he joined in a heated discussion about white racism in the U.S. military. The truck driver was frustrated because he had heard from African American soldiers that most black workers were being sent to labor battalions, not combat units. But Hughes the interlocutor was skeptical. "Look at the pictures you see of colored soldiers in the papers," said the truck driver right back to Hughes, "always working, building roads, unloading ships, that's all. Labor battalions! I want to be a fighter!" In what would become his most typical conversational tactic in the Simple columns, Hughes played "devil's advocate" and said that he knew a black worker who went to Officers School and another who was learning to fight paratroopers. "I don't know none," the truck driver shot back.

> "And besides, if they don't hurry and take this blood test, I'm liable to lose my job. This Italian I work for don't care whether the draft board calls you or not, you better be to work on time. He ain't been in this country but six or seven years and owns a whole fleet of trucks, and best I can do is drive one of 'em for him. Foreigners can get ahead in this country. I can't."
> "Some colored folks get ahead some," I said.
> "You have to be a genius to do it," he argued.
> Another man in the line spoke up, older, dark brownskin, quiet. "Between Hitler and the Japanese," the other man said, "these white folks are liable to change their minds. They're beginning to find out they need us colored people."
> It was that third fellow who took the conversation all the way from the here of Manhattan Island to the yonder of Hitler, the Japanese . . .
> . . . But I hope, since he wants to be a fighter, Uncle Sam will give him a gun, not a shovel or a truck. A gun would probably help his morale a little—now badly bent by the color line.[43]

Hughes's role at the *Defender* as both an observant interlocutor and a deft conversationalist would take on many forms over the course of twen-

---

43. Hughes, "Why and Wherefore," 222.

ty years. When discussing language questions, Hughes assumed the role of "Ananias Boyd," a bourgeois who believes that the solution to white racial oppression rests on the shoulders of black folk and not progressive whites and who thinks that one of the greatest obstacles to African American equality is the persistent use of Black English Vernacular. In fact, Boyd frequents Simple's favorite Harlem bar solely "for literary purposes," he says.[44] He has never lived in the South and has no social life to speak of. His major concern is "contemplating how people play so desperately when the stakes are so little" (CW 7:31). Although several critics have argued that Boyd is Hughes's alter ego, there is no evidence that Hughes ever felt that white racism could be eradicated if African Americans would "extend a friendly hand" to whites, which is Boyd's standard answer to the question. On the contrary, Hughes's writings never let the "white race" off the hook. Hughes believed, as Simple does, that every time African Americans extended a friendly hand to whites they got put back in their place. At one point, Hughes has Simple recite a popular ditty for Boyd to make exactly this point:

> The black cat said to the white cat,
> "Let's sport around the town."
> The white cat said to the black cat,
> "You better set your black self down!" (CW 7:41)

At the same time, Boyd is a likable character. He often changes his opinions after Simple breaks down his argument, and the other African American patrons of the bar find Boyd remarkably different from the rest of the middle class. Harper has analyzed Boyd's role in the Simple columns suggestively: "Simple not only tolerates the foil's education, he draws upon it. On the other hand, he feels comfortable reprimanding his bar buddy when he perceives an exaggerated erudition or any other offensive air surfacing. The foil, then, emerges as a sympathetically presented upwardly mobile, college-educated persona."[45] In this respect, Harper notes that

44. On the language question, Hughes's "Wooing the Muse" column is instructive. Here, Simple shares some of his "poetries" with Boyd. Instead of commenting on Simple's poems, however, which were written at Orchard Beach the previous weekend, Boyd insists on correcting Simple's grammar and encourages him to write more about nature and less about Jim Crow. In this light, it's probably absurd to suggest that Hughes would have himself given this same advice to a poetry-writing African American worker. Hughes, as usual, was showing the inanity of this advice—perhaps where the name "Ananias" came from in the first place.
45. Harper, Not So Simple, 5.

Hughes's use of Boyd in his play *Simply Heavenly* provides an even richer nuance to Simple's steady conversational partner. For example, in the play Miss Mamie appreciates the difference between Boyd and "Character," a minor figure in the play who is described as "that character trying to make people think he's educated." "One thing I like about Boyd here," she says, "even if he is a writer, he ain't always trying to impress folks. Also he speaks when he comes in a public place" (*CW* 6:190).

A view of Boyd that has not been put forth in the criticism is that Boyd represents for Hughes a fresh moment of possibility: an immersion of the African American literary artist in the vibrant language of the black working classes. As Harper has shrewdly observed, it is Boyd who learns from Simple and not the other way around. By the same token, Hughes wanted the "Here to Yonder" column to serve as an African American working-class forum for political education, and here Boyd is a great asset because he "conversates" on international affairs with Simple, whose position is that the whole world would be a much better place if African Americans were no longer under the boot of Jim Crow. This process of immersion, which takes place through an ongoing conversation between the middle-class Boyd and the working-class Simple, is the first level of Hughes's Simple strategy. The second level is that on which a new African American working-class consciousness is *produced*. Hughes's aesthetic innovation is to dialectically link the two levels, since any immersion in the everyday life of black workers by the African American literary artist is reduced to a routine academic exercise if no new literary culture arises from this vital interchange.

In terms of Antonio Gramsci's definition of "cultural politics," Hughes's task was to put in motion "a continuous adhesion and exchange between popular language and that of the educated classes." Moreover, the Simple columns put into effect what Gramsci termed "a deeper cultural substance": a way of thinking and feeling that exists "beneath the cosmopolitan expression of musical, pictorial and other types of language." A literary work is truly popular, Gramsci argued, when its

> cultural, moral and emotional content adheres to national morality, culture and feelings—these being understood not as something static but as a continually developing process. Immediate contact between reader and writer is made when the unity of form and content for the reader can presuppose a unity of poetic and emotional worlds. Otherwise, the reader must begin to translate the "language" of the content into his own language. The situation is rather like that of someone who has

learned English in a Berlitz speed course and then reads Shakespeare: the effort of literal comprehension, achieved with the constant aid of a mediocre dictionary, reduces the reading to no more than a pedantic school exercise.[46]

Hughes's April 26, 1947, column, "When a Man Sees Red," is one of the best examples of this strategy. In writing it, Hughes's conscious aim was "an adhesion and exchange between popular language and that of the educated classes." One interesting aspect of the column is its projection of an imaginary scene in front of the House Un-American Activities Committee (HUAC), something that would take place in reality for Hughes six years later. As Rampersad has noted, when Hughes arrived in Washington in March 1953 to appear in front of the committee, the scale of the anticommunist assault on the American left was already familiar to everyone. During his questioning of Hughes, McCarthy's chief counsel, Roy Cohn, actually cited a Simple column, "Something to Lean On" (November 22, 1947), as evidence that Hughes was a communist, since the column "thoroughly ridicules" the committee and its anticommunist objectives.[47]

The committee is also thoroughly ridiculed in "When a Man Sees Red," but Hughes goes even further by giving Simple the floor to declare why he thinks African American workers should begin seeing their interests through the color "red," not through "red, white and blue." Hughes the interlocutor has only two or three lines; the rest of the story is Simple's account of a recent confrontation he had on the job with his white boss. After the boss has tried to get him to work faster, Simple reaches his limit and tells the boss off:

"The boss said, 'You ain't doing as much work as you used to do.'
"I said, 'A Dollar don't do as much buying for me as *it* used to do, so I don't do as much for a Dollar. Pay me some more money, and I will do more work.'"
"What did he say then?"
"He said, 'You talk like a red.'
"I said, 'What do you mean, red?'
"He said, 'You know what I mean—*red, communist.* After *all* this country has done for you Negroes, I didn't think you'd turn out to be a red.'
"I said, 'In my opinion, a man can be any color except yellow. I'd be yellow if I did not stand up for my rights.'

46. Gramsci, *Selections from Cultural Writings*, 120.
47. Rampersad, *Life of Langston Hughes*, 2:213, 217.

"The boss said, 'You have no right to draw wages and not work.'

"I said, 'I have *done* work, I *do* work, and I *will* work—but also a man is due to eat for his work, to have some clothes, and a roof over his head. For what little you are paying me, I can't hardly keep body and soul together. Don't you reckon I have a soul?' I said.

"Boss said, 'I have nothing to do with your soul. All I am concerned about is your work. You are talking like a communist, and I will not have no reds in my plant.'" (*CW* 7:156)

Speaking in political symbols, as opposed to moral metaphors, had the added advantage of allowing Hughes's Simple figure to flourish in the role of trickster. This comes through strongly in the column:

"I said, 'It wasn't so long ago you would not have no Negroes in your plant. Now you won't have no reds. You must be color-struck!'

"That got him. That made him mad. He said, 'I have six Negroes working for me now.'

"I said, 'Yes, out of six hundred men. You wouldn't have them if you could've got anybody else during the war. And what kind of work do you give us? The dirty work! The cheapest wages! Maintenance department—which is just another way for saying *clean up.* You know you don't care nothing about us Negroes. You getting ready to fire me right now. Well, if you fire me, I will be a red for sure, because I see red this morning.'" (*CW* 7:156–57)

Hughes, under the ruse of the cautious bourgeois, warns Simple about using this kind of language in the workplace, which gets Simple even hotter. "Is it red to want to earn decent wages? Is it red to want to keep your job? And not want to take no stuff off a boss?" This puts the bourgeois on the defensive: "Don't yell at me. I'm not your boss. I didn't say a thing." At this point, Simple brings the whole issue back to the interlocutor's class position. "Just because you are not working for white folks," Simple tells his conversational partner, can he afford to steer clear of labor struggles. "There you go bringing up the race issue again," Simple's interlocutor responds. "I think you are too race-conscious." "I am black," Simple retorts, "also I will be red if things get worse. But one thing sure, I will not be yellow. I will stand up for my rights till kingdom come." Hughes the author then prepares the way for the imaginary scene in front of the House Un-American Activities Committee: "You'd better be careful," says the interlocutor, "or they will have you up before the Un-American Committee." Simple fires back: "I wish that old Southern chairman would send for me. I'd tell him more than he wants to know" (*CW* 7:157).

As Simple creates the scenario in the column, Hughes lays out a straight-forward argument, with concrete examples and anecdotes, of the relations between anticommunism and white racism. Simple forces the committee to admit that anticommunism draws no distinction between African American labor organizers and international communists. "You're both," the committee tells Simple. "Why?" asks Simple. "Because I want to drive a train?" "Yes, because you want to drive a train! This is a white man's country. These is white men's trains! You cannot drive one. And down where I come from, neither can you ride in a WHITE coach." This sets up Simple's most brilliant riposte:

> "'You don't have any coaches for Red Russians,' I said.
> "'No,' yells the Chairman, 'but we will have them as soon as I can pass a law.'
> "'Then where would I ride?' I asked. 'In the COLORED coach or in the RED coach?'
> "'You will ride nowhere,' yells the Chairman, 'because you will be in jail.'
> "'Then I will break your jail up,' I said, 'because I am entitled to liberty whilst pursuing happiness.'
> "'Contempt of court!' bangs the Chairman." (CW 7:158)

It would be easy to see Hughes's argument here as a kind of middle-class African American veiled threat against the U.S. ruling class. Yet even a cursory look at the debates over African American civil rights and communism in the 1930s shows a qualitative difference between Hughes's position and that of the African American press in general, in which the veiled threat was in fact regularly deployed. In the spring of 1932, for example, Du Bois undertook as editor of the *Crisis* the publication of a major symposium on communism. The participants were journalists and editors in the black press. At the time, the Scottsboro Boys death penalty case was at a decisive stage; the anti-eviction, unemployment, and sharecropper movements were gaining momentum; and the American Communist Party had nominated labor organizer James W. Ford as its candidate for vice president, the first time an African American had run for such a high office since Frederick Douglass was the candidate of the Equal Rights Party in 1872. In the main, the African American editors and journalists who took part in the symposium addressed themselves to the U.S. ruling class, not to African American workers. Journalist W. P. Dabney, for instance, wrote: "There will be no black Communists in America when fair play rules, merit is recognized, race prejudice ostracized. Will Pharaoh heed?"

P. B. Young of the Norfolk, Virginia, *Journal and Guide* elaborated this position more forcefully:

> The Communists in America have commendably contended for and have practiced equality of all races, and in their many activities, have accepted Negroes into their ranks in both high and lowly positions; more, they have dramatized the disadvantages of the Negro by walking in a body out of a jim-crow Pittsburgh hospital, by aiding ejected dwellers, and in industrial strikes directed by them fighting against the practice of excluding Negroes from labor unions. All these accomplishments go to the credit side for the Communists.[48]

Of all the editors and journalists featured in Du Bois's symposium, those representing the *Defender* were the least willing to sell out the Communist Party in exchange for new legitimacy. As historian Mark Solomon has shown in *Red and Black: Communism and Afro-Americans,* throughout the 1930s the *Defender* consistently argued that failure to support the efforts of American communists "would constitute an unprincipled accommodation to a racist society which expected loyalty but refused to justify such devotion by granting equality."[49] It was this principled stand in support of the Communist Party that separated the *Defender* from mainstream African American newspapers of the day and that would provide fertile soil for Hughes's aesthetic experiments with Simple more than a decade later.

To put it another way, whereas African American editors and journalists such as Dabney and Young saw in the American communist movement a prime opportunity to extend moral metaphors to the sphere of politics—"Will Pharaoh heed?"—the *Defender*'s tactic was to make the Communist Party into a political *symbol*. This important distinction between moral metaphor and political symbol was also a feature of Hughes's writings for the *Defender*. As in "When a Man Sees Red," the political *conditions* for activism are what matter most, not the moral persuasiveness of certain political tactics and strategies. Not only does Hughes have Simple defend American communists in front of McCarthy and his white anticommunist inquisitors, he goes even further by showing black labor's *internalization* of the communist answer. Simple discovers in political action

---

48. Du Bois, "Negro Editors on Communism," 156, 17. The symposium "Negro Editors on Communism" is discussed in Mark I. Solomon, *Red and Black: Communism and Afro-Americans, 1929–1935,* 522.
49. Solomon, *Red and Black,* 525–26.

a sphere reserved for symbols, not metaphors. It is the *symbol* of communism—the color "red"—that Simple deploys against his white racist boss and the anticommunist movement in general, not the familiar moral metaphor. As a metaphor, the association of communism with the struggle for black equality was for Hughes limited in that it implied a deceptive optimism, not realistic "pessoptimism" (to paraphrase the Palestinian writer Emile Habiby) à la the blues. As political symbols, communism and blackness can be easily interchanged, as Simple's white boss and HUAC agree alarmingly.[50]

In the main, the African American editors and journalists in Du Bois's historic symposium assumed political neutrality on the part of the state, as if they trusted the "bipartisan" state to choose reconciliation between classes and "races" over labor militancy and the broadening of the Communist Party's base. What Hughes's column argued is that this view of politics was opportunistic because it asserted that the intellectual's role in the public sphere was a contemplative one. Simple's role is active in that he articulates his demands through imagery and political symbols, interrupting his own activity as a worker to better take on this new role. In this sense, "Here to Yonder" was itself a political symbol. It referred to a shifting of the ideological ground on which African American writers lived and worked. Their task was to enter the new life of black workers not as distant observers but as professional image-makers involved in the everyday needs and aspirations of their own African American working-class communities. Thus, Simple the black worker is better suited to address congressional committees on behalf of organized labor than are "oppositional" (or public) intellectuals, because Simple speaks in symbols, images, and analogies, not moral metaphors, and because these symbols, images, and analogies are themselves generated from everyday class struggle, not contemplation.

Simple comes to see *red* and *black* as synonymous through his own daily struggles as an African American worker. Robin Kelley has termed this process "the making of black internationalists." In Kelley's words, "Black Communists were not blank sheets when they entered the movement. Instead, they were born and reared in communities with a rich culture of opposition—a culture that enveloped and transformed the Party into a movement more reflective of African-American radical traditions than anything else." His terminology refers specifically to Alabama commu-

50. *Pessoptimism* is Habiby's sarcastic term for the situation of Palestinian citizens of Israel, from his masterpiece *The Secret Life of Saeed, the Ill-Fated Pessoptimist.*

nists during the Great Depression, yet it speaks also to the literary projection of Simple's conversion to communism. For Hughes, the idea that
communist ideology was "foreign" to black workers—a false notion that
continues to distort even the most sympathetic accounts of the relations
between African Americans and communism—was absurd. The opposite
was true: African American workers were already communists because
of their enforced racial position in the U.S. class struggle. The task for
Hughes, then, was to produce African American communist ideology
through the imagery and political symbols of everyday life: through an
aesthetics of black equality.[51]

Aesthetics of Black Equality

> The thing to treat is the condition which makes the daily press insufficient
> for the needs of Negroes. The justification of the Negro press . . . is that it
> fights for goals which if attained would liquidate itself. Thus it proves its
> essential integrity. Its essential patriotism and Americanism. In sum, we
> shouldn't ask why this or that is printed by Negroes, but what it is that
> causes Negroes to want to read such and such.
>
> —Arna Bontemps, letter to Langston Hughes, April 22, 1939

In terms of political education, Hughes would extend Simple's conversion process in "When a Man Sees Red" to the sphere of memoir two
months later when he launched a seven-part series on detailing his im-
pressions of the Bolshevik Revolution and his own experiences with
socialist life in the Soviet Union. According to Rampersad, Hughes was
"badly shaken" after receiving a summons from McCarthy's Senate Permanent Sub-Committee on March 23, 1953, and one can safely assume
that this series had a lot to do with his being summoned.[52]

The first column was entitled "The Soviet Union." Its opening lines set
the tone for the columns that followed: "There is one country in the world
that has no JIM CROW of any sort, NO UNEMPLOYMENT of any sort,
NO PROSTITUTION or demeaning of the human personality through

---

51. Kelley, *Hammer and Hoe*, 99. In terms of distortion, Solomon's *Red and Black* stum-
bles over the issue of appropriation from start to finish. He rightly faults American
party leaders for pushing a Europeanized model of class struggle on to African American organizers, yet never once does he assess the African American response to this
attempted imputation, and the creative methods black communists used anyway to
popularize Leninist slogans and strategies.

52. Rampersad, *Life of Langston Hughes*, 2:209.

poverty, NO LACK OF EDUCATIONAL FACILITIES for all of its young people, and NO LACK OF SICK CARE or dental care for everybody. That country is the Soviet Union." Hughes's choice of topics is revealing. The first column is a prologue, yet it is not without a "current events" angle of its own. After listing what he considered the most important gains of the Bolshevik Revolution, Hughes shifted his attention to a statement made recently in the U.S. press by Senator J. William Fulbright. Fulbright was quoted as saying that "we are willing and able to fight whenever we believe any power threatens the right and opportunity of men to live as free individuals under a government of their own choice." Hughes put his own blues response in parentheses: "As if such freedom existed in Arkansas." Fulbright's call to arms against the Soviet Union was thus the occasion for Hughes's seven-part counternarrative. "Perhaps he is so willing to fight the Soviet Union," he concludes the first column of the series, "because he knows that once Soviet ideas spread over the world, people will get tired of poor schools, Jim Crow—and Senator Fulbright."[53]

As Hughes would go on to show in the next six columns, the signal advance made by the Bolsheviks in the struggle to abolish racism, sexism, and internal colonialism consisted in the Communist Party's understanding of racial oppression, gender oppression, and national oppression as organically interconnected forms of capitalist social control, imposed and maintained by the Russian ruling class to exploit labor, especially in the "brown" countryside. In other words, Hughes's underlying argument was that the Bolshevik Revolution disproved the notion that racism, sexism, and colonialism are permanent or "transhistorical" fixtures of modern social life, or that they are psychologically or culturally predetermined.

In this respect, Hughes was far ahead of his time. For as Allen has shown convincingly in *The Invention of the White Race,* in the field of U.S. historiography the notion that white racism is the product of "psychocultural" tendencies on the part of white Americans to racially dominate not-whites has gone persistently unchallenged. Allen observes that the "liberating impulses set loose by World War Two, and the impact of the United States civil rights movement in particular brought official society for the first time in American history to acknowledge racism to be an evil in itself." But then, as he documents, it was the all too familiar "White Blindspot" that led white American historians down a neoconservative path in explaining the historical origins of white racial oppression. Rather

53. Hughes, "The Soviet Union," 167, 168.

than recognizing the Anglo-American capitalist foundation of white racism, white historians opted for psychological and cultural explanations, such as the so-called unthinking desire of Euro-Americans to racially dominate not-whites, which had created, the white historians so claimed, "the discriminatory social atmosphere of the early seventeenth century." The main exponents of the discredited psychocultural model are Winthrop Jordan, in *White over Black: American Attitudes toward the Negro, 1550–1812* (1968), and Carl Degler, in *Neither Black nor White: Slavery and Race Relations in Brazil and the United States* (1971). The conclusion that follows from the psychocultural theories is that there is little, if anything, anyone can do to change racism. Writing several decades before white American labor historians set out to "prove" the psychocultural hypothesis, Hughes was already exposing its fallacies and urging his readers to take heart, for the seizure of state power by the Bolsheviks had ushered in a new period of radical abolitionism.[54]

The second column, "The Soviet Union and Jews," begins with Hughes reminiscing about his days as a child in Kansas, when his grandmother used to read to him from the daily paper and the *Defender* on hot summer nights on the front porch. In the daily paper were accounts of pogroms against Jews in Russia, the Ukraine, and Poland, and in the *Defender* were reports of lynchings of African Americans in the South. In his "child mind," he says, the connections between Jewish suffering in Europe and white racial oppression in the U.S. were made concrete through these nightly readings. In fact, he believed that "the Jewish people's problems were worse than ours." Taking his readers through his high school experience in Cleveland, where he celebrated along with his Jewish American peers the triumph of the Bolsheviks, he wrote, "Among the Jewish students in my American high school there was much jubilation because, they said, the Soviets did not believe in anti-semitism, and that there were Jews high in the government now." He then recounted several conversations he had with Russian Jews during his yearlong stay in the Soviet Union—June 26, 1932, to June 17, 1933—and many of his own firsthand observations as a visiting artist: "In the new Soviet Union I found no Jewish problem. I found no towns or cities from which Jews were still barred. I found no schools that refused to admit them. I found no more pogroms against Jews, and no one who dared openly insult or spit on Jews as was done in the old days. In *less than fifteen years*, I found that Soviet Russia

54. For a demolition of the psychoculturalist argument, see Allen's introduction to *Invention of the White Race*, 1–24.

had gotten rid of the Jewish problem." Presciently, he finished the column with an explanation of how the Bolsheviks eradicated anti-Jewish discrimination in such a short time, anticipating the epic struggle of the African American civil rights movement twenty years later. For the communists, Hughes wrote, it was not enough to pass laws prohibiting discrimination against Jews. Quoting several Communist Party members in Moscow, he concluded the column suggestively:

> The Russians said, "In the Soviet Union, we *make* [anti-discrimination laws] work. Here nobody dares insult or spit on or hurt a Jew simply because he is a Jew any more. If any one does that, he is put in jail. After he stays in jail a while, he does not come out and soon insult or harm a Jew again, not very likely. But if a person persists in his racial prejudice, then he is put in jail for a *long* time. So people have stopped insulting Jews here—that is, the people who still might wish to do so. But no Communist, no real Soviet citizen would think of doing so anyway, nor would any child educated in our schools. Such a thing would be uncomraderly—not to speak of being bad manners."[55]

The third column in the series, "The Soviet Union and Color," extends the discussion of how the Communist government fought racist discrimination against Jews through a personal account of life in Tashkent, the regional capital of the republics of Soviet Central Asia, and Ashkhabad, the capital of Turkmenistan. Hughes described the citizens of Tashkent and Ashkhabad as "brownskin." Like the Jews in czarist Russia, brown-skin nation-peoples in Central Asia were treated as second-class citizens. They were forced to ride in segregated trolleys and barred from using public parks. "I thought to myself," Hughes recalled,

> how many white Americans say it will take a hundred years, or two or three generations, to wipe out segregation in the South. But in Tashkent it had taken only a few years—and a willingness on the part of the government to enforce decent racial laws. . . . The Soviet government has wiped out all of these restrictions. People who less than 30 years ago had to travel under Jim Crow conditions, now travel as freely as anyone else. People who could not vote because of their race or colonial status, now vote as freely as others, and elect members of their own group to the Soviet law-making bodies. Whole groups of people whom the Tzars never permitted to have schools, now have schools—even colleges and

---

55. "The Soviet Union and Jews," 169, 170.

medical schools. . . . So there is a clear example in the world to prove to our American "experts" in race relations that it DOES NOT TAKE A HUNDRED YEARS, it does NOT take generations to get rid of ugly, evil, antiquated, stupid Jim Crow practices—if a country really wants to get rid of them.[56]

In his next column, "The Soviet Union and Women," Hughes argued that the Bolsheviks had also proved that gender oppression is homologous with racial oppression and class oppression. Continuing in his "here to yonder" mode of explanation, he wrote:

In many great cities of the capitalist world, I have seen poor girls of high school age selling their favors as cheaply as a pair of stockings. And I have seen women too old to be appealing to men still trying to earn a few dollars with their bodies. During the American depression, the streets of our big cities were full of such women. Poverty, the economic root of prostitution, is gone in the Soviet Union.

In the Tzarist days in Russia, only women of the top middle and upper classes received an education. It was almost unheard of for poor working girls to have a chance to go to school. Educational opportunities for poor people were far more limited in Imperial Russia than they are even in Mississippi today. And when a family could afford to send one child to school, it was the boy who got the chance, not the girl. Now all that is changed, and girls are educated equally with boys in the Soviet Republics. Jews and colored Asiatics, formerly hindered by quotas or no-admittance policies in Tzarist schools, are no longer so restricted, which means that women and men of minority groups have the same educational advantages as other Soviet citizens.

He concluded the column by turning to women's participation in Soviet culture, in particular the women of Central Asia. Before the revolution, he wrote, "Art and culture were not for women. Custom did not permit them to appear in public except heavily veiled. A woman was only for her husband's harem pleasure." He then provided a fascinating anecdote about the Uzbek dancer Tamara Khanum, who told Hughes in an interview that for her first several performances in Central Asia she had to be accompanied by soldiers, "to keep the reactionary men-folks from tearing her from the stage." Hughes added, "But today hundreds of women take part in Uzbek plays and concerts, so soldiers are no longer necessary."[57]

56. "The Soviet Union and Color," 171, 172.
57. "The Soviet Union and Women," 172–73, 174.

The last three columns of the series deal with the building of socialist institutions in the Soviet Union: the new dam at Chirchikstroy, public medical schools, health clinics and hospitals, schools and youth clubs, theaters, museums, cinemas, newspapers and radio stations, and public housing and transportation facilities. Hughes offered constructive criticism. In the area of health he was "deeply impressed," but in the areas of newspapers, housing, transportation, and especially the theater, he was sadly disappointed. Hughes identified a lack of condensed serial novels, a sports page, and comic strips as weaknesses in the Soviet daily press. Ironically, these are the same commercial elements of American newspapers that many left-liberal critics often associated with depolitization. Hughes wished that the Soviet press covered sports and had a comics section, and the lack of condensed serial novels, as well as the total absence of big and splashy pictures from around the world, compounded the problem of their unreadability. Hughes also found Soviet streetcars and trains overcrowded and inefficient, and good houses and apartments too hard to get. But these problems appeared surpassable; the problems with the daily press, however, would require a special effort. In this aspect, Hughes sounds a lot like Gramsci, who had found the success in Italy of foreign books in translation symptomatic of the Italian educated class's detachment from the popular classes, "not because the latter has not shown and does not show itself to be interested in this activity at all levels, from the lowest (dreadful serial novels) to the highest—indeed it seeks out foreign books for this purpose—but because in relation to the people-nation the indigenous intellectual element is more foreign than the foreigners." Hughes's critique of the new Soviet press follows these same lines and serves—as does all of his Soviet series—as an argument for developing a new anti–white supremacist popular-democratic politics in the United States—*mirroring the triumphs and failures of Soviet Russia.* Simple himself is a symbol of this new politics—a representative of the "lay forces" (in Gramsci's terms) that could elaborate "the intellect and the moral awareness of the people-nation."[58]

To conclude the seven-part series, Hughes ended with another political symbol: light. The last column, "Light and the Soviet Union," revolves around a conversation that Hughes had with an "unpreposing looking little guy of unknown ancestry, maybe Tartar, maybe Tajik." Described throughout the piece as "the meriney guy"—a reference to his complex-

58. Hughes, "Faults of the Soviet Union," 177; Gramsci, *Selections from the Cultural Writings,* 210.

ion—he took Hughes on a tour of Chirchik River Dam in the heart of Central Asia. "At the end of my rickety auto ride," Hughes wrote, "I was to hear in five short symbolic words the meaning of all that projected around the world and forward into time beyond our day." The five words spoken by his guide—"Then there will be light"—are an ingenious attempt by Hughes to elaborate a kind of "modern humanism," in Gramsci's sense of the term. The five symbolic words evoke the biblical Creation myth and function in the column as a sort of popular hook, since the process of electrification is felt by Hughes's guide on the level of a religious belief. Following the lead of his guide, Hughes sees in electrification the stuff of scientific popular literature—"a generic element of life and national strength," as Gramsci said of the Italian peasantry's interest in modern science, industrial production, and work.[59]

Always tuned in to the aesthetic preferences and intellectual interests of workers and peasants, Hughes lets his enthusiastic guide have the last words of the series, a flight of oratory that would have had Simple buying the next round of drinks:

> He said, "Then there will be light." He told me how there was only candles and lanterns and tallow flares now, and most of the villagers in the mud huts scarcely had those. "But," he said, "when the dam is built, there will be light! And not just for us," he said, "but for all the world, too, because this dam will be so powerful that we can send light over the borders into India and into China! That is why we do not mind giving our labor after hours to build this first building here—this workers' barracks—and we will give many extra hours to that dam, too—because when it is done—tell your people in your America—when it is done, there will be light! Light to study by and to see—and it won't be dark any more!"[60]

Reintegrationism

> The social expression of the liberated work instinct is *cooperation*, which, grounded in solidarity, directs the organization of the realm of necessity and the development of the realm of freedom. And there is an answer to the question which troubles the minds of so many men of good will: what are

59. Hughes, "Light and the Soviet Union," 179; Gramsci, *Selections from the Cultural Writings*, 211.
60. "Light and the Soviet Union," 179–80.

the people in a free society going to do? The answer which, I believe, strikes at the heart of the matter was given by a young black girl. She said: for the first time in our life, we shall be free to think about what we are going to do.

—Herbert Marcuse, *An Essay on Liberation*

An African American migrant laborer from the South, self-transplanted in the streets of New York, Simple always makes sure when he speaks of his origins to include his American Indian ancestry. Many of Simple's ideas about "race" are in fact fully developed concepts that can be traced back to Hughes's experiments with the mestizo trope during the 1920s and 1930s. For example, Hughes's emphasis in *A New Song* on the dehumanizing effects of white supremacy on the minds and bodies of Euro-American workers is explained later, from Simple's point of view, in rich, everyday detail. In one column, "Soul Food," Simple raises the question of integration in relation to African American cooking. Speaking ironically about the "drawbacks of integration," Simple recounts a story of an African American woman in Washington, D.C., "who went downtown one day to a fine white restaurant to test out integration." After finding that the restaurant did not have a single African American dish on the menu, the woman tells the waiter on her way out, "I knowed you-all wasn't ready for integration. I just knowed you white folks wasn't ready" (*CW* 8:230).

The story enables Simple to speak specifically on the importance of African American hospitality and fresh cooking for black workers in Harlem and to describe many of the joys of eating that Euro-American workers are deprived of due to their own white racism. "It's too bad white folks deny themselves that pleasure," says Simple, "because there is nothing better than good old-fashioned, down-home, Southern Negro cooking. And there is not too many restaurants in Harlem that has it, or if they do, they spoil everything with steam tables, cooking up their whole menu early in the morning, then letting it steam till it gets soggy all day. But when a Negro fries a pork chop *fresh,* or a chicken *fresh,* or a fish *fresh,* I am telling you, it sure is good" (*CW* 8:230–31). At this point, Simple breaks into a critique of a fried fish joint on Lenox Avenue, where "hateful help can spoil even soul food" (*CW* 8:233). The two women who run the fish joint are mean to their black working-class customers and consequently lose their patronage, and along with it their restaurant, one of the few soul food eateries for black workers in Harlem.

Rampersad has noted, "All of Hughes' life experiences as a Black American, all of his intimate knowledge of how Blacks lived, and all his love of

African Americans went into the Simple saga."[61] This can be seen in Simple's observations: they are precise, open-ended, antagonistic, and logical. More than anything, their conversational structures allow for a call and response with readers. As in "Soul Food," the pretext for speaking on issues important to Harlem's black working class, such as fresh cooking and good service, is often a national question, such as integration. This pleases the middle-class narrator, Boyd (whom Rampersad somewhat hastily identifies as Hughes himself), but as soon as Simple turns the issue around to examine what it means to black workers, Boyd accuses Simple of being obsessed with race. This dialogue between the black working class and the black middle class is perhaps the most complex aspect of the Simple stories, and also one of the main reasons for their popularity. For inside each Simple story are an infinite number of departure points for a discourse on race, class struggle, and black popular culture, all of which Boyd must be able to address in order to maintain his close relationship to Simple.

Hughes accomplished this complexity through recourse to a conversational mode of literary journalism—in the "from roots" sense given it by Mumia Abu-Jamal.[62] In *The Weary Blues, Fine Clothes to the Jew,* and *A New Song,* the blues mode enabled a political critique of everyday life and also an elevation of the blues to the status of high literary expression. But the "continually developing process" that Gramsci associated with "national-popular" art and literature was limited in Hughes's poetry due to the institutional time lag between the writing of his blues poems and their eventual publication and dissemination. As we have seen, *A New Song* improvised within the institution of high art through the chapbook form. But with Hughes's first two volumes, the circuits of bourgeois literary production governed the dissemination of his poetry. The poem "The Weary Blues," for instance, was written in 1923, three years prior to its publication in volume form. In another aspect of disconnect, the title of his second volume, *Fine Clothes to the Jew,* was denounced by mainstream critics as "anti-Semitic," reflecting the ever widening gap between the popular language of Harlem—"fine clothes to the Jew" referred to a worker being laid off and then having to sell his best clothes to the local pawnshop to avoid eviction—and New York's intellectual establishment. It is revealing in this context that Hughes was insistent that his Simple stories had nothing to do with "art." He wanted to stress that with Simple a *deep-*

61. Rampersad, *Life of Langston Hughes,* 2:81.
62. Mumia Abu-Jamal, "Interview with Mumia Abu-Jamal," 190.

er cultural substance was being expressed. As Hughes had it: "I put down on paper exactly what he [Simple] said."[63]

In the Simple columns, the institution of art is both circumvented and directly challenged, creating the political conditions for its objectification. That is, the limits of bourgeois art are clearly revealed through Simple's understanding of language as a form of total expression. Complex literary narratives grow out of simple conversations, and conversation itself is the basis of Hughes's journalistic mode of writing. In this way a set of new social relations arises from the Simple columns. Without dialogue, there are no Simple stories; without Simple, there is no social relationship between the educated class and the working classes. As Gramsci formulated the problem, "in oratory the words are not the only element: there are also gestures, tone of voice, and so on, a musical element that communicates the leitmotiv of the predominant feeling, the principal passion, and the orchestral element: gesture in the broad sense, which scans and articulates the wave of feeling and passion."[64]

Hughes manifested his aesthetics of black equality in a 1964 *Defender* column entitled "Coffee Break," which appeared one year later in *Simple's Uncle Sam*. In the story, Simple tells Boyd about how his white boss is always tracking him down during coffee breaks to ask him "just what does THE Negro want." As did many of the Simple stories, "Coffee Break" provided Hughes with a prime opportunity to revisit national (as well as international) debates over so-called race relations in which he himself had participated, or in which no response was solicited from any African American intellectuals. The question "What does the Negro want?" had been posed to Hughes and other prominent African American intellectuals in 1943 by the editor of the University of North Carolina Press, William T. Couch. According to Rampersad, Couch commissioned Hughes, Du Bois, A. Philip Randolph, Roy Wilkins, and Mary McLeod Bethune to write on the topic, but once he read their essays Couch canceled the project. If the authors were right about the Negro's wants, Couch said, "then what he needs, and needs urgently, is to revise his wants." Eventually the book was published under the title *What the Negro Wants*, with a reactionary introduction by Couch.[65] In "Coffee Break," Hughes returned to this debate, which had been transformed over the course of twenty years from an academic discussion between African American and white intel-

63. Quoted in Donna Akiba Sullivan Harper, ed., *The Return of Simple*, xix.
64. Gramsci, *Selections from the Cultural Writings*, 123.
65. Couch quoted in Rampersad, *Life of Langston Hughes*, 2:81–82.

lectuals into a regular topic of workplace conversation. This Simple story offers an excellent example of an ongoing adhesion and exchange between the popular language and the language of the educated class.

Simple's gestures in the story are what make the column so enlivening, from the way Hughes capitalizes "the" whenever it comes from the mouth of the white boss in reference to black folks, to the italicization of pronouns such as *she, me, you, this,* and *him.* Simple's most impassioned gesture, though, is a single idea. After avoiding his white boss for several weeks—itself an important gesture—he finally gives in to his incessant query. To the question "What does THE Negro want?" Simple replies, simply, "I am not THE Negro. I am *me.*" Simple then takes his white boss on several detours, since the boss does not want to see Simple as anything other than his factory's official "Negro representative." Simple points out that, although he is proud to have Dr. King and Ralph Bunche represent him, they have private telephone numbers and do not drink at his bar and therefore cannot really be said to represent black workers like himself. But if you want to know what THE Negro wants, Simple tells his boss, go ask *them.* "I cannot get to them," says his boss. "Neither can I," says Simple, "so we both is in the same boat" (*CW* 8:207).

But this does not deter the white boss. He continues to press Simple, which leads Simple through another set of detours, from a remark about the last time James Farmer was seen at the Apollo to a Moms Mabley stand-up routine about "Little Cindy Ella" and her prom date with the president of the Ku Klux Klan. After wearing magic slippers that turn her into a blonde princess, Little Cindy Ella returns to her black self at the midnight hour, landing in jail. Simple's clever parable of token integrationism passes right over the head of his white boss, who insists that Simple is not in jail, so what does he want now that he is no longer oppressed? "To get out of jail," he tells the boss.

"'What jail?'
"'The jail you got me in.'
"'Me?' yells my boss. 'I have not got you in jail. Why, boy, I like you. I am a liberal. I voted for Kennedy. And this time for Johnson. I believe in integration. Now that you got it, though, what more do you want?'
"'Reintegration,' I said.
"'Meaning by that, what?'
"'That you be integrated with *me,* not me with you.'
"'Do you mean that I come and live here in Harlem?' asked my boss. 'Never!'
"'I live in Harlem,' I said.

"'You are adjusted to it,' said my boss. 'But there is so much crime in Harlem.'

"'There are no two-hundred-thousand-dollar bank robberies, though,' I said, 'of which there was three lately *elsewhere*—all done by white folks, and nary one in Harlem. The biggest and best crime is outside of Harlem. We never has no half-million-dollar jewelry robberies, no missing star sapphires. You better come uptown with me and reintegrate.'"

Many of Hughes's literary strategies with Simple can be gleaned in this particular column, expressed lucidly in Simple's enlivening new concept of "reintegration." First, Simple's discourse is advanced and popular at the same time; that is, it partakes in a current debate ("What does the Negro want?") but from the perspective of African American labor. Second, it goes "to the roots"—in a journalistic sense—by presenting a key new concept from the point of view of a distinctly black working-class sensibility. Simple's boss's unwillingness to accept his astute analysis allows Hughes to complete its elaboration:

"'Negroes are the ones who want to be integrated,' said my boss.
"'And white folks are the ones who do *not* want to be,' I said.
"'Up to a point, we do,' said my boss.
"'That is what THE Negro wants,' I said, 'to remove that *point*.'
"'The coffee break is over,' said my boss." (*CW* 8:208)

The column ends here, with Simple having introduced the concept of "reintegration" and sent his white boss back to his office empty-handed and bewildered. Simple's gestures are essential, because they show possession and control of the issue at hand—from the standpoint of a crafty underdog. In this way Simple is exactly like the archetypal antagonistic "signifyin' monkey" that Gates conceptualized. Through Simple's gestures, Hughes gave immediate expression to the strong feelings of black workers toward the civil rights leadership.

Throughout the Simple columns are points of ideological contention between black workers and the African American intelligentsia. One is the language question, which turns on the opposition to the use of "broken English" or Black English Vernacular by the middle class, which sees it as an embarrassing sign of backwardness rather than as a brilliantly subversive popular language. Another is the critique of American liberalism, which forces the middle class to side with black workers over who will determine the course of the civil rights movement. There is also the question of the cold war and U.S. imperialism, where Simple calls for a similar taking of sides. And there is the overarching issue of black workers joining the struggle for international socialism, to which Simple offers his solidarity. In each instance, Boyd represents the middle class and Simple the black worker. The point of contention is over the concept of America itself and what political strategy is the most effective for making the United States live up to its endlessly broken promises to black folk and its grand claims about freedom and democracy for all. In this respect, Hughes's concept of "reintegration" in the "Coffee Break" column—one of the nodal points in his construction of the mestizo archetype, as we have seen—is associated with communist ideology, for the middle class's ambivalence to communism is the other side of white America's resistance to the African American civil rights movement. Just as the middle class sees in the color *red* an ideological threat and a political challenge to its control of workers, black and otherwise, white America sees in the political color *black* a total loss of white-skin privileges.

In subtle contrast to the poetry of *A New Song*, Hughes's Simple columns argue for American socialist nationalism through the popular language of the African American laborer. In *A New Song* this argument had been voiced in the language of the race-free communist poet and was framed as a work of party literature. With the Simple columns, Hughes deepened the mestizo image precisely by making it more commonplace, through the mode of dialogue. If the North American mestizo is a new archetype, which is Hughes's argument in *A New Song*, then it needs a popular art form through which to express itself. Hence, the popular language of the North American mestizo laborer is also the language of the African American working class, since the socialist joy of workers is, by the logic of the Simple columns, to speak directly (to "gesture in the broad sense") to those who claim to represent their class interests. When Simple's language is objected to by Boyd, a corresponding restraint is placed by the middle class on the self-assertion of black workers. But Simple's popular language cannot be restricted in this way—through moral suasion—which leaves Boyd and the middle class in a state of limbo, since their ambivalence to both the resistant popular culture of the black working class and the politics of socialism frustrates their efforts to properly represent African Americans in the public sphere. Hughes's great innovation in the Simple columns is to *simplify* (or popularize) civil society by giving it over to black workers. Any conversation between the middle class and black workers has to take account of Simple's discourse.

For Hughes, having a weekly newspaper column in the *Defender*, a major outlet of information and analysis for African Americans, offered a prime opportunity for reshaping the popular language into a specifically African American political language, since this form of journalistic communication—a grounding with black workers, to paraphrase Walter Rodney—could involve intellectuals, artists, students, and teachers directly in revolutionary activism. The newspaper column was transformed by Hughes into a forum for the whole black working class, including especially African American women workers, whose interests were voiced by a variety of women characters in the Simple columns, from Simple's hardworking wife, Joyce, to his cousin Minnie, whose participation in an uprising of black workers in Harlem was discussed in several different columns.[66] Simple quoted and paraphrased the black workers he met, giving their speech patterns distinctive intonations and rhythms and the literary *space*—perhaps that "ancestral matrix" Baker named—within which he could respond and elaborate new countermyths and aesthetic preferences.

In this way the writer (Hughes) became a producer, and the product (Simple) became a new producer in his own right. In the Simple columns, everyday life was posed as a political problem. It follows that the antagonistic imagery and language of African American workers were put to creative use—as a cooperative place where liberation could be achieved day by day.

66. See for example "Wigs for Freedom," *CW* 8:248–52.

4

The Collage Aesthetic

The Writer as Teacher

> You don't make things popular just because you want them to be simple,
> but because you want people to understand them. But when people under-
> stand things, then they demand more. And so I think the question is, how
> do you combine the advanced with the popular?
>
> —Amiri Baraka, *Conversations with Amiri Baraka*

In 1952 Langston Hughes told friends that his books were getting "simpler and simpler and younger and younger." Besides describing the
audience for his latest work, the statement announced Hughes's own aesthetic preferences, for it was during the 1950s that he returned to children's literature and Jesse B. Semple, producing his five "Simple" books
as well as seven histories for young people.[1] But the announcement also
revealed the social and political circumstances that he faced as a professional African American writer. Despite an outpouring of writing in every
genre and literary form at his disposal, more than a hundred appearances
on the lecture circuit in the United States and Canada, and canonization

1. Hughes quoted in Berry, *Langston Hughes,* 320. The works of children's literature
are *The First Book of Negroes* (1952), *The First Book of Rhythms* (1954), *Famous American
Negroes* (1954), *Famous Negro Music Makers* (1955), *The First Book of Jazz* (1955), *The First
Book of the West Indies* (1956), and *Famous Negro Heroes of America* (1958).

by the American Academy of Arts and Letters, he remained unable to support himself as a writer. Ironically, it was a one-thousand-dollar cash grant from the academy—according to Arnold Rampersad, the largest single sum he had received during his career—that provided the down payment on his first permanent residence, a Harlem town house he settled into in July 1948.

His few funds had not come from proceeds from his publications, which by 1948 included twenty works of literature, a broad range of magazine and journal articles, a host of short stories, a Broadway play, a Broadway musical, a Hollywood screenplay, eight radio scripts, and more than a dozen song lyrics. By comparison, William Faulkner was making $1,250 a week as a professional writer during the 1930s and by the 1940s was bringing in thousands of dollars at a time for screenplays and for the movie rights to his short stories and novels, in one case $50,000 for *Intruder in the Dust*. While Faulkner was securing a lucrative writer-in-residence position at the University of Virginia, Hughes was being denied a poet-in-residence post at Texas Southern—a position offered and then withdrawn after threats and intimidation from white supremacist and anticommunist groups at the university. In fact, Hughes was an early victim of the kind of political firing that would eventually force hundreds of left-wing U.S. college and university professors from the academy. Hughes came up with his own term for this sort of dual antired and antiblack political repression: "literary sharecropping."[2]

The term drew attention more to the persistence of white racial oppression in the United States than to the punishing effects of the anticommunist movement on socialist writers and artists, since for Hughes "blacklisting" was something that African American writers had been victims of long before the creation of HUAC. "Negro writers, being black, have always been blacklisted in radio and TV," he told the Authors League of America in 1951. Rampersad suggests that Hughes was unwilling to accept that his participation in the American communist movement of the 1920s and 1930s made all subsequent attempts to enter the U.S. mainstream triply hard, but that he pushed forward anyway, taking on projects that he was less than passionate about or that he had a hard

2. David Minter, *William Faulkner: His Life and Work*, 220; Rampersad, *Life of Langston Hughes*, 2:196–97; Charles H. Nichols, ed., *Arna Bontemps–Langston Hughes Letters, 1925–1967*, 292. A 1958 study by Paul Lazarsfeld and Wagner Thielens Jr. of the anticommunist movement's success inside the academy showed that, of 165 colleges and universities surveyed, 102 reported political firings (Lawrence S. Wittner, *Cold War America: From Hiroshima to Watergate*, 124).

time finishing. His literary agent in the 1950s, Ivan von Auw, character-ized Hughes's response: "He didn't concentrate enough on just one proj-ect. Instead, he seemed easily distracted, always running all over the place. He honestly believed that the way to get ahead was to take on everything offered. I think he was wrong; but perhaps he had no choice, really."[3] To say that Hughes "had no choice really" is misleading, how-ever; in fact, the choices he did make during the cold war were based on a systematic approach to writing, teaching, and producing literature.

Three decades after announcing famously in "The Negro Artist and the Racial Mountain" that his purpose as a writer was to help win self-determination for African American writers, Hughes found himself at an impasse. Writing geared for the mass market brought harsh criticism from the literary establishment, while writing from the left was greeted by mainstream publishers with one rejection slip after another. To make mat-ters worse, his opportunities on the lecture circuit dried up. According to Faith Berry, the cause was the persistent propaganda campaign against him by the anticommunist white supremacist group America First. The anticommunist right's aim was twofold: to force Hughes, one of the world's most popular left cultural workers, to renounce socialism and to undermine the important links he had begun to forge between African American writers and a new African American reading public. As George Cunningham has noted, "He hoped that his readings would help to build a Negro reading public for the works of Negro authors, and at the same time, to stimulate and inspire the younger Negroes in the South toward creative literature, and the use of their own folklore, songs, and racial background as the basis for expression."[4] With his situation as a writer deeply circumscribed by a nexus of antiblack and anticommunist ideo-logical forces, Hughes returned to work on two unfinished projects: his Simple saga and a series of popular histories for young people. That the Simple stories saved his career is certain; less clear are the relations be-

---

3. Rampersad, *Life of Langston Hughes,* 2:198, 196.

4. Berry, *Langston Hughes,* 316; Cunningham, "Afterword," 35. James Baldwin, as well as literary critic Robert Bone, strongly criticized Hughes's writing for a mass au-dience. Reviewing Hughes's *Selected Poems* in the March 29, 1959, issue of the *New York Times Book Review,* Baldwin opined, "this book contains a great deal which a more dis-ciplined poet would have thrown into the wastebasket." Bone accused Hughes of "merchandising" African American literature in his review of Hughes's anthology *Best Short Stories by Negro Writers* (both cited in Rampersad, *Life of Langston Hughes,* 2:418). As for rejections, in 1949 Blanche Knopf rejected both *Montage of a Dream De-ferred* and *I Wonder As I Wander.*

tween popular culture and literature in his writing during the height of
the cold war.

Both projects offer insights into how Hughes responded to cold war issues both as an African American socialist writer and as an intellectual.
Hughes's shrewd point in his Simple columns about the dual function of
the color line—to keep not only blacks down and out but reds too—could
be easily applied to popular culture and socialism. For it was during
the early stages of the cold war that U.S. anticommunist intellectuals
launched their first systematic attack on American popular culture. On
trial were specific art forms, styles, genres, mediums, and aesthetics, since
the sole criterion for determining guilt or innocence was the subject's popularity. Under interrogation were sporting events, gossip columns, comic books, concerts, children's literature, photographic essays, the "New
Hollywood," writing workshops, Broadway musicals, detective fiction,
popular periodicals, coffee table books, esoterica, soap operas, sick jokes,
movie queens, religious literature, "race" records, touring artists and
chamber groups, hipsterism, cults, radio news broadcasts, the Book-of-
the-Month Club and Modern Library, pornography, celebrity watching,
television quiz shows, and documentaries. As the 1954 U.S. Army pamphlet *How to Spot a Communist* revealed, the attack on popular culture by
the anticommunist intelligentsia was a logical corollary of the political
right's intention to destroy all forms of popular democracy in American
society. For example, the pamphlet asserted that a communist could be
identified by his or her "predisposition to discuss civil rights, social and
religious discrimination, the immigration laws, [and] antisubversive
legislation" and by a use of the terms "chauvinism," "book-burning,"
"colonialism," "demagogy," "witchhunt," "reactionary," "progressive,"
and "exploitation."[5] For creative artists such as Hughes, the anticommunist movement's narrowing of themes, subjects, and genres to only those
that affirmed God, family, and country helped create the political conditions for a systematic, negative critique of U.S. society. Later in this chap-

5. David Caute, *The Great Fear: The Anticommunist Purge under Truman and Eisenhower,* 296. For an example of systematic attack, see the seminar sponsored jointly by
the Tamiment Institute and *Daedalus,* the journal of the American Academy of Arts and
Sciences, held at Tamiment-in-the-Poconos in June 1959. In 1964, the collective work
of the seminar's participants was published in a pocket-size edition edited by Norman Jacobs entitled *Culture for the Millions? Mass Media in Modern Society,* announcing
their specific targets for attack. The list of participants resembles an all-star ballot for
the league of U.S. anticommunists: Arthur Schlesinger Jr., Irving Kristol, Sidney Hook,
Edward Shils, William Phillips, and Daniel Bell, among others.

ter I will explore how Hughes used the idea of negative critique in his writing for young people. For now, what is important is that the foreclosure of "affirmative culture" by U.S. reactionaries—that is, the foreclosure of anything that affirmed equalitarianism and interracial harmony on U.S. soil—left wide open whole fields of popular culture through which the ideals of high art, such as rupture and dissonance, could be carried on by popular artists.

Hughes's output during the high period of the cold war illuminates the sea change from "affirmative culture" to the arts of "negative resonance." In addition, it illustrates the fresh line of intervention by which socialist intellectuals and artists could make a political alliance between the U.S. working classes and emergent popular-democratic movements, such as the struggle for desegregation and the international alliance of scientists and cultural workers whose goal was the dismantling of atomic weaponry in the United States and Europe. For Hughes, the task was to attract workers to socialism with an advanced artistic technique and a steady diet of aesthetic forms and structures that raised their standards while meeting their desires and reflecting their own way of seeing and feeling the world.

In 1942 Hughes described succinctly his intellectual formation. When read next to the anticommunists' condemnation of popular culture, his list of influences and favorite public figures amounted to a total self-indictment:

My chief literary influences have been Paul Laurence Dunbar, Carl Sandburg, and Walt Whitman. My favorite public figures include Jimmy Durante, Marlene Dietrich, Mary McLeod Bethune, Mrs. Franklin D. Roosevelt, Marian Anderson, and Henry Armstrong. I live in Harlem, New York City. I am unmarried. I like *Tristan*, goat's milk, short novels, lyric poems, heat, simple folk, boats, and bullfights; I dislike *Aida*, parsnips, long novels, narrative poems, cold, pretentious folk, buses, and bridge. . . . My writing has been largely concerned with the depicting of Negro life in America. I have made a number of translations of the poems of Negro writers in Cuba and Haiti. In 1931–32 I lectured throughout the South in the Negro schools and colleges there, and one of my main interests is the encouragement of literary ability among colored writers. The winter of 1934 I spent in Mexico, where I translated a number of Mexican and Cuban stories. I was the only American Negro newspaper correspondent in Spain, in 1937—for the Baltimore *Afro-American*. I am executive director of the Harlem Suitcase Theater, the only Negro Worker's Theater in New York. I received the Palms Intercollegiate Poetry Award in 1927, the Harmon Award of Literature in 1931, in 1934 was selected by Dr. Charles A. Beard as one of America's twenty-five "most interesting" personages with a "socially conscious" attitude, and in 1935 was granted a Guggenheim Fellowship for creative work.[6]

In 1953 Dwight MacDonald denounced children's literature (a genre that would figure prominently in Hughes's career during the 1950s) in his openly jingoistic essay "A Theory of Mass Culture." MacDonald's problem with the children's literature of the 1930s and 1940s was that it had "adultized children" by replacing the popular symbol of Uncle Sam with that of Peter Pan. Under the aegis of anticommunism, MacDonald's attack on juvenile literature was both a realignment of the ideologies of patriarchy and American empire and a thinly veiled argument for reversing the democratic gains made in American literature and culture during the Popular Front period, the popularization of children's literature being one such gain.[7] Christopher Lasch has argued perceptively that the principal strategy of American anticommunism during the 1950s was to conflate the aims and ideals of bourgeois-democracy with those of revolutionary socialism. For fellow travelers such as MacDonald, Lasch suggested, anticommunism

represented a new stage in their running polemic against bourgeois sentimentality and weakness, bourgeois "utopianism" and bourgeois materialism. That explains their eagerness to connect Bolshevism with liberalism—to show that the two ideologies sprang from a common root and that it was the softness and sentimentality of bourgeois liberals which had paradoxically allowed communism . . . to pervade Western society in the thirties and early forties.[8]

In his classic critique of U.S. cultural imperialism, *The Empire's Old Clothes*, Ariel Dorfman inverts McDonald's whole thesis. In his final chapter, "The Infantilizing of Culture," Dorfman suggests that the effect of U.S. children's literature, television, and film has been to produce in the North American popular classes "the feeling of being reborn at every crossroads . . . [and] the belief that growth and power need not relinquish, let alone

6. Quoted in Stanley J. Kunitz and Howard Haycraft, eds., *Twentieth Century Authors*, 684.
7. MacDonald, "A Theory of Mass Culture," 66.
8. Lasch, *The Agony of the American Left*, 68.

destroy, innocence." As Dorfman stresses, it is not simply a question of American economic power and the control of production and distribution by American multinational corporations.

> The history of America, of the very particular sort of empire it became, seems to have allowed the process of infantilization of the adult to be accompanied by images or intimations of innocence that were reinforced by the magical, fairy-tale, ubiquitous quality of the media themselves, which could instantaneously transmit dreams and beliefs. The mass media added a new frontier, an unlimited, nonviolent one, to the prior unrelenting expansion of physical boundaries over a vast territory that could not be defended forever by its native inhabitants. Communication is a "peaceful" way of extending, of reaching out to those planetary outposts where military interventions previously had been the preferred way of ensuring free trade.[9]

Thus, the claim that Hughes's response to the rise of U.S. anticommunism was to choose a less "political" kind of writing—children's literature and the "Simple" stories, among other popular literary forms—is contradicted by the fact that the anticommunist movement considered these genres and forms to be no less political than were radical organizations such as the American Labor Party or the National Council of American-Soviet Friendship. To be sure, Hughes took no chances with the anticommunist right, severing ties with leftist organizations, including the American Labor Party and the National Council of American-Soviet Friendship, that had come under investigation by the FBI and the Special Committee on Un-American Activities.[10] In fact, his turn toward popular literature and culture can be read in this same light: not as an escape from politics but rather as a reentry into the political through a different opening. This was a new reality Hughes was reminded of constantly.

Rampersad points out that when the first book-length collection of Simple stories, *Simple Speaks His Mind*, went to press in the spring of 1950, Hughes's editor at Simon and Schuster made a concerted effort to disguise the politics of the book, describing it as a "charming portrayal" of Negro life in Harlem. The editor dismissed Hughes's objections to the advertisements, insisting that Simon and Schuster could not afford to "frighten prospective readers away by indicating that it is, in any sense, a

---

9. Dorfman, *The Empire's Old Clothes: What the Lone Ranger, Babar, and Other Innocent Heroes Do to Our Minds*, 54.
10. Rampersad, *Life of Langston Hughes*, 2:198.

tract." In terms of his own stated position on American popular culture, since the 1930s Hughes had been outspoken in his criticism of white racism in Hollywood and on the air. In 1945, for instance, he responded to a query from Columbia University Professor of Communications Erik Barnouw about race and radio thus: "Radio furnishes some very good Negro entertainment, but comparatively little more, seldom touching on the drama or the problems of Negro life in America. . . . And it continues to keep alive the stereotype of the dialect-speaking, amiably moronic Negro servant as the chief representative of our racial group on the air." As Barnouw acknowledged at the time, not only had Hughes expressed a strong interest in writing a daytime serial about an African American family, but his name was always the first mentioned whenever the subject was raised in radioland. Indeed, Hughes's first impulse was to make the Simple stories into a radio program, not short fiction or a novel; the networks, however, remained either indifferent or openly hostile to such a proposal. His unaired 1945 radio drama, "Booker T. Washington in Atlanta"—an experimental piece based on the forms and concepts of arena theater— makes it clear that American radio listeners, as well as the medium itself, suffered a serious loss when Hughes was banished de facto from the airwaves.[11]

Aesthetically, "Booker T. Washington in Atlanta" is interesting for Hughes's use of multiple narrators. Through the blues trope of a train ride to an unknown land, Hughes has Washington retell his children about how he came up from slavery. As the children gather around their father in a railroad car headed for Atlanta, Washington acts as a vessel through which his grandparents, his parents, and his former fellow mine workers can speak. From the voice of Washington's grandmother during storytelling sessions and the auditory effects of workers laboring in salt furnaces, to the sounds of children learning how to read and write at the "pay school" where Washington was a student, Hughes's radio drama is based on the daily rhythms of work and family life. Washington's Atlanta speech is actually an afterthought, taking up only two or three minutes of the play. The effect that Hughes was seemingly after was a kind of theater-in-the-round, with the audience participating in a type of call-and-response. In this communal form, longer speeches and monologues are difficult to sustain, as is the case with Washington's Atlanta speech. One reason for the speech, perhaps, is that the big radio networks would air an African

11. Ibid., 2:178; Barnouw, ed., *Radio Drama in Action*, 284; Rampersad, *Life of Langston Hughes*, 2:285.

American program only if it had a "special interest" angle—that is, a commemorative or retrospective emphasis, usually based on the life of a "safe" African American hero such Crispus Attucks, George Washington Carver, or Booker T. Washington. In "Booker T. Washington in Atlanta," the "special-interest" angle was used shrewdly by Hughes as a departure point for giving expression to his overriding interest: translating the theater-in-the-round form into radio for working-class audiences.[12]

Despite his forced exile from Hollywood, radio, and television, Hughes still managed a twenty-year march through major forms of American popular culture. His most popular works were the Simple stories and the histories for young people, but other conscious and purposeful interventions in popular culture laid the groundwork for those writings. In the 1950s and 1960s, for instance, Hughes worked on several collaborations that revealed the creative method through which he would carry out these multiple tasks. These methods are worth noting for what they reveal about the specific obstacles he faced as a socialist African American writer in cold war America.

The first collaboration of the 1950s was a photo essay with African American photographer Roy DeCarava entitled *The Sweet Flypaper of Life* (1955). The second, coauthored by Milton Meltzer, was *A Pictorial History of the Negro in America* (1956). Finding a publisher for *A Pictorial History* proved extremely frustrating for Hughes and Meltzer, as more than ten firms turned down the project. According to Meltzer, "Two or three even said that blacks don't read, so why bother with them? And a few suggested going to a foundation, since no normal publisher would take on such a pointless task." In the case of *The Sweet Flypaper of Life*, a publisher was not hard to find; the problem was that Simon and Schuster had cut costs on the book by printing pocket-size paperbacks rather than the big and glossy coffee-table books that were standard for works of popular photography. In the mid-1960s Hughes worked again with Meltzer, producing *Black Magic: A Pictorial History of the Negro in American Entertainment* (1967)—arguably the most comprehensive history of African American popular culture ever published.[13]

Black Magic is a breathtaking account of the origins of virtually every African American popular art form, from major components such as hand-clapping, feet-stomping, stick-dancing, and drum-beating rhythms

12. "Booker T. Washington in Atlanta" was published for the first time in Barnouw's *Radio Drama in Action*, 283–94.
13. Rampersad, *Life of Langston Hughes*, 2:248.

of the eighteenth and nineteenth centuries, as well as the spirituals and folk culture, to constitutive elements such as homemade banjos and drums and a list of the first African American radio commentators and newscasters. The text is filled with a stunning array of esoterica—the stuff of any lasting book on popular culture—but has, unfortunately, been completely ignored in U.S. "cultural studies" projects. Hughes and Meltzer's ninth chapter, "Just About Everything," provides a fascinating history of the first African American "exhibits" in P. T. Barnum's traveling circus. Barnum's first set of Siamese twins—the fourteen-year-old Carolina twins Millie and Christina—is discussed, along with Barnum's first "Fat Ladies"—who were actually blues singers looking for steady work—Big Maybelle and Beulah Bryant. There is also a story about Barnum's first "Giants," one of whom was an African American Civil War veteran named Admiral Dot. Admiral Dot stood seven feet eleven inches tall and weighed six hundred pounds; the text is accompanied by a rare daguerreotype of him. There are also brief histories of forgotten pioneers, such as "the world's most beloved nightclub hostess," Ada "Bricktop" Smith Du Conge. Made into a celebrity in Paris during the early 1920s with the help of Louis Aragon, Bricktop ran the most popular nightclub in Paris for nearly twenty years. In addition to the brief histories of individual pathfinders, there are brief histories of institutions, such as the Lincoln Theater in Harlem, the Lafayette Players, and the American Negro Theater, which began in the basement of the New York Public Library. But perhaps the most delightful and useful aspect of the book is, not surprisingly, the graphics. Mixed throughout the text are playbills, posters, signed photographs, advertisements, rare photographs of artists at work, newspaper clippings, drawings, and diagrams.

These three texts—*Sweet Flypaper, Pictorial History,* and *Black Magic*—belong to the coffee-table book genre and as such constitute one of three main lines of work in popular literature chosen by Hughes in the postwar period. Critics have placed the other two—short fiction and juvenile literature—into the category of "high" literature, yet the relations between the final form of these works and the "wreckin' shop floor" whence they came have not been properly recognized nor explored.[14] A new concept—the "collage aesthetic"—can be used to account for the logic and direction

14. For example, in Hans Ostrom's *Langston Hughes: A Study of the Short Fiction,* there is barely a mention of Hughes's column for the *Chicago Defender,* the origin of his "Simple" stories. Ostrom begins his discussion of the Simple stories with a section entitled "The Genesis and Growth of Simple," but nothing is said about Hughes's *Defender* column.

of Hughes's astonishingly diverse literary output during the cold war. For the dialectic of Hughes's literary production during the 1950s and early 1960s is precisely the diversifying, or unfixing from within, of popular aesthetic forms, preferences, and practices in an increasingly monolithic, market-driven, and antipopular system of mass cultural production.

Poetry of the Negro: "A Supreme Feat of Reconnaissance"

> Our brains are dulled by the incurable mania of wanting to make the un-known known, classifiable. The desire for analysis wins out over the sentiments.
>
> —André Breton, *Manifestoes of Surrealism*

> The destruction of the past, or rather of the social mechanisms that link one's contemporary experience to that of earlier generations, is one of the most characteristic and eerie phenomena of the late twentieth century.
>
> —Eric Hobsbawm, *The Age of Extremes*

The main component of Hughes's literary technique in the cold war period can be described provisionally as *anthological*. During the late 1940s and through the 1950s and early 1960s, Hughes produced ten anthologies.[15] Although each of the anthologies put in motion a "collage aesthetic," and relied on that aesthetic for its organizing logic and basic structure, three in particular define this aesthetic most clearly and represent its fullest expression and development.

The first anthology, *The Poetry of the Negro, 1746-1949* (1949), was produced in collaboration with Hughes's best friend and closest comrade, Arna Bontemps. The two had worked together on numerous projects before *Poetry of the Negro,* including the play *When the Jack Hollers* in 1935, the short stories "Bon Bon Buddy" and "Boy of the Border" in 1934, and the children's book *Popo and Fifina* in 1932, and they would collaborate again in 1958 on *The Book of Negro Folklore.* Among their various collaborations, *The Poetry of the Negro* required the most time and energy to com-

15. Hughes's anthologies are: *The Poetry of the Negro, 1746–1949; An African Treasury: Articles, Essays, Stories, Poems; Anthology of Negro Poets in the USA—200 Years; The Best Short Stories by Negro Writers: An Anthology from 1899 to the Present; The Book of Negro Humor; The Langston Hughes Reader; New Negro Poets USA; Poems from Black Africa: Ethiopia, South Rhodesia, Sierra Leone, Madagascar, Ivory Coast, Nigeria, Kenya, Gabon, Senegal, Nyasaland, Mozambique, South Africa, Congo, Ghana, Liberia,* and *Selected Poems.*

plete. It also provoked the most ambivalent response from critics. Most significant is the fact that the mixed response was due explicitly to the logic and structure of the text.

In his biography of Hughes, Arnold Rampersad provides a perspicacious summary of the book's reception in 1949.

> *Poetry of the Negro*, which sold briskly from the start, was a historic anthology that would not become outmoded in the lifetime of its editors, who had shown an internationalist understanding of blackness, and a deep pride in their race without a limiting chauvinism. They were the first editors to bring to the attention of North Americans the new Caribbean writing that would flower in the work of V. S. Naipaul and Derek Walcott. . . . *Poetry of the Negro* also boosted the morale of black American poets. . . . As it was intended to do, *Poetry of the Negro* brought black poets to the attention of a wider audience.[16]

The collection was historic for these reasons and also for the fact that no previous anthology of African American poetry had used so elastic an organizing structure or featured so many nonacademic, noncanonical, and, in several instances, previously unanthologized writers and artists. This broad reach played a part, no doubt, in the bewildering reception the book received in 1949. But the more obvious source of bewilderment was the inclusion of European, European American, and West Indian poets. According to Rampersad, white American reviewers hotly objected to the inclusion of West Indian writing in the anthology, while several West Indian writers criticized the volume's inclusion of whites. The *New Yorker* lamented that Hughes and Bontemps had not included a section on African American folklore, and a reviewer for the *Saturday Review of Literature* snidely second-guessed their motivation behind putting Euro-American writers in an anthology of Negro writing. In a letter to Bontemps, Hughes characterized tersely the *Saturday Review* critic's attitude: "My feeling is that they are still for strict segregation when it comes to poetry—as most 'white' anthologies attest—since they leave us out entirely."[17]

The white critics' attack on the inclusion of nonblacks in *Poetry of the Ne-*

16. Rampersad, *Life of Langston Hughes*, 2:160–61.
17. Ibid., 2:160. Before *Poetry of the Negro*, four anthologies of African American poetry had been published in the United States: James Weldon Johnson's *The Book of American Negro Poetry* (1922); Robert T. Kerlin's *Contemporary Poetry of the Negro* (1923); Countee Cullen's *Caroling Dusk* (1927); and Beatrice Murphy's *Negro Voices: An Anthology of Contemporary Verse* (1938). Needless to say, none of these texts includes white poets or West Indian poets.

gro is especially vexing given the stated purpose for their presence in the book. The anthology is divided into four sections: "Negro Poets of the U.S.A.," "Tributary Poems by Non-Negroes," "The Caribbean," and "Africa," with the white poets of course falling into the second category. As for the charge that the anthology was deficient because it lacked a section on Negro folklore, this too was a maddening objection since one would be hard-pressed to come up with an African American poet who failed to draw on or help popularize African American folklore in his or her poetry. In fact, the Hughes and Bontemps anthology argued against this kind of classification of art: the "white" way of partitioning popular forms of black culture from the African American literary tradition. Indeed, a resistance to classification, or "localized formalism," to use Timothy Brennan's useful concept, is the organizing principle of the volume as a whole.[18]

The fact that many white critics were stupefied by the structure of the anthology—that they saw it as surreal, or to use the Surrealists' own terminology, that they experienced an "intensification of the irritability of the faculties of the mind" when confronted with the book—is revealing and provides a departure point for understanding its aesthetic logic.[19] Clearly, the two editors rejected identity politics as a literary or cultural method of struggle against the ideology of white supremacy. As Hughes and Bontemps noted in the preface:

> If the compilers had sought for a racial idiom in verse form among Negroes, they should have concerned themselves with the words of Negro spirituals, with folk rhymes, with blues, and other spontaneous lyrics. These song materials, no doubt, suggest a kind of poetry that is racially distinctive, that lies essentially outside the literary traditions of the language which it employs. But the present anthology consists of poems written within that tradition, by Negroes as well as others. (*CW* 9:486)

In opposition to racial identity politics, Hughes and Bontemps advanced a politics of identification, in the sense that the term is used by A. Sivanandan in his essay "All That Melts into Air Is Solid": wars of position that counter and overwhelm the propagandists of the bourgeois state and that directly challenge coercive power through the development of anticapitalist mass movements and specific nonviolent direct action strate-

18. Brennan, "Places of Mind, Occupied Lands: Edward Said and Philology," 81.
19. The phrase arises from Salvador Dalí's definition of "frottage," the technical side of collage; quoted in André Breton, *Manifestoes of Surrealism*, 274–75.

gies, such as boycotts and solidarity strikes.[20] This is the rationale behind the anthology's second section, "Tributary Poems by Non-Negroes," as well as its third, "The Caribbean"—by far the most straightforward aspect of the anthology. What is less obvious, and what requires attention, is the politico-literary method Hughes and Bontemps proposed through the specific arrangement of poets and their verse: that is, the method that enabled them to formulate a new kind of cultural identification and solidarity, while simultaneously breaking the localized formalisms that had internally segregated African American poetry on the one hand while on the other sealing off the popular-democratic Euro-American literary tradition, as well as the Caribbean tradition, from mainline African American literature and culture.

To arrive at a working definition and clear description of Hughes and Bontemps's method, it is necessary first to name what was not included in the anthology, as well as what is rhythmically juxtaposed and contrasted. In the first section, where the editors' main aesthetic preferences are advanced, there are no poems that rely on historical narration. Also, there are no rhetorical poems and no prosaic poems. Instead, there are elegies, chants, blues poems, conversation poems, documentary poems, epitaphs, sound poems, song poems, ballads, epistles, short lyrics, sonnets, free verse poems, speech poems, epigrams and, above all, *image poems*. Following the Surrealists, the image poem can be defined as verse that digs deeper the trench between poetry and prose, relying most of all on *metaphor*. Thus, another reason for leaving out African American work songs, folktales, blues, and spirituals from the volume—although unstated by Hughes and Bontemps in the preface—has to do with the dependence of these forms on instrumentation, dance, rhythm, and rhyme. For what the poetry they assembled affirms is what the Surrealists called "the primordial virtue of poetic language": it does not subordinate the sentiments to sound and is "free of any sort of practical end."[21] Conversely, the logic for leaving out long narrative poems, rhetorical poems, and prosaic poems is that these forms raise barriers between languages, between the language of history, say, and the language of everyday life, or the language of persuasion and that of lyricism—barriers that would foreclose any attempt at literary collage.

Staying true to the total scale of the anthology, the preface is brief and

20. Sivanandan, "All That Melts into Air Is Solid: The Hokum of New Times," 41.
21. For my definition of the image-poem, I have had recourse to André Breton's 1935 essay "Surrealist Situation of the Object," in his *Manifestoes of Surrealism*, 262.

unforthcoming. Hughes and Bontemps mention only one or two details about the structure of the text. Like the poets and poems themselves, the editors treat their own words with the respect given to good conversation. Less than three pages, the preface talks not about itself but instead casts out lines of inquiry. The editors say that whereas the Caribbean section and the "white" section are ordered according to "historical, sometimes dramatic" determinations, the African American section follows a chronological order "based on the date of the poet's birth, or the closest estimate that could be made of it" (*CW* 9:486). The elasticity of this ordering principle—unheard of in literary anthologies of the day—gives way dialectically to a tightly knit literary pastiche or, better, *collage,* since the various forms of poetry presented are not combined incongruously as in pastiche but are layered and juxtaposed according to one overarching theme: the Du Boisian triad of work, culture, and liberty. It is worth quoting Du Bois at length, since so many of the poems in *Poetry of the Negro* give individual expression to, and begin from, the basic tenets of his magisterial discourse:

> Work, culture, liberty—all these we need, not singly but together, not successively but together, each growing and aiding each, and all striving toward that vaster ideal that swims before the Negro people, the ideal of human brotherhood, gained through the unifying ideal of Race; the ideal of fostering and developing the traits and talents of the Negro, not in opposition to or contempt for other races, but rather in large conformity to the greater ideals of the American Republic, in order that some day on American soil two world-races may give each to each those characteristics both so sadly lack. We the darker ones come even now not altogether empty-handed: there are to-day no truer exponents of the pure human spirit of the Declaration of Independence than the American Negroes; there is no true American music but the wild sweet melodies of the Negro slave; the American fairy tales and folklore are Indian and African; and, all in all, we black men seem the sole oasis of simple faith and reverence in a dusty desert of dollars and smartness. Will America be poorer if she replace her brutal dyspeptic blundering with light-hearted but determined Negro humility? or her course and cruel wit with loving jovial good-humor? or her vulgar music with the soul of the Sorrow Songs?[22]

Hughes and Bontemps projected Du Bois's thematic triad into the making of the anthology in two ways: first, in the selection of individual po-

22. Du Bois, *Souls of Black Folk,* 52.

ets and their poems; second, through the layering or collage-style arrangement of the poetry itself.

For the African American section, Hughes and Bontemps selected poets without regard for their academic reputation or place in "Negro Literature" or their records of publication. The criterion for inclusion seems to have been based solely on their organic relationship to the popular-democratic tradition of American literature. For example, three poems are included by Effie Lee Newsome—a writer who, like many in the anthology, had never before been anthologized. Newsome herself was so touched and surprised by Hughes and Bontemps's request for permission to use her work that she wrote back to Hughes, "It is a waste of postage for you or Mr. Bontemps to ask permission to use verse of mine, to say nothing of trimming off some of its Victorianism."[23] Born in 1885 in Philadelphia, Pennsylvania, Newsome lived her life at Wilberforce, Ohio, and wrote mainly for children. The first of her three poems in the anthology, "Morning Light: The Dew Drier," is about the exploitation of African children by European colonial settlers. The Du Boisian dialectic of the forces of conquest—"brutal dyspeptic blundering"—and those encircled by it—"the sole oasis of simple faith and reverence"—is unmistakable in her verse:

> In Africa little black boys,
> "human brooms," are sent before the explorers
> into jungle grasses that tower many feet
> to tread down a path
> and meet sometimes
> the lurking leopard or hyena.
> They are called Dew-Driers.

> Brother to the firefly—
> For as the firefly lights the night,
> So lights he the morning—
> Bathed in the dank dews as he goes forth
> Through heavy menace and mystery
> Of half-waking tropic dawn,
> Behold a little black boy,
> A naked black boy,
> Sweeping aside with his slight frame
> Night's pregnant tears,
> And making a morning path to the light
> For the tropic traveler!

23. Quoted in Rampersad, *Life of Langston Hughes*, 2:160.

Also illustrative of this principle of selection—the projection of African American organic intellectuals into the American national-popular culture—are the poems of Bruce Wright. Best known today as a former New York Criminal Court judge and New York State Supreme Court justice, as well as the author of the classic *Black Robes, White Justice* (1987)—a powerful exposition of how white racial oppression continues to operate in federal, state, and local courts—the Honorable Bruce Wright was thirty-one at the time of the anthology's publication and unknown in U.S. poetry circles. He was among many young African American poets in the volume to find access for the first time to a U.S. poetry-reading public. While serving in the U.S. Army overseas during World War II, he authored his first book of poetry, which was published in Wales as *From the Shaken Tower* in 1944. Both of his poems in *Poetry of the Negro* were written overseas: one juxtaposes images of war in Europe with images of European civilization as taught in his New York City public high school, while the other speaks in metaphors of blackness. In both poems the tension between the forces of reaction and those of progress is renewed through a string of images of exterior objects: "the cow stinking in the street"; "a woman sweeping dung"; "pillows trimmed in *böhmisch* lace"; "thatched temples"; "carved ebon-wood"; "dead statues in a frieze." The second poem, "The African Affair," is composed of four metaphors of blackness: a prison, a creviced wall, a burning desert, and a sacred temple.

The dominant image of both poems, however, is a rifle turned to a ground decimated by war. This image is the first image of the first poem, "Journey to a Parallel: Summer, 1947." Adjacent to the image of a rifle turned down is that of Miss Upjohn's geography class "and all the things she never taught" her students about the world, to better preserve her own white innocence or detachment from the world. For the poet, the end of the war is a not a new beginning but, rather, an unloosing of the unconscious so that a crystallization of images formerly "blacked-out" in the U.S. imagination could be articulated:

> I should have known of Omaha
> And Utah—
> American Indian hinterlands—
> as French as Bar-le-Duc;
> But Miss Upjohn was a virgin,
> then a spinster;
> she shied away from Flesh and French facts,
> she disapproved of certain acts:

Between us there can be no bond,
Now that I can teach Upjohn.

What the poet can teach Miss Upjohn is that which he now understands about himself, his own people, and the centrality of their history in the United States and the world, which is the subject of the second poem. The last two metaphors of "Journey to a Parallel" constitute Wright's lesson plan:

black is where the deserts burn,
The niger and Sasandra flow,
From where the Middle Passage went
Within the Continent of Night
From Cameroons to Carisbrooke
And places conscience cannot go;
Black is where thatched temples burn
Incense to carved ebon-wood;
Where traders shaped my father's pain,
His person and his place,
Among dead statues in a frieze,
In the spectrum of his race.

The idea about American education that Wright proposes in "Journey to a Parallel" shares much with V. F. Calverton's main argument in *The Liberation of American Literature* (1932): that every limitation of American literature is a product of the country's own "colonial complex." "American universities," wrote Calverton, "were constructed so completely upon the English style, even to the point of modeling their curricula upon exactly the same pattern, that little influence of the mother country was lost in the change."[24] Speaking of the British educational system's effects on Afro-Caribbean youth, Bajan scholar and poet Kamau Brathwaite offers a more precise analysis:

What our educational system did was to recognize and maintain the language of the conquistador—the language of the planter, the language of the official, the language of the Anglican preacher. It insisted that not only would English be spoken in the anglophone Caribbean, but that the educational system would carry the contours of an English heritage. . . . People were forced to learn things that had no relevance to

24. Calverton, *The Liberation of American Literature,* 10.

themselves. Paradoxically, in the Caribbean (as in many other "cultural disaster" areas), the people educated in this system came to know more, even today, about English kings and queens than they do about our own national heroes, our own slave rebels—the people who helped to build and to destroy our society.[25]

At the structural level—the selected poems of a single poet within a single section of the anthology—the technique used by Hughes and Bontemps is to juxtapose images of exterior objects and to choose poems that use metaphors in which a strengthening of the poet's conscious will takes place. As editors they put aside that which is irrelevant and embraced works that ennoble the spirit of the people—that defy the despair imputed to them and heroize their desire for self-emancipation.

Poetry of the Negro is one of the few poetry anthologies to feature W. E. B. Du Bois in its pages. More interesting is that Hughes and Bontemps chose not from among Du Bois's published poetry but an excerpt from his autobiography *Darkwater* (1920). A speech-textured piece, Du Bois's "A Litany at Atlanta" is placed between an elegy to Paul Laurence Dunbar by James David Corrothers and a song poem called "Miss Melerlee" by John Wesley Holloway, who was a member of the Fisk Jubilee Singers. Surrounding these two poems is a constellation of poetry by George Moses Horton, Frances E. W. Harper, James Weldon Johnson, and Paul Laurence Dunbar. The arrangement of poets preceding and following this grouping suggests that Hughes and Bontemps arranged these poems to constitute one "strip" of a larger collage. Before Horton is Phillis Wheatley, and after Dunbar is William Stanley Braithwaite. For both of these poets, the process of canonization within the African American literary tradition had been controversial, disputed on the grounds that their writing amounted to nothing more than a flat imitation of established English literary models. In his 1962 essay "The Myth of a Negro Literature," Amiri Baraka argued that Phillis Wheatley is symptomatic of the African American middle class's failure to produce "any art that would attempt to describe or characterize some portion of the profound meaningfulness of human life with any finality or truth." The reason for this failure, he wrote, "is that in most cases the Negroes who found themselves in a position to pursue some art, especially the art of literature, have been members of the Negro middle class, a group that has always gone out of its way to cultivate any mediocrity, as long as that mediocrity was guaranteed to prove

25. Brathwaite, "History of the Voice," 262–63.

to America, and recently to the world at large, that they were not really who they were, i.e., Negroes."[26] Elsewhere, Baraka has written of Wheatley's verse with brutal sarcasm:

> Ms. Wheatley writing in the eighteenth century is simply an imitator of Alexander Pope. It was against the law for black slaves to learn to read or write, so Ms. Wheatley's writings could only come under the "Gee whiz, it's alive" category of Dr. Frankenstein checking out his new monster! Also Wheatley's writing abounds with sentiments like "'Twas mercy brought me from my pagan land," evincing gratitude in slavery— that the European slave trade actually helped the Africans by exposing them to great European culture: which be the monster remarking how wise how omniscient be her creator![27]

Hughes and Bontemps did not seem to subscribe to such a view, but in terms of the overall structure of the anthology—the collage aesthetic— their specific placing of Wheatley and Braithwaite does produced a deliberate clashing of what we might call "high-affect poetic forms."

Horton's and Harper's poetry came out of the militant antislavery movement. Punctuated with exclamatory and anaphoral turns of phrase and structured according to a strict rhyme scheme (rhymed quatrains), their poems—next to the neatly packaged closed couplets of Wheatley and the odes and sonnets of Braithwaite—are an irruption of the popular-democratic tradition in African American literature. Braithwaite's verse comes directly after eight poems by Paul Laurence Dunbar and one by his wife, Alice Dunbar Nelson. The eight Dunbar poems are a mix of his so-called dialect verse and verse written in traditional English forms: an epitaph, a Horatian ode, an epigram, and an open couplet à la Milton.

The notable and felicitous feature of this collage is that it defies a linear conception of African American literary development. In African American poetry anthologies it is customary to place Dunbar's "dialect" poems before his verse in the English manner, in order to show his ostensible "development" as a poet, from folk forms to those of poetry proper, meaning English poetry. Conversely, Dunbar's poetry is often included in anthologies under biologistic or evolutionary categories such as "The Planters"[28]—the kind of classification that tries to isolate a particular

26. Baraka, "The Myth of a Negro Literature."
27. Baraka, "Revolutionary Tradition," 313.
28. "The Planters" is how Arthur Davis classifies Dunbar's verse in *From the Dark Tower: Afro-American Writers, 1900–1960* (his other categories are "First Fruits," "To-

stage of African American poetry in which the seeds of its own development are said to have been sown. Since Hughes and Bontemps were motivated by the total scale of African American poetry and not by its "stages" of growth, they avoided such naturalistic classifications, within a poet's own work and for the tradition as a whole. Instead, they looked for the sudden bursts and booms, the summits and the depressions, the overlaps and intersections, and, above all, the interstices. In this way the aesthetic and the historical interact dialectically, as nothing separates or blocks their productive tension: neither sterile chronologies nor a linear perspective; not liberal pluralism, not formalism, and not the ideology of cultural nationalism.

Du Bois's "A Litany at Atlanta" is at the center of this bold, percussively contrastive arrangement or "strip" of poems. It is at this point in the anthology that Hughes and Bontemps moved directly into the oral tradition, the so-called dialect poetry of African American literature. "A Litany at Atlanta" is the nexus, since Du Bois's poem is a post-Reconstruction sermon delivered in a call-and-response mode. The opening two stanzas establish the tenor of the piece and are followed by twenty-three stanzas of differing lengths and intensities:

> O Silent God, Thou whose voice afar in midst and mystery hath left our ears an-hungered in these fearful days—
> *Hear us, good Lord!*
> Listen to us, Thy children: our faces dark with doubt are made a mockery in Thy sanctuary. With uplifted hands we front Thy Heaven, O God crying:
> *We beseech Thee to hear us, good Lord!*

The trope of the old-time Negro preacher takes center stage, placed in the interstice between the poetry of the antislavery movement and the "dialect" poetry of the early twentieth century. A strictly linear account of African American poetry could not include Du Bois's poem. Instead, the short lyrics of James Weldon Johnson are typically made to fill the

---

ward the Mainstream," and "Integrationists and Transitional Writers"). Although "Forerunners"—Dudley Randall's classification in his seminal anthology *The Black Poets*—is not a biological metaphor, a tendency to show a linear development in African American poetry is still evident. Hughes and Bontemps's point is that African American poetry has always been deep and diverse, filled with class conflict just like any other literature, and that to "partition" it according to a slowly unfolding narrative of literary evolution betrays this characteristic of the tradition.

gap between the poetry of radical abolitionism and that of the post-Reconstruction period, specifically his widely anthologized "O Black and Unknown Bards." Hughes and Bontemps also anthologized this poem; however, they included it not to glorify vernacular literature nor to signify a smooth, straightforward transition from folk forms to the literary but rather to mark the irruption of a new way of feeling or appreciating the folk itself. Du Bois's sermon poem is precisely *that* irruption into modernity.

James Weldon Johnson broke new ground in American literature with his 1927 book of old-time Negro preacher poems, *God's Trombones*. Du Bois's preacher poem, however, is a different kind of writing altogether. Whereas Johnson's task in *God's Trombones* was to assert the literariness of African American vernacular expression, Du Bois's aim in "A Litany at Atlanta" was broader: he sought a literary form that could directly involve African American intellectuals and cultural workers in the daily struggle against the mounting forces of political reaction—"the counter-revolution of property." For this he went to the Psalms, where "the peculiar ethical paradox," as Du Bois phrased it in *The Souls of Black Folk*, facing African Americans at the turn of the century—namely, the paradox of the bitterness and despair of African American sharecroppers and migrant workers who nonetheless remained steadfast in their belief in God's deliverance—could be felt historically. Du Bois recognized the force of this contradiction in the everyday lives of African American workers for whom religion, he wrote in *Souls*, "instead of worship, is a complaint and a curse, a wail rather than a hope, a sneer rather than a faith."[29] For Du Bois, a new form of communication was necessary that could seize the moral high ground and then radically change the terms of national redemption for the masses of African Americans.

The problem for Du Bois was that these terms were being set not according to the requirements of national redemption but according to those of white racial oppression: the political restoration of the White Republic and the social reconstruction of white-skin privileges, or Lynch Law and Jim Crow. The Psalms provided the form through which complaint could be transformed into social organization. Yet this was accomplished only through a radical revision of the psalm form itself. Du Bois replaced the subjective "I" of the Psalms with an objective "We"—objective in the sense that the response to the horrors of post-Reconstruction society was collective and issued from outside the preacher's own subjectivity; objec-

29. Du Bois, *Souls of Black Folk*, 149.

tive in that the collective's constant enemy, the "white race," was thereby objectified:

> Bewildered we are, and passion-tost, mad with the madness of a mobbed and mocked and murdered people; straining at the armposts of Thy Throne, we raise our shackled hands and charge Thee, God, by the bones of our stolen fathers, by the tears of our dead mothers, by the very blood of Thy crucified Christ: *What meaneth this?* Tell us the Plan; give us the sign!
> *Keep not Thou silence, O God!*
> Sit no longer blind, Lord God, deaf to our prayer and dumb to our dumb suffering. Surely, Thou too art not white, O Lord, a pale, bloodless, heartless thing?
> *Ah, Christ of all the Pitties!*

The faith that Du Bois dwells on in the poem, on whose behalf he speaks a prayer, is faith in human progress, in the constructive movement of history as a dialectical process. The poem is also a projection of the view that faith in human progress must become *popular*—must become a regular form of secular worship—if the struggle for self-emancipation in the United States is to have a chance of succeeding.

By the logic of Hughes and Bontemps's anthological method, Du Bois's psalm poem is that fragment of the collage where a solution to the separation between the intellectuals and the people is proposed. This is borne out by the poem the editors chose to close the first section: a short tribute for Du Bois on his eightieth birthday by Bette Darcie Latimer. If Du Bois's psalm poem introduces to African American poetry a conception of the world through which writers and the masses of African Americans could converse on a daily basis—through which popular religious sentiments could be animated and then take hold as aesthetic preferences in the nation's secular literature—then Latimer's tribute to Du Bois is a rephrasing of this concept, serving both as the conclusion of the first section and as a bridge connecting Hughes and Bontemps's concept of African American poetry to the verse forms of European and Euro-American writers. The Latimer poem takes from Hughes and Bontemps's Du Boisian concept of art and politics that which is most useful for the development of a popular-democratic tradition of American literature, namely the creation of national heroes or historical figures. Du Bois is the anthology's hero not because of his literary achievements and his enormous international stature but because of how he entered, and continued to guide, the intellectual life of all African Americans. This is the subject of Latimer's "For William Edward Burghardt Du Bois on his Eightieth Birthday":

> He does not lounge with the old men
> on their thrones in the sun . . .
> I have awakened from the unknowing to the knowing
> hoping to see the fathomless . . .
> But I saw the old men
> on their thrones in the sun,
> with aged eyes
> and dust in their beards.
>
> Mixed with the shadows,
> veiled and unthroned,
> the brown one smiles.
> I meet them at the turnpike,
> but they point signward,
> waving the crutches of empty years.
>
> The brown one, smiling, led me on
> with wisdom as a sturdy cane.
> "The masterpiece is there," he said—
> and the dread beauty of living
> crushed us into reverence.

As is also the case with the second and third sections of the anthology, the editors assembled the first section according to a layering or "pasting" procedure. First, one set of high-affect poetic forms was selected—for example, Wheatley's "On Imagination" alongside Horton's "On Liberty and Slavery." Second, the pattern of this set of poems was repeated in an adjoining strip of poems—for example, Paul Laurence Dunbar's "A Death Song" alongside Braithwaite's "White Magic: An Ode." Third, both strips were carefully aligned, "preempting any assumption of accident"—to use Robert Farris Thompson's precise formulation in his classic study of West African aesthetics, *Flash of the Spirit*[30]—in relation to the section's major accent—for example, Du Bois's psalm poem. Fourth, one strip was staggered in relation to an adjoining strip through inclusion of unpatterned pieces—for example, James David Corrothers's "Paul Laurence Dunbar" and John Wesley Holloway's "Miss Melerlee."

In terms of the dialectical tensions between the historical and the aes-

---

30. Thompson, *Flash of the Spirit: African and Afro-American Art and Philosophy*, 210.

thetic, the collage structure privileges certain aesthetic approaches over others. For example, the love of aesthetic intensity through bold contrasts and offbeat phrasing is preferred over the aesthetics of what we might call "slating": the process by which an art form's inner logic is disciplined according to strict time and space management, creating socially quantifiable and hence controllable units of creative activity. To put it another way, by projecting the collage structure as a popular aesthetic preference, Hughes and Bontemps rejected the market trends in postwar American culture that sought to capitalize on the further integration of everyday life in the realm of aesthetics. In *American Civilization*, C. L. R. James understood this new dialectic with great clarity when he argued that "Gasoline Alley and its prototypes, the soap-operas, the 'realist' stories of the old *True Confessions* can be abused on the score of vulgarity, triviality, exploitation by manufacturers, etc. But when all of that type that can be said, has been said, there remains an immense social and artistic movement—which points a broad arrow to the future and the integration of the social and aesthetic aspects of life."[31]

By arranging a work of literature exclusively for popular tastes during the conjuncture described by James—the war period and the years immediately after—Hughes and Bontemps moved to the aesthetic forefront of this movement by showing the full scope of its political possibilities. For Hughes and Bontemps, poetry provides a refuge when daily distractions and hardships become too much to bear. It is a personal refuge that, because it is based on the sharing of knowledge and feelings, very soon grows into an underground site of collective image making, information preservation, and shaping of definite aesthetic preferences. Against all odds, the underground goes on to produce the worst possible scenario for the corporate source of those distractions and sublimations: a whole new relationship between the producers, technicians, and performers of popular culture and the communities of people who provide the support necessary for their survival. In other words, the contradictory relations between civil society and the state provide the raison d'être for the collage technique itself, as the political status of each depends on the other's relative position in the struggle for equalitarian social change: for a strong labor party and trade union movement, for instance; for black equality; and for the liberation of women—social advances that are the collage form's condition for popular appreciation.

Politically, Hughes and Bontemps's collage aesthetic is a kind of African

31. *American Civilization*, 139–40.

American popular-frontism, while at the level of mass culture it intervenes as a disruptive form of American Surrealism. The latter move is made from the standpoint of popular aesthetic preferences (for example, for the short lyric and the image poem over long narrative and historical poems); the former, from a new site of civil rights struggle: the fight for desegregation. On the one hand, the collage does not need any historical antecedents: as we have seen, by "chronology" Hughes and Bontemps meant arranging the poets by their birth dates, not by their places in a literary checklist of artists and their works. As André Breton once put it, what Surrealism makes possible is "a supreme feat of reconnaissance." In Breton's terms, the task is not to criticize long narrative poems but, rather, to put an end to them altogether—to steer political thought itself "back onto the path of total comprehension . . . to its original purity," and for intellectuals and creative artists to engage in "the perpetual excursion into the midst of forbidden territory."[32] For African American writers and intellectuals in cold war America, that territory was writing itself. As Hughes stated in 1959 at the First Conference of Negro Writers: "commercial white culture would rather allow a colored writer a book than a job, even fame rather than an ordinary, decent, dependable living." To make a living as a writer in America, he told his audience, "you must have white skin." Moving quickly to ease the pain of his incisive words, in his familiar blues style, and also to motivate his listeners to action, he concluded with a sarcastic rhyme: "Of course, to be highly successful in a white world—commercially successful—in writing or anything else— you really should *be* white. But until you get white, *write*" (CW 9:383).

In *Poetry of the Negro,* Hughes and Bontemps's "feat of reconnaissance"—their excursion into the midst of forbidden white territory—was to produce an anthology of writing, in this case, poetry, by artists and intellectuals for whom writing was a primary source of income as well as of institutional funding and support, either from private foundations and endowments or directly from the state. Of the 145 writers in the anthology, more than half were employed as academics, journalists, or commercial editors and writers—a majority of whom belonged to cultural clubs, trade unions, teachers unions, editorial collectives, and writers' associations. About a third were employed by the state in a range of fields: as librarians, musicologists, public schoolteachers, translators, writing teachers and literature professors, job training instructors, youth home directors, physicians, lawyers, judges, and legislators. This balance between

32. Breton, *Manifestoes of Surrealism,* 124, 137.

civil society and the state gave the collage structure its rationale. The literary outcome is an arrangement of writers whose affiliation is with a fundamental social group—with either the working class or the bourgeoisie. There are no solitary writers in *Poetry of the Negro*, nor are there writers on the margins or writers in-between the margins and the center. In addition, the "negative resonance" regularly associated with art produced *against* society or as a result of "disinvolvement," to use Armand and Michele Mattelart's useful term, was for Hughes and Bontemps the aesthetics of preference, in that it was an aesthetics in which each writer was free to make his or her own choices.[33]

That there is no contradiction here, no new Manichaeanism in which aesthetic choices are reduced to two—art for the mass market or art for the few—raises two important questions. In what cultural category do we place the collage aesthetic? An "African" or "black" aesthetic goes a long way in helping describe the tendencies, strategies, structures, and patterns of this American collage, and indeed this type of analysis has been encouraged by Africanist scholars and intellectuals. To cite one example, Robert Farris Thompson's analysis of West African aesthetic structures in *Flash of the Spirit* establishes a strong link between the West African tendency toward metric play and the staggering of accented elements, as well as the preference for multistrip, multidecorative compositions—for "visual syncopation," in Thompson's terminology—and the dominant aesthetic preferences in African American culture.[34] What Hughes and Bontemps achieved was to advance this West African–based aesthetic preference through an anthological form of African American literary collage.

By presenting a popular aesthetic preference for "rhythmized writing," *Poetry of the Negro* superseded the laws, procedures, and myths of "high" literary art by rejecting its "natural" terms of classification, structure, periodization, and arrangement. This can be seen in Hughes and Bontemps's first order of business: to provide a negative shock to the episteme of bourgeois art by completely disregarding it. Their next task was to give, dialectically, an answer to the popular preference for collage by introducing at the level of high literary production new kinds of writing that the collage aesthetic directly enables. In place of the European bourgeois model, they advanced a Du Boisian framework: that the collage earns its broad appeal from the thesis that *all* art is committed art. Further, because

33. Mattelart and Mattelart, *Rethinking Media Theory*, 112.
34. Thompson, *Flash of the Spirit*, 210–11.

the collage technique is based on juxtaposition and contrast, class juxtapositions and contrasts are brought easily into view—"easily" in the sense that the weight of anticommunist ideology, in which class conflict is submerged beneath the rhetoric of white American patriotism, is promptly set aside to make space for the collage. The literary collage, then, is in effect taking political sides, since the selection process itself is both the content and form of the collage aesthetic.

For the projection of writing as an essential site of political struggle, there has to be a form through which the contending forces in society can be called forth, so that "state writers," for instance—writers employed by state agencies and institutions—can be seen as just as crucial to society as are "civil society" (or commercial) writers. Hughes and Bontemps accomplished this through a kind of roll call or "shout-out." In this way, the pleasures of the collage are in recognizing all the intellectuals struggling for the Du Boisian ideal: the democratic flourishing of work, culture, and liberty. In the early 1980s, at the beginning of the second cold war, the shout-out became popularized through the work of commercial artists and cultural workers of the hip-hop movement, which spread quickly to Europe and Japan in the late 1980s and early 1990s.[35] This same sort of internationalization of African American art is powerfully present in *Poetry of the Negro*, in the form of the shout-outs that Hughes and Bontemps send across several seas and continents.

Du Boisian in conception, the shout-out has the aim of recognizing those who labor on behalf of the three freedoms: the freedom of life and limb, the freedom to work and think, and the freedom to love and aspire. At the underground level, hip-hop culture still includes all three freedoms in the shout-out technique; in the U.S. mass media, the shout-out usually selects only the freedom to love and aspire, leaving the other two for philosophes and left academics. The great virtue of *Poetry of the Negro* is that it includes all three, which is also its "supreme feat of reconnaissance." For to go back over war-torn literary terrain from the standpoint of the present, where two new wars were underway simultaneously—the cold war and the African American civil rights movement—required of Hughes and Bontemps an ideological realignment of social forces. The argument they made is that the three freedoms must be fought for togeth-

35. On the internationalization of hip-hop music and culture, see David Toop's *The Rap Attack II: From African Rap to Global Hiphop* and Brian Cross's *It's Not About a Salary: Rap, Race, and Resistance*. On the three freedoms and hip-hop culture, see James Spady and Joseph Eure's marvelous *Nation Conscious Rap*.

er, not successively—as Du Bois had cautioned in *Souls*—if the object of this freedom struggle (the fostering of the traits and talents of African Americans in conformity to "the greater ideals of the American Republic") is to be successfully advanced.[36] In this way, Hughes and Bontemps rejected the prevailing liberal bourgeois anticommunist ideology of the state—the notion that the state is abstract and civil society active and concrete—by showing that the state is just as much a part of society as is the market and that the struggle for a democratic society involves both spheres simultaneously rather than simply one against the other in a zero-sum game. As Christopher Lasch observed sharply in his analysis of cold war U.S. culture, McCarthyism's concept of the state as opposite to civil society derived from a populist mode of legitimation, which rested on a double-edged sword, that of populist ideology and utopianism:

> Whereas the elitism of European intellectuals expressed itself in a cult of charismatic leadership, the American variety based its distrust of the masses precisely on their susceptibility to extreme political solutions; that is, to the same utopianism which the Europeans attacked as a vice of deluded intellectuals. Thus a neat twist of logic permitted those who opposed McCarthyism to argue that McCarthyism was itself a form of populism.[37]

Poetry of the Negro had to circumvent the terms of this polarity—the state versus civil society; the public versus the private—to find its own form, since the existing forms did not allow "white" writers to be included in an anthology of African American writing—or, more to the point, for the cultural coexistence of "commercial" or popular writers and "state" or public writers. Thus, rather than setting one against the other, as in the bourgeois concept of the state (the popular versus the public, or the masses versus the elite), Hughes and Bontemps juxtaposed the two spheres "contrapuntally" to achieve what bourgeois art could not: popular avant-garde aesthetics in the form of a mass-market poetry anthology.

The collage structure also allows for other aesthetic preferences. One is an aesthetics of *lateral mobility*. For example, a subway or bus rider could take in one poem per stop, or a worker could enjoy four or five poems during a break in a day's hectic schedule. At once a basic component of the collage structure's functionality and a specific aesthetic preference, the

36. Du Bois, *Souls of Black Folk*, 52, 62, 54.
37. Lasch, *Agony of the American Left*, 69.

brevity of the poems in the first section also animates the aesthetic of high-affect poetic forms by deliberately clashing with the poetry of the second and third sections. Although the second section does not include long narrative poems, rhetorical poems, or prosaic poems, the verse there tends to be much longer. In the main, the ode, the elegy, and the epistle are the favored forms, owing to the thematic focus of the section: poems written by Europeans and Euro-Americans on behalf of black self-emancipation. For example, William Ellery Leonard's twenty-one-part "The Lynching Bee" covers thirteen pages of the anthology; Vachel Lindsay's jazz poem "The Congo" is five pages long; Kay Boyle's "A Communication to Nancy Cunard" is slightly less than five pages; and Elizabeth Bishop's four-part lyric "Songs for a Colored Singer" is four and a half. By contrast, the longest poem of the first section is Margaret Walker's three-part ballad "Harriet Tubman," which covers less than four pages. In the Caribbean section, Hughes and Bontemps stayed true to the collage aesthetic of the first section but used a different ordering principle. The third section is arranged according to the poets' countries of origin: Jamaica, British Guiana, British Honduras, Barbados, Trinidad, Haiti, Martinique, French Guiana, or Cuba. This organizing principle functions structurally as the juxtapositions in section one did compositionally—that is, as a multipatterned "strip."

More to the point, all schematisms have to be forced out for the total visual design of the collage to reemerge. Thus the "nation logic" of the third section, like the thematics of black-and-white-unite-and-fight in the second, need to be superseded by an aesthetic that can hold them all. Also, the major theme of the anthology reappears in the final section as the anthology's theme-of-all-themes: that African American poetry belongs to a greater, "non-American" tradition, an all-embracing popular-democratic ideology of literature that brings into contact three continental peoples: African Americans, European Americans, and Africans. Hughes and Bontemps defined this ideology and described its overall scale with the inclusion of one section, one poet, and three entries.

The entries, which compose the entire "Africa" section, are by the West African woman poet Aquah Laluah, who was a teacher in the Girl's Vocational School of Sierra Leone. The text's collage structure is redesigned spontaneously through her poetry in two ways: first, Africa is represented, simple and plain, without fanfare or rhetoric; second, Africa is presented as an essential player in the fight to overthrow U.S. racial oppression. Laluah's sonnet "The Souls of Black and White" shows a way that has always been there—an "old" path to a new level of comprehension:

The souls of black and white were made
By the selfsame God of the selfsame shade.
God made both pure, and He left one white;
God laughed o'er the other, and wrapped it in night.

Said He, "I've a flower, and none can unfold it;
I've a breath of great mystery, nothing can hold it.
Spirit so illusive the wind cannot sway it.
A force of such might even death cannot slay it."

But so that He might conceal its glow
He wrapped it in darkness, that men might not know.
Oh, the wonderful souls of both black and white
Were made by one God, of one sod, on one night.

The return to Africa in this final section involves all the techniques, themes, and basic logic of *Poetry of the Negro:* the aesthetic preference for short and boldly contrastive poems; the intercontinental links among Africa, Europe, and America; and the collage technique itself. Moreover, as Hughes and Bontemps began with Africa in the first section—with the African-born poets Lucy Terry and Phillis Wheatley—they ended here, completing the outer strip of the their elegant multistrip literary collage.

Art for the Sake of Conscious Youth: Chuck D and Langston

He made proposals. We
Carried them out.

—Bertolt Brecht, *Poems, 1913–1956*

When literary scholars and critics mention Hughes's writings for young people, his juvenile poetry and short fiction are ranked above the popular histories he wrote for youth, if the latter are acknowledged at all. Indeed, until the publication of *The Collected Works of Langston Hughes,* all but two of his histories for young people had been out of print for several decades, whereas a fair number of his works of poetry and prose for children had remained in constant circulation, while others had been republished as the market for children's books expanded. As with his radio scripts in the 1940s and 1950s, it can be argued that Hughes's histories for young people are neglected today *in spite* of their certain success in the marketplace. Understanding these writings in the context of the cold war will highlight the vitality of Hughes's relationship with socialist politics and popular avant-garde aesthetics. A close analysis of two works—*The First Book of Rhythms* (1954) and *The Sweet Flypaper of Life* (1955)—will better reveal his overriding purpose.

In 1996 the veteran rapper Chuck D issued a blueprint on the topic of African American youth culture and political education entitled "Ten Resentments of the Industry," which he placed as a hidden track on *The Autobiography of MistaChuck: Report from the Commissioner.* Chuck D is a founding member of the rap group Public Enemy (PE), which was formed in Long Island, New York, in 1982. In 1987, PE released on the newly established Def Jam record label its debut album *Yo! Bum Rush the Show,* and then a year later *It Takes a Nation of Millions to Hold Us Back.* Both works are considered masterpieces in hip-hop as well as catalytic texts in the international expansion of its distinctive cultural styles and practices. PE helped to accomplish the globalization of hip-hop in the late 1980s through extensive worldwide tours, which introduced to European, Asian, and African audiences the latest in a long line of world-historical African American arts movements.

The ten resentments are enunciated by Chuck D in a voice heavily altered through computer modulation and stimulate a series of questions. Given the persistence of white racial oppression in U.S. society, which has given us a white racist mass culture, how do African American popular artists manage to develop their own audiences and independently carry out their own artistic plans and projects? To phrase the problem differently, how do African American artists create popular art independent of white-run mass culture? Moreover, how could independent African American voices be raised up (Chuck D's concept of "voice leadership") in a system designed at every level to reduce them to an undifferentiated sameness? For Chuck D, every constraint on African American popular expression, and every form of exploitation and co-optation obtaining in the U.S. entertainment industry, is a result of "white Americanism," in the sense given it by Du Bois in *Souls:* the glorification of "dollars and smartness" at the expense of "light-hearted but determined Negro humility."[38]

I suggest that Chuck D's ten-point critique of U.S. media culture is Hughesian in aim and conception. Chuck D's type of analysis, as well as Public Enemy's whole iconoclastic cultural practice, is precisely what Hughes was laying the groundwork for during the 1950s. Although each of Chuck D's resentments could easily generate separate research projects

---

38. Du Bois, *Souls of Black Folk,* 52.

in American popular culture, three in particular serve as departure points for an analysis of Hughes's popular histories for youth, including most significantly his writing workshops, which I will turn to in a moment.

> One, I resent the fact that between ownership and creativity in the entertainment and music industry, blacks are not presented the options on how they can participate in it, besides singing, rapping, dancing, telling jokes or acting. . . . Four, I resent the pedestal that we human beings place on others based on minimal manufactured achievements. The illusion of so-called stars has created, through culture, the imaginary perception of falling off. You never fall off if you know where you are. Star spelled backwards is rats. And the attitude of a rat is what many have adopted and portrayed to its public: slam-dunking, rhyming, singing when it meant nothing a hundred and fifty years ago in the United States. So what's the big deal now? . . . And ten, I resent the fact that we do not keep and store facts about us, leaving others to create facts about us. Television and radio has a serious imbalance of entertainment and information, imbalances of show and business, therefore steering youth culture to focus goals on only that of being an athlete or entertainer.

First, the need to independently store facts about African Americans in order to counter the white media's inventions (Chuck D's tenth point) is the basis for Hughes's "First" books about African American heroes and the premise for *The First Book of Rhythms,* among his other works for children. Second, because the whole "star system" of U.S. media culture helps reproduce pernicious antiblack tropes and images, from the one-sided projection of sports stars such as O. J. Simpson and Dennis Rodman or political stars such as former Detroit mayor Coleman Young (a constant target of the white media throughout the 1980s) and Washington, D.C., mayor Marion Barry (the target of the 1990s), this system must be undermined (Chuck D's fourth point). Third, because "the imbalance," as Chuck D puts it, "between ownership and creativity in the entertainment and music industry" has forever delimited "the options on how [aspiring African American creative artists] can participate in it, besides singing, rapping, dancing, telling jokes or acting" (his first point), a new relationship between popular aesthetics and independent intellectual and political work is in order. As I will show, Hughes accomplished this task through his role as a teacher of writing.

The need to independently store facts about African Americans was always linked for Hughes to the nurturing and development of politically active and independent African American popular audiences. What is at stake is the writer's method. As we have seen, Hughes approached writing during the 1930s and 1940s from two angles simultaneously. Politically, he served as a black national advocate for international socialism, mainly through his poetry and his journalism. As an artist, he influenced American popular culture through the formation of consciously "reintegrated" tastes and preferences. Unlike black communists such as Claude McKay and Richard Wright, Hughes approached literature as a site from which these two battles could be fought at the same time—"not singly but together, not successively but together, each growing and aiding each," in Du Bois's famous words. Especially in his popular histories for youth, Hughes set out to answer Du Bois's call, through literary forms newly accessible to the masses of American society.

As Cedric J. Robinson observed in *Black Marxism*, what distinguished McKay and Wright from their black radical coworkers such as Du Bois and Hughes was the fact that they came to communism directly through black nationalism: McKay through Garveyism and Wright through the African American working classes of the rural South. According to Robinson, this is why they ended up rejecting the communist solution to white racial oppression.[39] Yet had he studied Langston Hughes—in fact, not a single mention is made of Hughes in *Black Marxism*—he might have reached a different conclusion: that communism and black radicalism are far from irreconcilable ways of seeing the world and are therefore not doomed to mutual distrust and indifference but, rather, are one of the more successful crossovers of recent times—a far more successful crossover than those between, say, white American trade unionism and communism, environmentalism and communism, or feminism and communism. Moreover, that these supposedly antithetical worldviews could find common ground in popular literature—in the literary collage form and in children's literature—calls into question Robinson's thesis. Indeed, Hughes's enormous success as an African American socialist writer goes a long way toward explaining his omission from Robinson's study.

Although the conclusions drawn in *Black Marxism* cannot be adequately addressed here, they do provide a useful starting point for understanding Hughes's writings for youth. Namely, Hughes's emphasis on the worldliness of African American culture circumvented the polar opposition between black nationalism and communism by presenting and promoting a way of thinking that depended on both for its "historical unique-

---

39. Cedric J. Robinson, *Black Marxism: The Making of the Black Radical Tradition*, 297–98, 417–18.

ness," to use one of Robinson's central terms. Also, his writings for children raised up as a distinct front of political struggle the task of winning America's youth over to socialism. The fact that many of these works left out Du Bois—a point repeated needlessly in the scholarship on Hughes since the works in question were not about intellectuals—or that several were grossly censored by anticommunist editors is, of course, an excellent reason to study them.[40] That they have not been studied tells us two things: that Chuck D's resentments of U.S. media culture speak directly to a failure of method and not as much to questions of media access and representation, nor to the commodification of African American culture, which have been the focus of antiracist media critique; and that, more transparently, a good deal of work remains to be done on the writing of Hughes.

As Chuck D stresses, the opportunity to partake in the mass production of popular art has worked insidiously by "steering youth culture to focus goals on only that of being an athlete or entertainer." The saturation of the U.S. media with affirmations of narrow images of blackness made doubly easy the task of regulating all the racially iniquitous social relations needed to continue white racial oppression. In the critical vocabulary provided by Chuck D, the pillars of the imaginary relations of the United States are four white supremacist tropes, reinvented as necessary: (1) African American contentedness (singing); (2) fear of, and lust for, blackness (rapping); (3) loyalty and patriotism of ex-slaves (dancing); and (4) African American incompetence and buffoonery (telling jokes and acting). If Du Bois's concept of black America's "three gifts"—the gifts of story and song, of sweat and brawn, and of cheer—is kept in mind, the missing trope here is straightforward: "sweat and brawn," or labor power. Less clear is the creative path on which African American labor could be made into a new American archetype while at the same time abolishing the reigning four. This would open up new creative methods for *all* American writers. As Ishmael Reed has nicely put it in *19 Necromancers from Now,* "the inability of some students to 'understand' works written by Afro-American authors is traceable to an inability to understand the American experience as rooted in slang, dialect, vernacular, argot, and all of the other put-down terms the [English department] faculty uses for those who have the gall to deviate from the true and proper way of English."[41] By

40. On the censorship and suppression of Hughes's writing during the cold war, see Rampersad, *Life of Langston Hughes,* 2:230.
41. Du Bois, *Souls of Black Folk,* 275; Reed, *19 Necromancers from Now,* 3.

"deviate" Reed means to teach in the U.S. academy detective novels and dime-store westerns, a point that helps illuminate Hughes's path during the 1950s. The liberation of American literature, to invoke the title of V. F. Calverton's work of literary history and criticism from the 1930s, has to come by way of the popular in order for an authentic national culture to emerge in the United States. For Hughes, that path of the popular was the ground held by young people.

Dynamic Conformism

> In place of the old bourgeois society, with its classes and class antagonisms, we shall have an association in which the free development of each is the condition for the free development of all.
>
> —Karl Marx, *The Communist Manifesto*

> In the school, the nexus between instruction and education can only be realised by the living work of the teacher.
>
> —Antonio Gramsci, "On Education"

"There is no rhythm in the world without movement first" says Hughes in the first chapter of *The First Book of Rhythms,* the second of six children's books he wrote for Franklin Watts during the 1950s and 1960s (*CW* 11:255). The first, *The First Book of Negroes,* had been criticized by some African American intellectuals for leaving out any mention of Du Bois or Paul Robeson, a criticism that Hughes never responded to publicly. In 1965, however, he explained the circumstances he had faced at the time: "It was at the height of the McCarthy Red baiting era, and publishers had to go out of their way to keep books, particularly children's books, from being attacked, as well as schools and libraries that might purchase books. . . . It was impossible at that time to get anything into children's books about either Dr. Du Bois or Paul Robeson." According to Rampersad, "it was taken for granted by [Hughes's] various publishers that even brief references to Du Bois and other radicals were out of the question in a text aimed at children. Such books were virtually indefensible when attacked by the right wing." Rampersad points out that the first edition of *The First Book of Negroes* had featured a picture of Josephine Baker, but after a New York columnist threatened to attack the book unless all references to her were removed—on the grounds that Baker was a communist—she disappeared from the text in the next printing. Not only were Hughes's children's books vulnerable to anticommunist attack, as Rampersad has documented, but his critically acclaimed poetry suffered as well.

> Just about everyone at the firm of Henry Holt who had been involved in publishing Hughes' *Montage of a Dream Deferred* in 1951 and *Laughing to Keep from Crying* in 1952 had been summarily fired and various contracts canceled. Stock of the books, including *Montage,* was sold off cheaply—all because of pressure, Langston was told, from reactionary groups backed by oil-rich conservatives. "That Texas oil money suddenly found them *their* list!" Hughes joked desperately about the fired editors. "All due to a few little poetries."[42]

Montage of a Dream Deferred and *Laughing to Keep from Crying* were indeed "little poetries" compared to his series of "First" books and his photo-essay with Roy DeCarava, as well as his history of the NAACP, *Fight for Freedom.* The children's books brought Hughes a much wider audience, as did *The Sweet Flypaper of Life.* More important, the whole mode of writing was different. *The First Book of Rhythms* came directly out of Hughes's teaching experiences at the Laboratory School in Chicago, where in 1949 he led interdisciplinary writing workshops for eighth graders. In contradiction to Ivan von Auw's opinion that Hughes's method during this period was scatterbrained, the project demanded rigorous planning and execution. Hughes scholar Robert G. O'Meally has noted: "According to his carefully wrought lesson plans, Hughes led a series of discussions of rhythm in plants, animals, and the universe, as well as rhythm in human body movements, speech, music, visual arts, and, of course, poetry. His notes indicate that for homework students were to prepare reports comparing rhythms they had observed. One was scheduled to make a presentation on music and baseball, another on swimming and modern dance."[43]

Like his 1929 cultural studies project at Lincoln University, his cross-disciplinary venture twenty years later gives a sense of Hughes's purpose as an intellectual and of how he understood his own role as a writer in the world. I use the term *cross-disciplinary* rather than *interdisciplinary,* since the latter would not have required of his students a dialectical approach to culture; instead of seeing in baseball, for example, the same logic of development and change that one finds in popular music, they would have witnessed a formal encounter between two distinct partners. At the Chica-

42. Rampersad, *Life of Langston Hughes,* 2:230–31.
43. O'Meally, "Afterword," 50.

go workshops, Hughes's role was to assist in the intellectual and moral development of youth. In Gramsci's concept of the common school, Hughes's function was similar to that of the humanist grade school teacher. As Gramsci put it in "On Education," "The common school, or school of humanistic formation (taking the term 'humanism' in a broad sense rather than simply in the traditional one) or general culture, should aim to insert young men and women into social activity after bringing them to a certain level of maturity, of capacity for intellectual and practical activity, and of autonomy of orientation and initiative." The fact that the Laboratory School was conducted in Chicago is also a Gramscian point of departure. City children, Gramsci wrote, "already know and develop their knowledge of the literary language, i.e. the means of expression and knowledge, which is technically superior to the means possessed by the average member of the school between the ages of six and twelve. Thus, city children, by the very fact of living in a city, have already absorbed by the age of six a quantity of notions and attitudes which make their school careers easier, more profitable, and more rapid."[44]

The most germane Gramscian point of contact, though, is that the common school he describes is designed to prepare the way for the most decisive phase of learning and instruction, where the "creative method" of dialectical thinking and acting in the world—what Gramsci called "the active school"—is mastered. Arguably one of the most complete blueprints of how to organize a national public school system, Gramsci's proposal is worth quoting at length:

In the first phase the aim is to discipline, hence also to level out—to obtain a certain kind of "conformism" which may be called "dynamic." In the creative phase, on the basis that has been achieved of the "collectivization" of the social type, the aim is to expand the personality—by now autonomous and responsible, but with a solid and homogeneous moral and social conscience. Thus creative school does not mean school of "inventors and discoverers"; it indicates a phase and a method of research and of knowledge, and not a predetermined "programme" with an obligation to originality and innovation at all costs. It indicates that learning takes place especially through a spontaneous and autonomous effort of the pupil, with the teacher only exercising a function of friendly guide—as happens or should happen in the university. To discover a truth oneself, without external suggestions or assistance, is to create— even if the truth is an old one. It demonstrates a mastery of the method,

44. Gramsci, "On Education," 29, 33.

and indicates that in any case one has entered the phase of intellectual maturity in which one may discover new truths. Hence in this phase the fundamental scholastic activity will be carried on in seminars, in libraries, in experimental laboratories; during it, the organic data will be collected for a professional orientation.[45]

In this regard, the contents page of *The First Book of Rhythms* is instructive: it indicates some of the old truths that Hughes wanted the students of his experimental laboratory to discover newly on their own. Each of the seventeen chapters proposes a different line of inquiry. The first chapter, "Let's Make a Rhythm," presents the method of discovery, which is the object of the book's first half. The second half, which begins with the ninth chapter, "Athletics," constitutes the book's "organic data," such as the operation of industrial equipment and other mass-organized activities, as well as their result: the artifacts of mass production. Indeed, to see a chapter entitled "Furniture" in a book on rhythm and writing is an experience much like the one shared by those intemperate attackers of *Poetry of the Negro:* an "intensification of the irritability of the faculties of the mind." Here, though, Hughes is interested not so much in deconstructing and "rephrasing" the bland schematisms of Anglo-American English studies—in this case, the relations between literary language and the rhythms of mass social life—as in laying the groundwork for a kind of "dynamic conformism," where young people could be socialized into what Hughes termed in his Simple columns the art of "listening fluently." In this context, however, the verb *to listen* is replaced by the verb *to move,* for as he plainly states in *The First Book of Rhythms,* "rhythm comes from movement" (*CW,* 11:255).

To move fluently requires coordination skills first and foremost. Since the workshops were writing workshops, Hughes's students started with pad and pencil. "Make a point of a triangle, then a smaller one, then a smaller one than that, then a still smaller one, so that they keep on across a sheet of paper, all joined together," he instructs. "Again you have made a rhythm. Your hand, your eye, and your pencil all moving together have made on the paper a rhythm that you can see with your eyes." Then shifting quickly to other sensory skills, the aural and the aerobic, he prepares them for the second part of this start-up exercise. "You can make a rhythm of sound by clapping your hands or tapping your foot," Hughes tells them. "You can make a body rhythm by swaying your body from side to

45. Ibid., 31.

side or by making circles in the air with your arms." At this point, the students go from making triangles to making circles:

> Now make a large circle on a paper. Inside your circle make another circle. Inside that one make another one. See how these circles almost seem to move, for you have left something of your own movement there, and your own feeling of place and roundness. Your circles are not quite like the circles of anyone else in the world, because you are not like anyone else. Your handwriting has a rhythm that is entirely your own. No one writes like anyone else. (*CW* 11:255)

This first writing exercise is also the first lesson of dynamic conformism: the exercise is common, as are the tools and the procedures, yet the outcome is idiosyncratic. In other words, to arrive at the axiom "no one writes like anyone else," the student has to first engage in a collective writing activity and then follow, in his or her own way, the teacher's general directive to all. But before this can happen, students must learn how to write.

"How do you write?" begins the next section of the first chapter. Verb-subject agreement is not the focus, nor are the rules for avoiding run-on sentences or using punctuation and capitalization—the typical concerns of the English composition instructor. Instead, Hughes has his students create their own illustrated rhythm patterns. "Make a rhythm of peaks, starting from the bottom of one peak," he instructs. "Make another rhythm like it, but start from the top. Then do the same thing again, but put one rhythm over the other, and you have a pattern. Fill in with your crayon and you have a pattern of diamond shapes. Rhythm makes patterns" (*CW* 11:256).

It is appropriate here to make a connection between Hughes and Bontemps's collage method in *Poetry of the Negro* and Hughes's goals in *The First Book of Rhythms*—not only because the rhythm workshops took place the same year Hughes and Bontemps completed the anthology, but also because the workshop exercises themselves often produced a collage aesthetic. Recall that the main method of the literary collage was the use of "multistrip" patterns. As Thompson has it in *Flash of the Spirit*, one of the signal features of multistrip composition is a strategy "for recovering a special West African spontaneity in design, without which there can be neither vividness or strength in aesthetic structure."[46]

In this respect, Hughes's fourth chapter, "Sources of Rhythm," includes

---

46. Thompson, *Flash of the Spirit*, 211.

an emphasis on bold rhythmic contrasts. Hughes prefaced his remarks on the sources of rhythm by saying, in his typical fashion, that when it comes to rhythmical design, no race—to riff on Aimé Césaire—has a monopoly on beauty, strength, and intelligence: that there is room for *everybody's* rhythm at the rendezvous of victory:

> Artists have used animals, trees, men, waves, flowers, and many other objects in nature for rhythms.
> In France 25,000 years ago the cave men made animal drawings on the walls of their caves.
> Later the flag lily, *fleur-de-lis*, became a rhythmical design that is the national symbol of France.
> African artists a thousand years ago made beautiful masks with rhythmical lines. (*CW* 11:261)

Thompson says that this kind of rhythm strategy confirms "a love of aesthetic intensity." What we can say in Hughes's case is that it also establishes a departure point for the instructor of writing. Hughes's method is an ingenious way of getting students to think in terms of the rhythms of prose writing; of lyrical flow; of word sequences, transitions, cadences, and caesuras. Already there is the room to start and stop as suits the writer, but in a disciplined, rhythmized way. In other words, all the frustrations of the college writing instructor—run-on sentences, improper use of punctuation, and so on—are answered in this simple exercise: how to give life to the rhythms of the natural world (in this case, moisture) on paper. Even great novelists have a hard time putting these rhythms to words, so the task is simply to draw them. And here the elaborateness of the design belies the claim that the task is too "elementary." Indeed, knowledge of rhythms is a prerequisite for great architectural design, as Hughes so convincingly explains in the closing lines of "The Sources of Rhythm":

> Perhaps the curve of a waterfall or the arching stripes of the rainbow suggested the rhythms for the arches of the houses and temples and tombs and bridges of men long ago—the arch of Tamerlane's tomb at Samarkand, the arch of a bridge in ancient China, or the Moorish arches at Granada.
> When the Egyptians built their tombs and temples over a thousand years before Christ, they knew how to combine the rhythms of nature with the possibilities of stone and sun-dried brick in the structure of their buildings. And the more harmoniously they did this, the more beautiful were their buildings. In splendid palaces the pharaohs lived.

The Greeks, hundred of years before Christ, knew the rhythmical beauty of the soaring line in a column. The rising lines of its many columns made the Parthenon one of the most beautiful buildings ever created.

The columns of Greek temples go upward.

The pyramids of the Egyptians point upward.

The skyscrapers of American cities rise into the skies.

Like the blades of grass and the stems of flowers and the trunks of trees, the houses and temples and other buildings of man rise toward the sky where the sun is. Almost nobody builds a house, church, or any kind of building underground. (*CW* 262–63)

Hughes uses a mode of explanation that emphasizes the secular power of rhythm. His one-line paragraphs in this passage serve as a figurative homology of the physical columns they describe, which Hughes suggests involve a kind of secular worship. He also allows us to see the practical importance of rhythms in terms of building a common school curriculum. If to make far-flung connections between disparate histories, ancient and modern alike, as well as between world civilizations, also ancient and modern, is the occupation of the philologist, then the process by which young people internalize both the method and the values of such secular generalism is the work of the teacher of writing rhythms. Hughes's sweeping account of the role of rhythms in the construction of more than a thousand years' worth of architectural landmarks, from bridges in ancient China to skyscrapers in New York, was motivated precisely by his nonspecialized method, which must strike today's U.S. reader as alien, even sentimental. As Brennan has nicely put it with respect to the generalism of Edward Said, "In the United States today, such a gesture is a calculated rebuke to technological panaceas and professionalist poses in the academy and in official public culture."[47] Yet for Hughes, a generalist method for teaching young people about world history and geography, about great civilizations and their historic contributions to human progress, was not a calculated rebuke but a beginning point—a means by which youth could be fully socialized into the dynamic rhythms of everyday secular life, which was for Hughes the consummate worldly sphere of existence.

"Rhythms in Daily Life," the fourteenth chapter of *The First Book of Rhythms*, serves as a transition from his guidelines, suggestions, and enu-

47. Brennan, "Places of Mind, Occupied Lands," 82.

merations in the earlier sections of the book to their concrete application in the last part. Until this point, Hughes has made the case well for the universality of rhythms. To briefly summarize his argument, through a few of his most pregnant phrases and formulations: (1) "Rhythm begins in movement"; (2) "Rhythm makes it easier to use energy"; (3) "The rhythm of the heart is the first and most important rhythm of human life"; (4) "Machines move in rhythm"; (5) "You, your baseball, and the universe are brothers through rhythms"; (6) "Nature is rhythm"; (7) "Each artist makes his own rhythms out of the things he sees around him and sees in his dreams and mind"; (8) "The rhythm of music and of words cause people to want to move, or be moved, in time to them"; and (9) "There are unseen rhythms that we cannot see, but which we can chart and measure by scientific instruments and by mathematics." What Hughes aims at in the last four chapters—"Rhythms in Daily Life," "Furniture," "How Rhythms Take Shape," and "This Wonderful World"—is getting his students to think about the new relations between intellectual and industrial work, "not only in the school," to return to Gramsci, "but in the whole of social life." This task Gramsci called "the comprehensive principle": the transformation of "all the organisms of culture" by giving to them a new, working-class content.[48]

Hughes understood the dialectic between the social and the natural orders through a study of rhythms and tested his hypotheses in the experimental writing laboratory. As Gramsci had insisted more than two decades earlier in his program for transforming Italy's national public schools, city life was essential for the success of avant-garde writing workshops like the one Hughes taught in 1949. But perhaps the most compelling parallel between Gramsci's national education program and Hughes's experimental writing lab is their mutual rejection of the distinction between "instruction" and "education," which is how the new relations between intellectual and industrial work are often twisted in order to rehierarchize them, according to a lost precapitalist social order. Perpetuated mainly by "idealist educationalists," the reorganization of public education on the basis of this distinction was, for Gramsci, inept and absurd:

> For instruction to be wholly distinct from education, the pupil would have to be pure passivity, a "mechanical receiver" of abstract notions—which is absurd and is anyway "abstractly" denied by the supporters of

48. Gramsci, "On Education," 33.

pure educativity precisely in their opposition to mere mechanistic instruction. The "certain" becomes "true" in the child's consciousness. But
the child's consciousness is not something "individual" (still less indi-
viduated), it reflects the sector of civil society in which the child partic-
ipates, and the social relations which are formed within his family,
his neighborhood, his village, etc. The individual consciousness of the
overwhelming majority of children reflects social and cultural relations
which are different from and antagonistic to those which are represented in the school curricula: thus the "certain" of an advanced culture
becomes the "true" in the framework of a fossilized and anachronistic
culture. There is no unity between school and life, and so there is no au-
tomatic unity between instruction and education.[49]

And so it was for Hughes. To put it more accurately, as the learning of
Latin was for Gramsci, the learning of rhythms was for Hughes. A glance
at the last four chapters of *The First Book of Rhythms* shows how. Even
more, it helps illustrate Gramsci's concept of *a mastery of the method:* the
bringing of *labor* into the field of knowledge at an early age.

As alluded to above, Gramsci had found in the idealist answer to the
national question of public education an obvious contradiction. If the lofty
goals and objectives of public education are deliberately raised beyond
the reach of newly emergent social groups, such as city-dwelling youth,
the concrete tasks of socializing young people into democratic civil society will fall into the hands of "traditional" (in the bad sense of reactionary
and provincial) intellectuals and teachers, making the work of national
education policy purely rhetorical (or idealistic) and, worse, a big and
clumsy target for right-wing corporate hacks who seek a radically decen-
tralized public education system to better control it, exclusively for the
business classes. As any observer of current U.S. politics can verify, we are
now seeing in public education exactly what Gramsci warned about in the
early 1920s, when the successful mobilization of right-wing minorities by
the reactionary parties of Italy—in the United States this would be right-
wing white ethnic minorities—had prepared the way for the fascist
seizure of power in October 1922. Gramsci's solutions should warrant a
careful review, then, in the U.S. context.

For our purposes, Gramsci's main point is that the concept of labor
must take center stage if any progress is to be made politically in the struggle for universal and free public education. For Gramsci, this meant an
emphasis on civic consciousness: "an awareness of the simple and fun-

49. Ibid.

damental fact that there exist objective, intractable natural laws which are the product of human activity, which are established by men and can be altered by men in the interests of collective development."

> The discovery that the relations between the social and natural orders are mediated by work, by man's theoretical and practical activity, creates the first elements of an intuition of the world free from all magic and superstition. It provides a basis for the subsequent development of an historical, dialectical conception of the world, which understands movement and change, which appreciates the sum of effort and sacrifice which the present has cost the past and which the future is costing the present, and which conceives the contemporary world as a synthesis of the past, of all generations, which projects itself into the future.[50]

The national scale of Hughes's writing workshops is easily discernible: the representation of America as a worldly place, as belonging to world history and not merely to a "peculiar" continental history, as well as his all-embracing definition of "American" baseball through the nonchalant pairing of Satchel Paige and Stan Musial—in 1949, no small thing. Less obvious is how he introduced the concept of labor as a solution to the contradiction between the social and natural orders on the one hand and as an attempt to unify school and life, instruction and education on the other.

Since everyday life is the locus of late capitalist society, the manifold tasks of reorganizing social life along democratic lines begin with harmonizing the concepts that are passed along by traditional intellectuals (folklore) with those that come with citizenship (social rights and duties). Hughes's emphasis on the role that the rhythms of nature play in the advancement of architectural design and construction is one example: that the living of life "upward," or out in the open, was inspired by the climbing rhythms of "growing things." Also insightful are his cues concerning the relation between spiritual upliftment and the sun. He draws an analogy between the pull of plant life toward the sun and the "common sense" observation that, when people are happy, "they generally walk with their heads up. When they are sad and days are dark and sunless, their heads are often down" (CW 11:264). Seemingly too pat, the analogy is meant to work dialectically, for the conclusion Hughes wants his students to draw is not merely that sunny days are usually happy days and sunless ones miserable, but also that social life organized around the universal rhythm patterns of the sun offers the greatest diversity of personalities, which are

50. Ibid., 35, 34.

held together by each individual's consciously understood social relationship to those patterns.

An analogy of the vital relation between civil society and the state under socialist or popular-democratic governance—a legal order that, in Gramsci's terms, "organically regulates men's life in common" and that is respected "through spontaneous assent, and not merely as an external imposition"—the sun metaphor is also an ingenious way of instilling in the minds of youth, and impressing upon their social consciences, the principles of dynamic conformism. For dynamic conformism gets its name precisely by rejecting every form and method of social control that reduces all individual members of certain groups—targeted on the basis of race, gender, sex, nationality, religion, and/or class—to one undifferentiated social status, "a status beneath that of any member of any social class within the colonizing population," as Allen has termed it in *The Invention of the White Race.* In Hughes's terms, the colonizing population comprises those who never made the transition from conscious fidelity to the rhythms of nature to conscious fidelity to the social rhythms of secular everyday life. In the enlightening words of Baraka, "They think Humans are food."[51]

In *The First Book of Rhythms,* Hughes elaborates a challenge to white racial oppression—which, as Allen has shown, is homologous to each and every form of social oppression in modern capitalist society[52]—through another nature image: the rhythmic shapes of seashells. "The sun influences the moon," he begins, picking up on the previous analogy of sun rhythms and a joyful national civic spirit. "The sun and moon influence the sea. The tides of the sea influence the shell life of the sea, and each shell is molded into a rhythmic shape of its own by all the rhythms and pressures that bear upon it from the sea. These are a few of the many shell shapes." Arranged across two pages of text are illustrations of different seashells. "On the surface of each shell," he continues, "the lines of some additional rhythms are etched in graceful beauty. No one shell in the world is exactly like any other shell. There are millions of different shells. Even each shell of each family is different and the lines on each single shell are different, too" (CW 11:264).

51. Gramsci, "On Education," 36; Allen, *Invention of the White Race,* 32; Baraka, "Heathens," 213–14.

52. Allen argues convincingly that the apprehension of racial oppression as a *particular* system of oppression "preserves the basis for a consistent theory of the organic interconnection of racial, national, and gender oppression" (*Invention of the White Race,* 28).

The analogy with racial oppression is subtle: the rhythmic formation of seashells is a metaphor for the infinite, universal diversity of human figures and countenances, which can be suppressed only by systematic denial and willful misrecognition of their playful differences and idiosyncrasies. In this way, Hughes's emphasis on *rhythms of their own* is conceptual: for individual rhythms to flourish, equal recognition among citizens, and national self-determination for those currently denied the rights and duties of citizenship, is the absolute precondition. Hughes's seashells lesson is, in fact, a repetition of the workshop's very first exercise: "Your circles are not quite like the circles of anyone else in the world, because you are not like anyone else." This dialectical movement in his teaching strategy between the unique and the commonplace is motivated by the fact that, in a society where racism and sexism persist, worse than ever in many respects, the individual and the collective remain fixed at opposite poles of the same conceptual spectrum. This explains Hughes's return again and again to the binary. The seashells metaphor concludes by giving his students one of their most salient examples of dynamic conformism: the *answer*, in the workshop's own terms, to those forms and methods of social oppression that keep hegemonic its dull-witted twin or what we might call, in line with Du Bois, the *dyspeptic conformism* of United States mass culture:

> You, like the shells, are like no one else. Even the rhythm of each line in your hands is like that in no one else's hands.
> The rhythm of your walk is like no one else's walk. Some people walk with long easy steps, some trip along, some wobble. Soldiers learn to march in step together, with their walking rhythms at the same tempo, so that they all cover the same amount of ground in the same time at the same speed. They look better marching in rhythm. If one man gets out of step, he makes the whole company look bad. That is why all must follow the same marching rhythm. Forward, march! . . . One-two-three-four! . . . One-two-three-four! (CW 11:264)[53]

53. Is Hughes riffing on Du Bois's image of the Negro as Seventh Son? See *Souls of Black Folk*, 45. Hughes's comparison of shells to human hands, and his suggestive wording—"The tides of the sea influence the shell life of the sea, and each shell is *molded* into a rhythmic shape of its own by all the rhythms and *pressures that bear upon it from the sea*" (CW 11:264; my emphasis)—seem to suggest a Du Boisian imaginary. This could also be a blues trope: the weathering of U.S. racial oppression through individual stamina, genius, and cunning.

These lines bring to mind Margaret Walker's famous conclusion of her classic poem "For My People," written several years before Hughes's Chicago workshops: "Let the martial songs be written, let the dirges disappear. Let a race of men now rise and take control." For as Gramsci argued in "On Education," it is through the activity of the leaders of labor—in this case, the work of systematically reorganizing the teaching and guidance of youth—that human beings actively participate "in natural life in order to transform and socialize it more and more deeply and extensively."[54] In this way, Hughes's masses-in-movement trope prepares for the transition from understanding the rhythms of the natural world to internalizing them socially, through the classroom or in the experimental writing workshop. Here the task will be to convince youth that streamlined rhythms are preferable to all others.

The rhythms of work are for Hughes where the class distinction between instruction and education, and between intellectual and industrial work, is dissolved. The chapter "Rhythms in Daily Life" demonstrates how concepts about rhythms that are "stored" by traditional intellectuals could be harmonized or "streamlined," as Hughes says, with those advanced in civil society and then reinforced by the state. One method is through an aesthetic education of rhythms. This harmonizing theme is present in every section of *The First Book of Rhythms*, but in "Rhythms in Daily Life" he indicates its importance for the writing lab as a whole. "What is exciting about tomorrow," he begins, "is that it is always different from today. Back in the early 1900s the first airplane looked like a crate. But modern airplanes are streamlined." He defines streamlining as making an industrial object "more rhythmical, more like a stream flowing." "It is much more pleasing to look at a rhythmical, harmoniously shaped object than at an awkward thing," he says. "That is one reason industrial designers who create many of the things we use in daily life are paying more attention to rhythm and beauty" (*CW* 11:273–74). Hughes then gives three examples: refrigerator design, indoor plumbing, and durable and affordable mass-produced eating utensils. That many of his pupils were most likely first- and second generation city-dwellers whose roots were in the Black Belt is reflected in his definitions.

At the same time, he is insistent that these advances of modern industrial design and manufacture not be glorified for their own sake or for advertising. His move is to shift along the axis from the traditional to the

54. Gramsci, "On Education," 34.

modern, drawing on that which is socially progressive and rejecting the backward and the reactionary. Hughes goes back to the "traditional" concept of human self-betterment—"traditional" in the sense of applying human social intelligence to the rhythms of nature for the good of every individual, for example in handmade eating utensils that reproduce and simplify the complex, everyday movements of eating and drinking:

> In grandma's day in the country butter was put into a well to keep fresh. And cool water was drawn from the well in an "old oaken bucket." Thousands of years ago, before men learned to dig wells, they drank from springs or streams.
> The first bowl to hold water was a man's cupped hand, or a pair of cupped hands.
> Then the hands took clay and made a ball. A bowl is half of a ball, hollowed out. And a cup is just a bowl with a handle on it. A plate is just a bowl flattened out.
> The first bowls and cups and plates were made only to be useful. Now we make them to be beautiful as well. Today fine designers like Russel Wright make beautiful dishes that are reproduced by machine methods so that people may buy them cheap. The rhythms of the hands of many makers of bowls, cups, glasses, and plates have given us the thousands of beautiful and useful shapes from which we eat and drink. (CW 11:274)

As we have seen, this same concept played a major part in Hughes's conceptualization of Simple: that Jesse B. Semple pays no mind to the uses to which the crankshafts he makes are being put is what earns him his nickname and is the vehicle by which Hughes introduced Simple to his *Chicago Defender* reading public—as "my simple minded friend." Yet as we quickly learn, Jesse B. Semple does not care what the U.S. government—the purchaser of the crankshafts—is using them for because he sees no logic to a nation waging war against fascism in Europe that itself has already produced, to paraphrase Baraka, "the original American Nazi, the southern Himmlers & Goebbels, mad poseur posing as the mad doctor."[55]

The force of Hughes's critique of U.S. racial apartheid in his Simple columns has been already noted, but now another way of viewing it is possible: that the hallmark of Simple's antagonistic blues is his dialectical understanding of rhythms. Simple is methodical about a lot of things and takes pleasure in most everyday chores and responsibilities, but working at the plant is not one of them. The reason is that the foundation of U.S.

---

55. Amiri Baraka, "Y's 18," 230.

wartime production is a racially unequal working class, making assembly-line work broken, unharmonious, and therefore anti-rhythmical. As we saw, even, or especially, during Simple's coffee breaks did his white boss interrupt and harass him.

In *The First Book of Rhythms,* interruptions and useless harassments are treated as "awkward" moments in the progressive march of history, in the forward advance of America's working classes. For Hughes, modern machine methods have made possible the conversion of traditional means and techniques of everyday life—for example, the preservation of butter or the storing of clean drinking water—into instruments of mass-production, socializing in turn the "rhythms of the hands of the many makers" of these instruments, who have "given us the thousands of beautiful and useful shapes from which we eat and drink." The old icebox has been replaced by mass-produced freezers, the "old oaken bucket" at the bottom of a cool well by refrigerators, and the hand-crafted clay bowl by ceramic cups, glasses, and plates. By staying true to the dialectic of teacher and student, and that of instructor and writer, Hughes is able to express the relationship between labor power and economic production: they are harmonious and rhythmic when organized along equalitarian lines and for socially useful purposes, but when they are organized clumsily and unequally, without respect and recognition for the rhythms of everyday social life, "the results are ugly. Broken rhythms usually are not beautiful. . . . Machines cannot create beauty. They can only copy it" (*CW* 11:270).

Just as the student's own rhythmic writing is an "original," in the sense that no one else could have done it the same way, so must modern industry allow for originality if there is to be harmony and rhythm in secular everyday life. It is worth recalling that the blues artist's search for a form of harmonious living, which was made impossible in the post-Reconstruction period by the restoration of white supremacy, rode the edge of this dialectic. Whereas for the bluesman and blueswoman the commodification of all human activities, even leisure and rest, spelled doom especially for the African American worker, since the rhythms of black labor were not only disrespected and misrecognized but systematically (through Jim Crow) debased and denied, the pleasures of everyday life were treated in the workshops as liberating. Thus, if the blues trope of American democracy denied was Hughes's departure point in his race-free early poetry and drama, and also in the Simple columns, rhythms functioned in his writing workshops as American democracy's last chance. To put it differently, whereas the blues trope is a critique of everyday life under white racial oppression, the rhythms trope of everyday life is an attempt to prepare young people—many of whom were the children of blues people themselves—for post–white supremacy America. Following the logic of his workshops, an appreciation of African American rhythms requires an appreciation and respect for African American labor.

This is the essence of the rhythms project: to revise the white racist image of black labor as entertainment into one of black labor as everyday struggle. Hughes's point is that, like all everyday struggle, black struggle is based on the dialectics of work and leisure, of necessary labor and aesthetic beauty and grace ("streamlining," in Hughes's term). In the penultimate chapter, "How Rhythms Take Shape," Hughes uses the example of knitting and sewing, making women's work equal to the masculine labor of building and manufacturing:

> Rhythms always follow certain conditions. Knitting creates its own rhythmical patterns by the very way the needles work in wool. So does chain stitching, cross-stitching, or featherstitching in sewing. Threads in weaving follow a rhythmical pattern according to the kind of weave being made. Pleats in dressmaking—knife pleats, accordion pleats—have a rhythm growing out of the way they are folded. When mothers curl little girls' hair they simply put the hair into the rhythm of spirals. But curls do not look well on all girls. Each person should arrange her hair to suit the shape of her face, just as a well-dressed woman chooses her hats to suit the lines of her profile, or her gowns to go well with the lines of her body. (CW 11:275)

Hughes's strategy is once again to harmonize the methods of craft production with those of industrial capitalism. The hallmark is his example of a mother curling her daughter's hair, which gives the image a working-class content. In Hughes's description, the gifts of everyday craftsmen and craftswomen to the world of modern industry are identifiable, measurable, and verifiable. That these gifts have come to be shared by all is also something identifiable, measurable and verifiable. To have knowledge of this is a source of pleasure. And this seems to be the essence of the trope: that only when industrial production is consciously and purposefully socialized can there be pleasing, harmonious, and rhythmic relations between the makers of commodities and commodity production itself. For Hughes, this happens when the rhythms growing out of craft production, such as "natural" weaves and pleats in clothing, are not only emulated by industrial designers and producers but also enjoyed by the masses of workers and small producers who make them. That every mother can now "design" her daughter's hair according to the child's own distinct body rhythms is a symbol for this socialization process itself and an educative expression of the dialectic of craft and industrial production. The other sign of harmony is when "fashions in clothes and styles of decoration and design are everywhere influenced by other people and places around the world":

> That design on your father's tie may be from Persia. Your uncle's jacket is a Scotch plaid. The lines of your mother's dress are French. Her shawl is Spanish in design.
> The music on your radio now is Cuban, its drums are the bongos of Africa, but the orchestra playing it is American. Rhythms go around the world, adopted and molded by other countries, mixing with other rhythms, and creating new rhythms as they travel. (*CW* 11:275)

This trope of traveling rhythms is the international principle of *The First Book of Rhythms,* while the national principle is expressed in the image of an African American mother curling her daughter's hair. What links them—similar to Hughes's "Here to Yonder" concept in his *Defender* columns—is a third principle: the love of reality. This principle is the subject of his last chapter, "This Wonderful World."

Jesse B. Semple also wrote poetry; Boyd has frequent occasion to critique Simple's verse at drinking sessions. In his verse, Simple consciously refuses to allow racial oppression to pollute the natural rhythms of the sea—on the beach is where he writes—an insight that offends Boyd, who sees no connection between the social and the natural worlds. Likewise, Hughes wants his students not only to take time to "smell the roses," but also to discover a specific scientific method of social observation and data collection that is aesthetically pleasurable. As in the literary collage, there are no classificatory hierarchies, only universal rhythms:

> [Y]our own hand controls the rhythms of the lines *you* make with your pencil on a paper. And your hand is related to the rhythms of the earth as it moves around the sun, and to the moon as the moon moves around the earth, and to the stars as they move in the great sky—just as all men's lives, and every living thing, are related to those vaster rhythms of time and space and wonder beyond the reach of eye or mind.
> Rhythm is something we share in common, you and I, with all the plants and animals and people in the world, and with the stars and

moon and sun, and the whole vast wonderful universe beyond this wonderful earth which is our home. (*CW* 11:276)

Hughes's concluding sentences return to the task at hand: learning how to write. Just as the universal attachment between human beings was for Marx social labor, for Hughes it was social rhythms: the starting point of all writing and the source of all human pleasure. It is in this sense that Chuck D's call to all teachers and creative artists to reject the narrowing of options for how African American youth can participate in the rhythms of American cultural and social life, "besides singing, rapping, dancing, telling jokes or acting," was advanced by Hughes several decades earlier. The idea was utopian then and is even more so today, for as Fredric Jameson has recently argued, in our postmodernist moment "the weakening of the sense of history and of the imagination of historical difference" has been "intertwined with the loss of that place beyond all history (or after its end) which we call utopia." Although Jameson does not mention Hughes's work, his thesis about the politics of utopia finds plenty of supporting evidence in the writing Hughes did for young people, during one of the most brutally repressive eras in U.S. history:

> [I]t is difficult enough to imagine any radical political programme today without the conception of systemic otherness, of an alternative society, which only the idea of utopia seems to keep alive, however feebly. This clearly does not mean that, even if we succeed in reviving utopia itself, the outlines of a new and effective practical politics for the era of globalization will at once become visible; but only that we will never come to one without it.[56]

The Photo-Essay Collage

> I want to express that moment when a man going to work has meaning for that man and for me, not the fragment of the whole but the expression that sets it apart for all men going to work at that given moment, when that man ceases being one man but becomes all men.
>
> —Roy DeCarava, *Roy DeCarava: A Retrospective*

The collaboration in the early 1950s between Roy DeCarava and Langston Hughes was both logical and fortuitous. Both had devoted

---

56. Jameson, "The Politics of Utopia," 36.

much of their creative lives to "storing" the history and politics of every-day life in Harlem—Hughes through his popular histories, musicology, poetry, fiction, and *Defender* columns, and DeCarava in his painting, print-making, and photography. And both had worked in 1937 at the WPA-sponsored Harlem Community Art Center, which was part workshop for WPA art classes and part salon for Harlem artists and intellectuals. What made their eventual collaboration on *The Sweet Flypaper of Life* so com-pelling, though, was their mutual understanding of artistic work as also a social activity. As the curator of DeCarava's work, Peter Galassi, ex-plains it:

> DeCarava's conception of his work as a social art found a welcome en-vironment in postwar photography. If the American aesthetic of the twenties had been dominated by the cool precision of Weston and Stieglitz, the new wave of the thirties was the photography of the Farm Security Administration—pictures by Dorothea Lange, Walker Evans, and Russell Lee, among others, which approached the individual as a social being and implied sympathy for the disadvantaged. Moreover, institutions as diverse as the Photo League, a leftist group of photogra-phers in New York, and conservative magazines such as *Life* and *Look,* also were enlisting photography as a vehicle for the expression of social values. . . . DeCarava already had developed a fierce independence that made him equally wary of the ideological prescriptions of the Photo League and the corporate pretensions of the magazines. But, if his op-position to the compromises of applied photography helped to sharpen his artistic resolve, the liveliness of photojournalism in the postwar years enriched the hand-camera vocabulary from which DeCarava crafted his style.[57]

This felt antagonism between mass culture and the independent popular artist was also at the heart of Hughes's writing during the cold war, as we have seen. That Hughes and DeCarava's method for negotiating these contradictions was a shared one makes for a fruitful analysis, for it pro-vides another concrete example of Hughes's approach to method. To break up the "localized formalisms" of American studies, to develop new popular-democratic aesthetic preferences, and to carry out writing work-shops through which young people could learn, practice, and then inter-nalize these preferences required a dialectical understanding of life.

In *Sweet Flypaper,* the dialectical method was applied to another cultur-al front, that of photojournalism. For Hughes the task was once again "to

57. Galassi, ed., *Roy DeCarava: A Retrospective,* 30.

combine the advanced with the popular"; in Baraka's terms, to rhythmize the conceptions of the natural and social orders that came from the folk with those being advanced in society, in this case the concepts of the professional postwar photographer. Hughes achieved this task in three ways: first, by transforming forms of folk culture, such as rumor and gossip, into popular literary aesthetic preferences; second, by using techniques advanced by the photojournalist to break up the localized formalisms of the short story; and third, by making idiosyncratic an impersonal artifact of mass culture: the coffee-table book.

Structurally, *Sweet Flypaper* resembles a family photo album and thus partakes in the third aspect of Hughes's work on the project: the personalizing of mass culture artifacts. As noted earlier, DeCarava was upset that the publisher, Simon and Schuster, had decided to print *Sweet Flypaper* in a pocket-size edition, not in the coffee-table format standard for works of popular photography. Although Galassi does not mention it, the fact that DeCarava worked exclusively in the genre of black-and-white photography made Simon and Schuster's austerity measures even more indefensible, since printing costs were considerably lower for black-and-white photos than for color. Nevertheless, for the first printing Simon and Schuster published three thousand clothbound and twenty-two thousand paperbound copies. The success of the book was immediate, prompting Simon and Schuster to supplement the first printing with a second of ten thousand copies. With thirty-five thousand copies in circulation, with the five-by-seven-inch paperback editions selling at only one dollar each, and a chorus of enthusiastic reviewers behind the book—"no book by Hughes was ever greeted so rhapsodically," Rampersad has concluded—the publishing house's cost-cutting tactics served American working-class readers quite well, albeit crudely and unwittingly. While it is doubtless true, as Galassi says, that the small format "does not adequately represent DeCarava's achievement," his claim that the final form of *Sweet Flypaper* "masks the eloquence of photographs so complete in themselves that they require no elucidation" is probably overstated and misleading.[58] Hughes's text is not an "elucidation" of DeCarava's photography but rather a literary testimony. Moreover, that it was designed "spontaneously"—in the sense that the text responds, first and foremost, to the arrangement of photographs and not to the requirements of the short story form—provides a felicitous entry point into *Sweet Flypaper*, for in relation to the photo-

58. Rampersad, *Life of Langston Hughes*, 2:249; Galassi, ed., *Roy DeCarava*, 22.

graphs, Hughes's text is both an accompaniment (or response) and a lead (or call).

The narrator of the story is Sister Mary Bradley, a lifelong resident of Harlem who lives on 134th Street. In the opening pages, Sister Mary is visited by a messenger of the Lord who has come to take her "home to heaven." Herein lie the pleasures of the text, for Sister Mary, a righteous churchgoing woman, has prepared for herself a home in Harlem, not heaven. She is not ready to go just yet; even more, her love of Harlem and its people is much stronger than her spiritual need for eternal rest and fulfillment. "Boy, take that wire right on back to St. Peter," she tells the messenger, "because I am not prepared to go. I might be a little sick, but as yet I ain't no ways tired." As we soon learn, Sister Mary has a host of reasons for wanting to stay with the living in Harlem, among them the U.S. Supreme Court's epochal decision of May 17, 1954. "For one thing," says Sister Mary, "I want to stay here and see what this integration the Supreme Court has done decreed is going to be like." Just as important for Sister Mary, though—and the subject of the next ninety pages—are her complex social relations with family and loved ones in Harlem. "Come home!" Sister Mary chastises the messenger excitedly. "I got plenty time to come home when I get to be eighty, ninety, or a hundred and one. Of course, when I wake up some morning and find my own self dead, then I'll come home. But right now, you understand me, Lord, I'm so tangled up in living, I ain't got time to die."[59]

Sister Mary's "entanglement" with Harlem is complex, and in this sense DeCarava's photography is therapeutic: it helps sort out the everyday struggles that define her life in Harlem. There are Sister Mary's grandchildren (whom she helps raise), Ronnie Belle, Jerry Jr., Louetta, Ellen, Rodney, and Chickasaw; her great-granddaughter; her daughters, Melinda, Mae, and Ellen; her son, Fred; Sugarlee, the mother of Rodney's child; her friends across the hall, Sister Jenkins and her husband; and her son-in-law, Jerry Sr. Each person is a different reason for Sister Mary to keep on living and each relationship a separate source of pleasure, worry, strength, and encouragement. Yet the complexity of her life is due precisely to the difficulties she has in keeping these relationships together, for herself and for the ones she loves. Her main concern, though, is Rodney.

Rodney came into Sister Mary's life when his parents put him out, "so's they can keep on good-timing themselves, I reckon," she says drolly. Al-

59. DeCarava and Hughes, *The Sweet Flypaper of Life*, 3.

ways her favorite grandchild, Rodney accepts Sister Mary's invitation to stay at her apartment and is a constant source to her of both intense joy and overwhelming distress. We learn of all the people and places in Sister Mary's life through a running dialogue she has with the Lord—a conversation she starts the moment the Lord's messenger is summarily sent by her back to heaven. Her first subject is Rodney:

> Now, Lord, I don't know—why did I take Rodney? But since I did, do you reckon my prayers will reach down in all them king-kong basements, and sing with the juke boxes, and walk in the midnight streets with Rodney? Do you reckon, Lord? Because there's something in that boy. You know and I know there's something in Rodney. If he got lost in his youthhood, it just might not be his fault, Lord. I were wild myself when I were young—and to tell the truth, ever so once in a while, I still feels the urge. But sometimes, I wonder why the only time that boy moves fast is when he's dancing. When there's music playing, girls have to just keep looking to see where he's at, he dances so fast. *Where's he at? Where's he at?*[60]

The italicized expression seems to indicate Hughes's own voice, pointing directly to a DeCarava photograph. In this instance, the photo is of a woman dancer looking over her shoulder. As with every page in *Sweet Flypaper,* the text and the photo are juxtaposed according to a spatial logic, which includes the arrangement of the photo and text on each pair of facing pages. That is, the book's structure is based on two-page units or "strips," to keep with the terminology of the collage aesthetic: what I have been referring to, borrowing from Robert Farris Thompson, as "multistrip" or offbeat phrasing. The effect is a kind of aesthetics of the family photo album—itself a collage—since the story being told literally unfolds before the reader's eyes as he or she goes along. Once the page is turned, a whole new arrangement of texts and photos is the object of interest, yet the narrative itself is still there, climbing and descending, and starting and stopping according to the rhythms of Sister Mary's narrative.

While the layout of the photographs follows a logic of discontinuity, the text follows a logic of continuity. The two-page unit featuring the photo of the woman dancer and Sister Mary's account of Rodney's travails is an illustrative example: on the adjoining page is a four-by-six photo of a man and woman in a loving, sensual embrace. That they are either in their own home or at a friend's or family member's home is suggested by their cloth-

60. Ibid., 7.

ing: the man has on a wrinkled white T-shirt and the woman a casual blouse with thin straps. On the left-hand side is a page-sized photograph, with only three and half lines of text, while on the right-hand side is a two-and-a-half-by-three-and-a-half-inch photo with eleven lines of text. The content of the photo-texts, then, follows a dialectical logic: on the left-hand side is a scene of domestic intimacy, while on the right-hand side is a scene of "public courtship," or worldly intimacy—that is, flirtation on the dance floor. A similar pattern or structure can be seen on every two-page strip of *Sweet Flypaper.*

As in *Poetry of the Negro,* and as suggested by the lessons of *The First Book of Rhythms,* the aesthetic preference for "visual aliveness," to use Thompson's apt phrase, is a basic requirement of any popular-democratic art form. Willful, percussively contrastive, and bold arrangements are, in the terms of *Flash of the Spirit,* the most distinguishable feature of West African textile production. In Hughes's conception, this hallmark of West African aesthetics is the main method of American popular artists, whether they know it or not. As African American artist Carrie Mae Weems has described the underlying photographic idiom of American popular culture, "A black idiom is simply one that comes out of the peculiar social, economic, and cultural conditions that mold black people. If a photographer is sensitive and understands the idiosyncratic gestures and rituals of the culture and employs this understanding while shooting, then that person is working out of a black idiom or a black aesthetic."[61]

The particular flow of African American experience is the basis of the popular photographer's method precisely because of how African American life and culture are treated under racial oppression: as internally flat and amorphous yet externally bold and exaggerated. It is this white racist binary that Hughes and DeCarava sought to undermine on every page of *Sweet Flypaper.* They did this through two main strategies: by internally juxtaposing or contrasting sentimentality and militance, so as to collapse the white racist binary from within; and by presenting in external form—in visual images—an overall portraiture of African American life that features a wide gallery of interesting, eccentric people.

Galassi has noted astutely that *Sweet Flypaper* undercuts "the blanket assumption that black men neglect their families."[62] He points to a series of photographs of Jerry Sr. caring for his young children as a salient ex-

61. Thompson, *Flash of the Spirit,* 209; Weems quoted in Galassi, ed., *Roy DeCarava,* 26.
62. Galassi, ed., *Roy DeCarava,* 21.

ample. Hughes's fictional Jerry was in fact a man named Joe James, a member of DeCarava's family. Although it is misleading to call these photos the "family pictures" of *Sweet Flypaper,* as Galassi does, since every Harlemite in the book is treated with the same tenderness and subtlety, the photographs of Joe James and his family were of special interest to Hughes. According to Galassi, DeCarava used more than three dozen of them for *Sweet Flypaper.* What must be noted also is the fact that DeCarava's conception of "family" is not limited to a neighborhood block or to "blood" relatives: family for DeCarava, and for Hughes, is that place where the opacity of Harlem life is most fully expressed, not where it culminates or finds refuge. This is a key aspect of *Sweet Flypaper*'s dissonance, since Hughes and DeCarava's concept of "family" is quite antagonistic to that projected in the white American mind.

The section of Sister Mary's narrative in which Jerry, his wife Melinda, and their children are introduced is the heart of *Sweet Flypaper:* an eighteen-page portraiture of daily life in Jerry and Melinda's apartment that opens with Melinda feeding her baby girl and closes with her reading the *Daily News* at the kitchen table. In between we see Melinda looking after her children, the children playing, Jerry coming home from work, the preparation of supper, dishwashing, a late night get-together among friends and family, and the children getting themselves ready for bed. Hughes resists romanticizing Jerry and Melinda's family life, however. The last page of Jerry and Melinda's section shows Melinda alone in the kitchen reading the paper. The text reads:

> One of Jerry's faults is, he don't come home every night. Melinda got the idea she can change him. But I tells Melinda, reforming some folks is like trying to boil a pig in a coffeepot—the possibilities just ain't there—and to leave well enough alone. Long as Jerry brings his wages home, he don't always have to bring his self. And when he does come home—well, I do believe Melinda is getting ready to populate the colored race again.[63]

Before and after the section on Jerry and Melinda's family are scenes from Harlem life that involve the whole community: walks in Riverside Park; children running through open hydrants in the hot summer streets; street meetings on the corner; working men and women waiting for the downtown bus; men delivering ice and coal; nightlife at local juke joints and bebop clubs; people socializing at candy stores; young men lounging

63. DeCarava and Hughes, *Sweet Flypaper,* 57.

in basements; children doing their homework in tenement windows; workers constructing buildings; men and women fishing by the Harlem River; domestic workers coming home after a long day of labor; rush hour on the subways; stickball games in the street; street vendors selling their wares; workers walking picket lines; children relaxing on stoops; political parades; weddings; games of hopscotch; folk going to political meetings on apartheid in South Africa; and the janitor in Sister Mary's building playing hide-and-seek with her grandchildren.

Here the textual accompaniments are brief, often ending with an ellipsis, a colon, or a suggestive question, such as, about Rodney, "What do you reckon's out there in them streets for that boy?" Significantly, Sister Mary's question about her grandson's future in Harlem is not a rhetorical one. As suggested above, the streets of Harlem for DeCarava and Hughes are not undifferentionally bad nor good; they are many things. "Yes, you can sit in your window anywhere in Harlem and see plenty," says Sister Mary. "Of course, some windows is better to set in than others mainly because it's better inside, not that you can necessarily see any more. But back windows ain't much good for looking out. I never did like looking backwards no how. I always did believe in looking out front—looking ahead—which is why I's worried about Rodney."[64] Hughes's text points to a lugubrious photo of Rodney standing against a cement wall: all but his face is submerged in darkness. Sister Mary's window metaphor is, in this sense, a word of advice to Rodney and other young people of Harlem. Amid the hustle and excitement of everyday city life, as well as its fatigue and stress, the keys to survival are a clear vision of the future and an attainment of collective meaning from irreducibly personal hardship and strife. In a phrase, Harlem needs its Rodneys to make up their minds—to be decisive about the role they will play in its development and change.

Sister Mary's narrative depends precisely on the connections she makes between her own past struggles and the present struggles of Harlem youth. The presence of different women in Rodney's life—another case of his chronic indecision—is a suggestive example, because it crystallizes Hughes's narrative strategy into a single monologue:

He's my grandchild, but he seems more like my son which is why I worry so much about Rodney. Sugarlee don't worry her mind with him, and he's the father of her child. Caroline says she loves him. But she has to run and chase to find him, and he laughs. . . . And when she does get a

64. Ibid., 84–85.

hold of him, she's glad. . . . Rodney says he loves Ada, which is the only gal he'll ever take out anywhere much. And she is sweet. She works, and she works hard, and sometimes when that girl gets uptown Ada's so tired she goes to sleep . . . setting around waiting for Rodney to take her on home out of that basement where he hangs out with them beer-boys. Ada is a decent girl. But I think maybe Rodney'd do better to marry Mazie who is somewhat like Jerry who don't give a damn about paying Con Edison. Mazie works just enough to get along . . . which is *enough* for some people. And when Rodney takes her out, he never has to come and borrow a dollar from me. I asked him once why. Rodney said, "Mazie never hails no taxi. That girl can walk faster than me."

Mazie is already kinder beat up by life which is like I were—so she knows what it's all about. My first husband down in Carolina, which was Rodney's grandpa . . . as the Irish say, *God rest his soul*—he were cut up by life, too. But it never got him down. I never knowed him to go to sleep neither, like Ada do, when loving was around. Well, anyhow, I would not choose no girl for Rodney, as I would not want no one to choose a man for me. But our janitor: his wife is dead. Do you reckon I'm too old to get married again? When I were sick he come upstairs to see me, and he said, "Miss Mary, I hear tell you's down—but with no intentions of going out."

I said, "You're right! I done got me feet caught in the sweet flypaper of life—and I'll be dogged if I want to get loose."

He said, "It is sweet, ain't it?" And ever since that time, that man's been looking at me, sort of—well, you know.[65]

Sister Mary's monologue exemplifies the dialectical movement in *Sweet Flypaper* between the life experiences and conceptions of the folk and the mass socializing urban modes of everyday life. At once theatrical (in the modern sense of an interiorization of worldliness) and literary (the text reads as an epistolary tale), Hughes's writing here rests ultimately on the eye of DeCarava. Or to borrow the language of Third Eye of the Oakland rap group the Pharcyde, on "the invisible fresh eye": invisible because of his subject matter and fresh because of his technique. DeCarava's way of seeing arose from his membership in the community: he took his hand-held camera with him to work every day, and his visual intonations and syntactical phrasings of Harlemites capture an intimate bond that would have been unseen by an outsider.

Moreover, this dialectical, antagonistic interplay between the folk-literary and mass culture made possible a new bond between the artist

65. Ibid., 87–92.

and the people of working-class communities such as Harlem. Much like the hip-hop movement of tristate New York, which has relied heavily on the aesthetic preferences of subway-riding youth for support and innovation, the success of DeCarava and Hughes's artistic method depended on the support and innovation of black workers in Harlem, in the sense that they converted the socio-architectural landscape into a set of secular customs and rituals: windowsills into study tables; basements into a drinking clubs; vacant lots into picnic grounds; stoops into front porches; kitchens into reading rooms; bus seats into reading chairs; streets into ball fields; schools into political meeting halls; doorways and lampposts into trees; man-made ponds into rivers, lakes, and oceans; curbs into rocks and hillsides; and intersections into public gathering places.

Sister Mary's dilemma, then, is trying to explain to young folks like Rodney, who live the ways of the folk without knowing it, how important it is to combine the strengths and advances of the folk, such as their respect and appreciation for the natural world, as well as their transformation of it into a commonly owned and used community resource, with the political struggle to make everyday life better for everyone, especially for young black people coming up but most of all for the entire family of Harlem which works hard on their behalf. Sister Mary's most compelling example is the symbol of the subway:

> After Rodney got in trouble with Sugarlee, that were when his father put him out, and he come to live with me—his favorite grandma. And I done climbed up and down a million subway steps. . . . I done rid a million subway cars, and went back and forth to work a million days for that Rodney—because he be's my favorite grandboy. Why? I don't know why. Now, you take the subway. . . . It's lonesome at night. But at the rush hour—well, all it took was the Supreme Court to decide on mixed schools, but the rush hour in the subway mixes everybody— white, black, Gentile and Jew—closer than you ever are to your relatives. Now me, I always done day's work ever since I come to New York, with no extra pay for riding in the subway, which is the hardest work of all.[66]

Sister Mary wants her children, grandchildren, and great-grandchildren to take their own concept of family, which comes from folk ways, and put it to political use by socializing every aspect of secular life, not just those aspects with which they are most familiar. In this respect, underlying Sis-

66. Ibid., 27–28.

ter Mary's narrative is the fact that Rodney was put out of his home. It was the failure of Rodney's parents to maintain the ways of the folk family—their adoption, it turns out, of the ways of the folk family's polar opposite, the narcissistic middle-class family—that began all her worries in the first place.

Their failure gave birth to a new spirit within Sister Mary: a renewed sense of purpose, a love of life, and a passionate desire to spread this spirit among a new generation of Harlem family. "As for me," she says just before finishing her daily work and the photo-narrative itself, "well, if I do say so, I'm as good as new—back on my feet again and still kicking—with no intentions of signing no messages from St. Peter writing me to 'come home.' When I get through with my pots and pans . . . ever so once in a while, I put on my best clothes. Here I am."[67]

67. Ibid., 97.

Conclusion

Tired

I'm so tired of waiting,
        Aren't you,
For the world to become good
And beautiful and kind?
Let us take a knife
And cut the world in two—
And see what worms are eating
At the rind.

    —Langston Hughes, "Tired"

Amiri Baraka made the case in 1986 that the writing of Langston Hughes was ripe for rediscovery and that he was tired—if I can riff on a Hughes poem—of waiting for American studies "to become good and beautiful and kind" by finally offering Hughes proper respect and appreciation. Baraka's comments came on the occasion of the republication by Thunder's Mouth Press of *The Big Sea*, Hughes's first autobiography, which had been out of print for decades. The republication of *The Big Sea* opened the door to two kinds of inquiry, readily apparent to any student of Hughes's life and work. Baraka would reiterate this same point ten years later in an interview he gave with St. Clair Bourne, published in 1997 in the *Langston Hughes Review.* Hughes's "greatest contribution to literature," Baraka said, "was that he was principally a very skilled intellectual with a great deal of energy and optimism."[1]

Fredric Jameson has taken up recently this same kind of approach in his study of Bertolt Brecht. "Brecht would have been delighted at an argument," Jameson wrote in *Brecht and Method,* "not for his greatness, or his canonicity, nor even for some new and unexpected value of posterity (let alone for his 'postmodernity'), as rather for his *usefulness*—and that not only for some uncertain or merely possible future, but right now in a post–Cold War market-rhetorical situation even more anti-communist than in the good old days." In the midst of teaching, researching, and writing on Hughes, I was struck powerfully by Jameson's book. I thought, is there a better example of gift and counter-gift in the history of world literature than that between the German Brecht and the African American Hughes? I could be overstating things, but after all there are August Wilson's "Four Bs"—Baudelair, Brecht, the Blues, and Baldwin—which he always named as his most profound influences. But I think the most convincing parallel is that between Brecht's and Hughes's ideas about science and knowledge: that they are, in Jameson's words, "not grim and dreary duties but first and foremost sources of pleasure"—*popular* pleasures.[2]

The first line of inquiry opened by *The Big Sea* centers on the fact that, in contrast to his second autobiography, *I Wonder As I Wander* (1956), it was written more than a decade before his interrogation in front of the House Un-American Activities Committee. Much has been made in the scholarship on Hughes regarding the supposed "centrist turn" he took after his interrogation by the state. Doubtless the event itself was a defining moment in his literary career. Yet too often in the criticism on Hughes is there an unnecessary concession to anticommunist ideology, expressing itself in a too-eager willingness to periodize Hughes's life-course according to the requirements of what Christopher Lasch has termed "the cultural Cold War."

So students of Hughes are asked to treat the first half of his career, the communist years, as exciting yet "troubled" and the second half, post-communism, as "forward-looking" and thus much more satisfying. While there is some obvious truth to this kind of periodization—Hughes was blacklisted in U.S. publishing and academia before the term was popu-

1. Baraka's comments are in his foreword to *The Big Sea* (New York: Thunder's Mouth Press, 1986), and in his interview with St. Clair Bourne, "Amiri Baraka on Langston Hughes," 33.
2. Jameson, *Brecht and Method,* 1.

larized, and after disassociating himself from the American Communist Party in the 1950s his publishing opportunities increased—the scheme itself comes from a class ideology Hughes rejected and from an aesthetic style he found limiting, to say the least. "Inorganic," then, is one way to describe efforts to periodize Hughes's writing according to a cold war conception of literary change and development.[3] But a better way of putting it, I think, is to say that the cold war periodization is insufficient because it is undialectical, because it fails to grasp the other side of the equation. At the end of the crisis-heavy 1930s, and after two decades of travel around the world (his longest stays were in Cuba, Haiti, Mexico, and the Soviet Union), Hughes published *The Big Sea* as precisely the other side of the anticommunist binary: a way of looking at the United States that came from without. This "non-Americanism," in the sense given it by Amiri Baraka in *Blues People*, enabled Hughes to objectify his homeland's state ideologies, its enduring myths, and its persistently bad social relations.

The second line of inquiry opened by *The Big Sea* is its emphasis on travel. Today terms such as *diasporic, transnational, cosmopolitan,* and *globalization* register across a broad range of academic disciplines, from literary and cultural studies to history, anthropology, economics, and sociology, and of course in the mass media as well, where they are popularized daily on CNN, in stock market reports, and in arts and leisure columns. But a rediscovery of Hughes brings to light another side of travel. For Hughes, travel was an African American national trope, defining a whole people and the specificity of its historical experience. This "other side" signifies a socialist conception of travel, where the idea is to help along other working-class national struggles in whatever way one can. As Timothy Brennan has shown in *At Home in the World,* "One can hold on to such a nonparticularist view politically, while retaining a nationalist position. It is, in fact, the only way to do so."[4]

The concept of exile suggests a beginning from which Hughes's later aesthetic projects during the "cultural cold war" would depart. Given the close affinity between "exile" in the African American tradition and "exile" in the decolonizing world, it is essential to recognize and appreciate the points of contact as well as the radical discontinuities among nation-

3. Tobin Seibers argues perceptively in *Cold War Criticism and the Politics of Skepticism* that modern U.S. criticism is primarily "a Cold War criticism" characterized by "arbitrariness and dogmatism." He shows that modern U.S. literary criticism has embraced the basic tenets of cold war ideology "as a means of fleeing from politics" (vii).
4. Brennan, *At Home in the World: Cosmopolitanism Now,* 24.

al liberatory cultural resistance movements in the Caribbean, Latin America, Africa, and black America. The affinities between the national liberation struggles in these disparate lands are political before they are cultural. Hughes's own approach to both travel and exile illuminates the question in ways that have yet to be analyzed in the discipline of post-colonialist studies.

The dynamic relations between aesthetics and politics in the cold war period have only begun to be investigated. I have tried to make a modest contribution to this exploration, avoiding notions of literature that come from anticommunist ideology, such as the one-sided fixation on propaganda, artistic freedom, and the "politics" of this or that: in other words, a critical frame that stacks the deck in favor of the U.S. ruling class, since these questions are rarely raised in discussions about canonical white American writers such as Faulkner and Hemingway. In obvious ways, American studies has not yet had its Saidian revolution, in spite of Toni Morrison's giant oeuvre in that precise direction. Thus I have chosen to discuss Hughes's writing from the standpoint of method: his techniques, his aesthetic preferences, his major themes, his rhetorical strategies, and the specific sources from which he drew these aesthetic forms and preferences. This approach has the advantage of simultaneously rejecting cold war criticism and renewing that of the secular democratic tradition.

Hughes took his stand with the "North American mestizo," a new archetype he presented in his sixth volume of poetry, *A New Song*. While not a resolution of the contradictions between cultural nationalism, integrationism, and socialism, Hughes's concept of the North American mestizo served as a powerful countermyth to the cold war ideology of American pluralism, recast lately as "multiculturalism." This new archetype was a major component of his alternative "non-American" literary method. Although the conventional view is that Hughes made a retreat from socialism in the 1940s and 1950s and adopted American democratic pluralism as the last best hope for confronting white racism in the United States, in fact he became increasingly skeptical of reformist solutions to white racial oppression and instead looked back to the Bolshevik Revolution for a "new" answer.

The 1947 publication of Hughes's seven-part series in the *Defender* on the Bolshevik Revolution was strategic. Describing his travels throughout the Soviet Union, where he resided for a year in 1932–1933, the series was written at the beginning of the twentieth-century African American civil rights movement, proposing an approach to the epic struggle to overthrow white racial oppression. Thus, Hughes's "Soviet series" is a "be-

ginning," in the Saidian sense: "the main entrance" to what he would offer the world in his writings from the late 1940s through the early 1960s.[5]

Although studies of form and content or sociobiography are essential
in understanding any writer, formal analysis is not enough when it comes
to Langston Hughes. A glance at the recent scholarship on Hughes testi-
fies to the new horizons opened to Hughes scholars by Rampersad's
painstaking research and writing in *The Life of Langston Hughes.* His enabling scholarship includes extensive research into the Langston Hughes
Papers, composed of materials from the James Weldon Johnson Collection
at Yale University and Hughes's manuscripts and correspondences, as
well as research in the archives of Hughes's contemporaries, comrades,
and collaborators, among them Locke, McKay, Cullen, Du Bois, Jean
Toomer, Zora Neale Hurston, Carl Van Vechten, and Wallace Thurman.
Although this book would not have been possible without Rampersad's
two-volume biography, my intent was not to reinvent the wheel. Hence,
my close attention to Hughes's method rather than to the already well established biographical record.

One way to describe the method of Hughes's writing during the cold
war is to say that it was an internalization of socialism. As a concept, "the
collage aesthetic" presents the key terms (or critical vocabulary) of this
fascinating process. It is worth mentioning at this point that even in the
best critical studies of American socialist writing ("socialist" in the broad
sense of literatures of popular-democracy), this kind of emphasis has not
been the main one. This is not meant as a criticism, since the labors of
scholars such as Paula Rabinowitz, Alan Wald, Michael Denning, Linda
Kerber, and Penny Von Eschen have brought to light legions of American
socialist writings hitherto buried in university library annexes and private
collections across the county. While their scholarship is necessarily critical and archaeological at the same time, my work is less sweeping, focusing on particular works by one socialist writer, who not only has been canonized in the U.S. academy—in contrast to the socialist writers featured
in the work of the scholars above—but who is also, alongside Whitman
and Melville, arguably the most widely known and appreciated American writer in the history of the United States.

A study of Hughes's method is important precisely because of his "official" stature and reputation. What Du Bois called in *Black Reconstruction*
"the Blindspot" (he meant the "White Blindspot") has also pervaded the
minds of many U.S. literary critics, white and otherwise. Whereas even

5. Edward W. Said, *Beginnings: Intention and Method,* 3.

minor white American writers such as Jack Kerouac and Robert Coover have had volumes of nuanced criticism devoted to the particular aporias and interstices of their writing, the massive Hughes canon has been treated in U.S. literary criticism arbitrarily and without any suppleness or genuine intellectual interest.

Try to imagine a book of essays on Eudora Welty, each authored by a different Americanist, in which no mention is made of Mississippi or of any of the material sources of her short stories. Absurd in the context of Welty, or for any other canonical white American writer, this type of treatment is a commonplace in the Hughes criticism. For example, Hans Ostrom's *Langston Hughes: A Study of the Short Fiction* (1993) never acknowledges the fact that Hughes's "Simple" stories were first conceived for radio and then, when rejected by the networks, designed deliberately for African American newspaper subscribers as well as reading groups. Doubtless such odd omissions happen in criticism of white American writers, but the standards are usually raised when it comes to the giants of the white American tradition, whose preservation and defense as "great writers" is usually undertaken as a matter of "national security," as Ishmael Reed has it in his masterpiece *Mumbo Jumbo*. If, as historian Theodore Allen argued in *The Invention of the White Race*, the hallmark of white racial oppression is the reduction of *all* African Americans to an undifferentiated social status, a status beneath that of any white American, no matter how minor the white may be, then Langston Hughes appears to be another victim of the U.S. apartheid system.[6] But this system's success in keeping Hughes beneath a Coover or a Kerouac will not last forever. Baraka's 1986 call is, demonstrably, no longer falling on deaf ears.

In some of the recent criticism of Hughes, the tactic has been a straightforward omission of key facts and details that show his return to the basic artistic tasks and political interests he cultivated during the 1930s while a cultural worker in the American communist movement. Yet at least two of these tasks and interests—a socially "reintegrated" general education program for the American working classes and the nurturing and development of a self-supporting African American reading public—were in the 1930s major components of American Communist Party policy, planning, and strategy.

The purpose of this book, however, is not to claim Hughes for some socialist political tendency or worldview. My intention is to suggest a dif-

---

6. Allen's definition, which has been cited in Chapter 2 and relied on throughout this study, comes from *Invention of the White Race*, 32.

ferent kind of thought: that the staying power of Hughes's irreducible discourse derives from a dialectical approach to art and politics that was neither opportunistic nor ideological. In a society in which anticommunist ideology (and hence opposition to dialectical reason) still dominates popular culture as well the academy, terms such as *class struggle, socialist, ruling class,* and *working class* probably evoke ideological associations of a sort that make their use easy to dismiss as nostalgic and anachronistic. But considered outside this peculiar and enduring U.S. anticommunist frame of reference, the idea that Hughes succeeded very well at popularizing socialist ideas in literature is uncontroversial. The real controversy is much larger than Hughes. It involves the way in which nearly every trace of a whole intellectual tradition—dialectical reason and self-consciousness, or social democracy—has been in the United States during the past thirty years eradicated and replaced by a reactionary and deeply repressive political culture in which even mention of the word *socialism* or *socialist* now signifies an unfortunate former epoch and a way of thinking long dead and gone.

Yet if this is true—that social democracy in the United States was once a popular dream but has become today irrelevant and anachronistic—then one has to acknowledge that much of Hughes's oeuvre is also irrelevant and anachronistic. The aim of this book has been to illustrate, by focusing on several major Hughesian projects, that his writing is not only vitally relevant today in political terms, but also extremely useful for those involved with educational and other cooperative endeavors of many kinds, such as English composition curriculum design and pedagogy, cross-cultural studies, and the building of independent intellectual organizations and institutes committed to creating a popular democratic culture in U.S. society.

Thus, to the objection that my study tries to make Hughes into something he was not—an African American intellectual devoted to socialism—or conversely that I left out certain evidence that could have proved the "socialist thesis" more compellingly, it seems to me that this narrow American frame of reference is the real issue, rather than the analyses in this book. For in most other contexts—that is, non-American ones—the kind of discussion of Hughes's writing that I offer is straightforward and not prone to political controversy, or the charge of imputing the political onto literature. Rather than to provoke controversy, my desire has been the contrary. My analyses propose that Hughes's central place in American as well as world literature came from his highly skilled intellectual method, and that this method's salient characteristic, which he mastered over five decades of ceaseless writing activity, is precisely its refusal to temporize the political.

In this respect, Robin Kelley's main thesis in his classic work of American historiography, *Hammer and Hoe*, played an important role in shaping my approach to Hughes. Kelley demonstrated convincingly that the interpretation of communism "through the lenses of [the African American working classes'] own cultural world and the international movement of which they were now a part" was not the exception during the 1920s and 1930s but the hard and fast rule—a thesis that I believe is richly supported by the writing of Hughes. Kelley wrote:

> Far from being a slumbering mass waiting for Communist direction, black working people entered the movement with a rich culture of opposition that sometimes contradicted, sometimes reinforced the Left's vision of class struggle. The Party offered more than a vehicle for social contestation; it offered a framework for understanding the roots of poverty and racism, linked local struggles to world politics, challenged not only the hegemonic ideology of white supremacy, but the petit bourgeois racial politics of the black middle class, and created an atmosphere in which ordinary people could analyze, discuss, and criticize the society in which they lived.[7]

7. Kelley, *Hammer and Hoe*, 93.

Bibliography

Works by Langston Hughes

"Mexican Games." *Brownies' Book* (1921). In *The Collected Works of Langston Hughes, Volume 11, Works for Children and Young Adults: Poetry, Fiction, and Other Writing*, ed. Dianne Johnson, 19–21. Columbia: University of Missouri Press, 2004.

"Rising Waters." *The Workers Monthly* (1925). In *The Collected Works of Langston Hughes, Volume 1, The Poems: 1921–1940*, ed. Arnold Rampersad, 164. Columbia: University of Missouri Press, 2001.

"The Negro Artist and the Racial Mountain." *Crisis* (1926). In *The Collected Works of Langston Hughes, Volume 9, Essays on Art, Race, Politics, and World Affairs*, ed. Christopher C. De Santis, 31–36. Columbia: University of Missouri Press, 2002.

The Weary Blues (1926). In *The Collected Works of Langston Hughes, Volume 1, The Poems: 1921–1940*, ed. Arnold Rampersad, 13–62. Columbia: University of Missouri Press, 2001.

Fine Clothes to the Jew (1927). In *The Collected Works of Langston Hughes, Volume 1, The Poems: 1921–1940*, ed. Arnold Rampersad, 63–115. Columbia: University of Missouri Press, 2001.

Not without Laughter (1930). In *The Collected Works of Langston Hughes, Volume 4, The Novels*, ed. Dolan Hubbard, 13–209. Columbia: University of Missouri Press, 2002.

Scottsboro Limited (1931). In *The Collected Works of Langston Hughes, Volume 5, The Plays to 1942*, ed. Leslie Catherine Sanders, with Nancy Johnston, 116–29. Columbia: University of Missouri Press, 2002.

Popo and Fifina (1932). With Arna Bontemps. In *The Collected Works of Langston Hughes, Volume 11, Works for Children and Young Adults: Poetry, Fiction, and Other Writing*, ed. Dianne Johnson, 113–69. Columbia: University of Missouri Press, 2004.

"People without Shoes." *Haiti-Journal* (1934). In *The Collected Works of Langston Hughes, Volume 9, Essays on Art, Race, Politics, and World Affairs*, ed. Christopher C. De Santis, 46–49. Columbia: University of Missouri Press, 2002.

"To Negro Writers." *American Writer's Congress* (1935). In *The Collected Works of Langston Hughes, Volume 9, Essays on Art, Race, Politics, and World Affairs*, ed. Christopher C. De Santis, 131–33. Columbia: University of Missouri Press, 2002.

Don't You Want to Be Free? (1938). In *The Collected Works of Langston Hughes, Volume 5, The Plays to 1942*, ed. Leslie Catherine Sanders, with Nancy Johnston, 538–73. Columbia: University of Missouri Press, 2002.

A New Song. (1938). In *The Collected Works of Langston Hughes, Volume 1, The Poems: 1921–1940*, ed. Arnold Rampersad, 127- 50. Columbia: University of Missouri Press, 2001.

The Big Sea. (1940). In *The Collected Works of Langston Hughes, Volume 13, Autobiography: "The Big Sea,"* edited by Joseph McLaren. Columbia: University of Missouri Press, 2002.

"Need for Heroes." *Crisis* (1941). In *The Collected Works of Langston Hughes, Volume 10, "Fight for Freedom" and Other Writings on Civil Rights*, ed. Christopher C. De Santis, 223–29. Columbia: University of Missouri Press, 2001.

"Songs Called the Blues." *Phylon* (1941). In *The Collected Works of Langston Hughes, Volume 9, Essays on Art, Race, Politics, and World Affairs*, ed. Christopher C. De Santis, 212–15. Columbia: University of Missouri Press, 2002.

Shakespeare in Harlem (1942). In *The Collected Works of Langston Hughes, Volume 2, The Poems: 1941–1950*, ed. Arnold Rampersad, 13–72. Columbia: University of Missouri Press, 2001.

"Negro Writers and the War" (1942). In *The Collected Works of Langston Hughes, Volume 9, Essays on Art, Race, Politics, and World Affairs*, ed. Christopher C. De Santis, 215–19. Columbia: University of Missouri Press, 2002.

"Why and Wherefore" (1942). In *Langston Hughes and the "Chicago De-*

fender": *Essays on Race, Politics, and Culture, 1942–62,* ed. Christopher C. De Santis, 221–23. Urbana: University of Illinois Press, 1995.

"If Dixie Invades Europe" (1943). In *Langston Hughes and the "Chicago Defender": Essays on Race, Politics, and Culture, 1942–62,* ed. Christopher C. De Santis, 145–47. Urbana and Chicago: University of Illinois Press, 1995.

"My America" (1944). In *The Collected Works of Langston Hughes, Volume 9, Essays on Art, Race, Politics, and World Affairs,* ed. Christopher C. De Santis, 232–39. Columbia: University of Missouri Press, 2002.

"When a Man Sees Red" (1947). In *The Collected Works of Langston Hughes, Volume 7, The Early Simple Stories,* ed. Donna Akiba Sullivan Harper, 156–58. Columbia: University of Missouri Press, 2002.

"The Soviet Union" (1947). In *Langston Hughes and the "Chicago Defender": Essays on Race, Politics, and Culture, 1942–62,* ed. Christopher C. De Santis, 167–68. Urbana and Chicago: University of Illinois Press, 1995.

"The Soviet Union and Jews" (1947). In *Langston Hughes and the "Chicago Defender": Essays on Race, Politics, and Culture, 1942–62,* ed. Christopher C. De Santis, 168–70. Urbana and Chicago: University of Illinois Press, 1995.

"The Soviet Union and Color" (1947). In *Langston Hughes and the "Chicago Defender": Essays on Race, Politics, and Culture, 1942–62,* ed. Christopher C. De Santis, 170–72. Urbana and Chicago: University of Illinois Press, 1995.

"The Soviet Union and Women" (1947). In *Langston Hughes and the "Chicago Defender": Essays on Race, Politics, and Culture, 1942–62,* ed. Christopher C. De Santis, 172–74. Urbana and Chicago: University of Illinois Press, 1995.

"Faults of the Soviet Union" (1947). In *Langston Hughes and the "Chicago Defender": Essays on Race, Politics, and Culture, 1942–62,* ed. Christopher C. De Santis, 176–78. Urbana and Chicago: University of Illinois Press, 1995.

"Light and the Soviet Union" (1947). In *Langston Hughes and the "Chicago Defender": Essays on Race, Politics, and Culture, 1942–62,* ed. Christopher C. De Santis, 178–80. Urbana and Chicago: University of Illinois Press, 1995.

"Wooing the Muse" (1949). In *The Collected Works of Langston Hughes, Volume 7, The Early Simple Stories,* ed. Donna Akiba Sullivan Harper, 47–51. Columbia: University of Missouri Press, 2002.

The Poetry of the Negro, 1746–1949. Ed. with Arna Bontemps. Garden City: Doubleday, 1949.

Simple Speaks His Mind (1950). In *The Collected Works of Langston Hughes, Volume 7, The Early Simple Stories,* ed. Donna Akiba Sullivan Harper, 11–170. Columbia: University of Missouri Press, 2002.

The First Book of Negroes (1952). In *The Collected Works of Langston Hughes, Volume 11, Works for Children and Young Adults: Poetry, Fiction, and Other Writing,* ed. Dianne Johnson, 223–50. Columbia: University of Missouri Press, 2003.

Simple Takes a Wife (1953). In *The Collected Works of Langston Hughes, Volume 7, The Early Simple Stories,* ed. Donna Akiba Sullivan Harper, 171–379. Columbia: University of Missouri Press, 2002.

Famous American Negroes (1954). In *The Collected Works of Langston Hughes, Volume 12, Works for Children and Young Adults: Biographies,* ed. Steven C. Tracy, 13–108. Columbia: University of Missouri Press, 2001.

The First Book of Rhythms (1954). In *The Collected Works of Langston Hughes, Volume 11, Works for Children and Young Adults: Poetry, Fiction, and Other Writing,* ed. Dianne Johnson, 251–76. Columbia: University of Missouri Press, 2003.

The Sweet Flypaper of Life. With Roy DeCarava. New York: Simon and Schuster, 1955.

Anthology of Negro Poets in the USA—200 Years. Folkways Records, 1955.

Famous Negro Music Makers (1955). In *The Collected Works of Langston Hughes, Volume 12, Works for Children and Young Adults: Biographies,* ed. Steven C. Tracy, 109–97. Columbia: University of Missouri Press, 2001.

The First Book of Jazz (1955). In *The Collected Works of Langston Hughes, Volume 11, Works for Children and Young Adults: Poetry, Fiction, and Other Writing,* ed. Dianne Johnson, 277–321. Columbia: University of Missouri Press, 2003.

The First Book of the West Indies (1956). In *The Collected Works of Langston Hughes, Volume 11, Works for Children and Young Adults: Poetry, Fiction, and Other Writing,* ed. Dianne Johnson, 323–58. Columbia: University of Missouri Press, 2003.

I Wonder As I Wander. (1956). In *The Collected Works of Langston Hughes, Volume 14, Autobiography: "I Wonder As I Wander,"* ed. Joseph McLaren. Columbia: University of Missouri Press, 2003.

Simple Stakes a Claim (1957). In *The Collected Works of Langston Hughes, Vol-*

ume 8, The Later Simple Stories, ed. Donna Akiba Sullivan Harper, 11–142. Columbia: University of Missouri Press, 2002.

"Negro Writers Have Been on a Blacklist All Our Lives." *Mainstream* (July 1957): 46–48.

"Simple on Indian Blood." In *The Book of Negro Folklore,* ed. Langston Hughes and Arna Bontemps, 612–15. New York: Dodd, Mead, 1958.

Famous Negro Heroes of America (1958). In *The Collected Works of Langston Hughes, Volume 12, Works for Children and Young Adults: Biographies,* ed. Steven C. Tracy, 199–309. Columbia: University of Missouri Press, 2001.

The Langston Hughes Reader. New York: Braziller, 1958.

Selected Poems of Langston Hughes. New York: Vintage, 1959.

Simply Heavenly (1959). In *The Collected Works of Langston Hughes, Volume 5, The Plays to 1942,* ed. Leslie Catherine Sanders, with Nancy Johnston, 179–245. Columbia: University of Missouri Press, 2002.

"Writers: Black and White" (1959). In *The Collected Works of Langston Hughes, Volume 9, Essays on Art, Race, Politics, and World Affairs,* ed. Christopher C. De Santis, 380–83. Columbia: University of Missouri Press, 2002.

An African Treasury: Articles, Essays, Stories, Poems. New York: Crown, 1960.

The First Book of Africa (1960). In *The Collected Works of Langston Hughes, Volume 11, Works for Children and Young Adults: Poetry, Fiction, and Other Writing,* ed. Dianne Johnson, 359–93. Columbia: University of Missouri Press, 2003.

The Best of Simple. New York: Hill and Wang, 1961.

Ask Your Mama: 12 Moods for Jazz (1961). In *The Collected Works of Langston Hughes, Volume 3, The Poems: 1951–1967,* ed. Arnold Rampersad, 79–125. Columbia: University of Missouri Press, 2001.

Fight for Freedom (1962). In *The Collected Works of Langston Hughes, Volume 10, "Fight for Freedom" and Other Writings on Civil Rights,* ed. Christopher C. De Santis. Columbia: University of Missouri Press, 2001.

Five Plays of Langston Hughes. Ed. Webster Smalley. Bloomington: Indiana University Press, 1963.

A Pictorial History of Negroes in America. New York: Crown, 1963.

Poems from Black Africa: Ethiopia, South Rhodesia, Sierra Leone, Madagascar, Ivory Coast, Nigeria, Kenya, Gabon, Senegal, Nyasaland, Mozambique,

South Africa, Congo, Ghana, Liberia. Bloomington: Indiana University Press, 1963.

"Coffee Break." (1964). In *The Collected Works of Langston Hughes, Volume 8, The Later Simple Stories,* ed. Donna Akiba Sullivan Harper, 207–8. Columbia: University of Missouri Press, 2002.

New Negro Poets USA. Bloomington: Indiana University Press, 1964.

Simple's Uncle Sam (1965). In *The Collected Works of Langston Hughes, Volume 8, The Later Simple Stories,* ed. Donna Akiba Sullivan Harper, 143–275. Columbia: University of Missouri Press, 2002.

The Book of Negro Humor. New York: Dodd, Mead, 1966.

Black Magic: A Pictorial History of the Negro in American Entertainment. With Milton Meltzer. Englewood Cliffs, N.J.: Prentice-Hall, 1967.

The Best Short Stories by Negro Writers: An Anthology from 1899 to the Present. Boston: Little Brown, 1967.

"Soul Food" (1964). In *The Collected Works of Langston Hughes, Volume 8, The Later Simple Stories,* ed. Donna Akiba Sullivan Harper. 228–33. Columbia: University of Missouri Press, 2002.

Good Morning Revolution. Ed. Faith Berry. New York: Citadel Press, 1973.

The Return of Simple. Ed. Donna Akiba Sullivan Harper. New York: Hill and Wang, 1994.

Works about Langston Hughes

Ako, Edward O. "Langston Hughes and the Négritude Movement: A Study in Literary Influences." *College Language Association Journal* 28:1 (September 1984): 46–56.

Baldwin, Kate. *Beyond the Color Line and the Iron Curtain: Reading Encounters between Black and Red, 1922–1963.* Durham: Duke University Press, 2002.

Baraka, Amiri. "Amiri Baraka on Langston Hughes." Interview with St. Clair Bourne. *Langston Hughes Review* 15:2 (Winter 1997): 30–38.

———. Foreword to *The Big Sea,* by Langston Hughes. New York: Thunder's Mouth, 1986.

Barksdale, Richard. "Langston Hughes: His Times and His Humanistic Technique." In *Black American Literature and Humanism,* ed. R. Baxter Miller, 11–26. Lexington: University Press of Kentucky, 1981.

Barksdale, Richard, ed. *Langston Hughes: The Poet and His Critics.* Chicago: American Library, 1977.

Berry, Faith. *Langston Hughes: Before and Beyond Harlem*. Westport, Conn.: Lawrence Hill, 1983.

Berry, Faith, with Maurice A. Lubin. "Langston Hughes and Haiti." *Langston Hughes Review* 6:1 (Spring 1987): 4–7.

Burleigh, Robert. *Langston's Train Ride*. New York: Orchard Books, 2004.

Cha-Jua, Sundiata Keita. "'Lest Harlem See Red': Race and Class Themes in the Poetry of Langston Hughes, 1920–1942." *Afro-Americans in New York Life and History* 19:2 (July 1995): 53–81.

Cobb, Martha K. "Concepts of Blackness in the Poetry of Nicolás Guillén, Jacques Roumain, and Langston Hughes." *CLA Journal* 18 (1974): 262–72.

Cooper, Floyd. *Coming Home: The Life of Langston Hughes*. New York: Philomel, 1994.

Cullen, Countee. "Poet on Poet." *Opportunity*, March 4, 1926, pp. 73–75.

Cunningham, George P. "Afterword: Serious Fun." In *The Sweet and Sour Animal Book*, by Langston Hughes, 34–42. New York: Oxford University Press, 1994.

Davis, Arthur P. "Langston Hughes: Cool Poet." In *Langston Hughes: Black Genius*, ed. Therman B. O'Daniel, 18–38. New York: Morrow, 1971.

De Santis, Christopher C., ed. *Langston Hughes: A Documentary Volume*. Detroit: Thomas Gale, 2005.

———. *Langston Hughes and the "Chicago Defender": Essays on Race, Politics, and Culture, 1942–62*. Urbana: Illinois University Press, 1995.

Dickinson, Donald C. *A Bio-bibliography of Langston Hughes, 1902–1967*. New York: Archon, 1967.

Dixon, Melvin. "Rivers Remembering Their Source: Comparative Studies in Black Literary History—Langston Hughes, Jacques Roumain, and Negritude." In *Afro American Literature: The Reconstruction of Instruction*, ed. Dexter Fisher and Robert B. Stepto, 25–43. New York: MLA, 1979.

Dudden, Arthur Power. "The Record of Political Humor." In *American Quarterly* 27:1 (Spring 1985): 50–70.

Duffy, Susan. *The Political Plays of Langston Hughes*. Carbondale and Edwardsville: Southern Illinois University Press, 2000.

Emanuel, James. *Langston Hughes*. New York: Twayne, 1967.

Fowler, Carolyn. "The Shared Vision of Langston Hughes and Jacques Roumain." *Black American Literature Forum* 15:3 (Fall 1981): 84–88.

Gardullo, Paul. "Heading Out for the Big Sea: Hughes, Haiti and Constructions of Diaspora in Cold War America." *Langston Hughes Review* 18:1 (Spring 2004): 56–67.

Gates, Henry Louis, Jr., and K. A. Appiah, eds. *Langston Hughes: Critical Perspectives Past and Present.* New York: Amistad, 1993.

Gibson, Donald. "The Good Black Poet and the Good Grey Poet: The Poetry of Hughes and Whitman." In *Langston Hughes: Black Genius,* ed. Therman B. O'Daniel, 65–80. New York: Morrow, 1971.

Gold, Michael. "Introduction." In *A New Song,* by Langston Hughes. New York: International Workers Order, 1938.

Guillén, Nicolás. "El Camino de Harlem" (1928). In his *Prosa de Prisa: 1929–1972,* ed. Angel Augier, 1:3–6. Havana: Editorial Arte y Literatura, 1975.

———. "Conversación con Langston Hughes" (1931). In his *Prosa de Prisa: 1929–1972,* ed. Angel Augier, 1:16–19. Havana: Editorial Arte y Literatura, 1975.

———. "Recuerdo de Langston Hughes" (1967). In his *Prosa de Prisa: 1929–1972,* ed. Angel Augier, 1:314–16. Havana: Editorial Arte y Literatura, 1975.

Harper, Donna Akiba Sullivan. *Not So Simple: The "Simple" Stories by Langston Hughes.* Columbia: University of Missouri Press, 1995.

Haskins, James. *Always Movin' On: The Life of Langston Hughes.* Trenton: Africa World Press, 1993.

Jackson, Richard. "Langston Hughes and the African Diaspora in South America." *Langston Hughes Review* 5:1 (Spring 1986): 23–37.

———. "The Shared Vision of Langston Hughes and Black Hispanic Writers." *Black American Literature Forum* 15:3 (Fall 1981): 89–92.

Jemie, Onwuchekwa. *Langston Hughes: An Introduction to the Poetry.* New York: Columbia University Press, 1976.

Jones, Harry L. "Rhetorical Embellishment in Hughes' Simple Stories." In *Langston Hughes: Black Genius,* ed. Therman B. O'Daniel, 132–44. New York: Morrow, 1971.

Leach, Laurie F. *Langston Hughes: A Biography.* Westport, Conn.: Greenwood, 2004.

Martin-Ogunsola, Dellita L. "Langston Hughes and the Musico-Poetry of the African Diaspora." *Langston Hughes Review* 5:1 (Spring 1986): 1–17.

———. "Langston Hughes's Use of the Blues." *CLA Journal* 22 (1978): 151–59.

McLaren, Joseph. *Langston Hughes: Folk Dramatist in the Protest Tradition.* Westport, Conn.: Greenwood, 1997.

Medina, Tony. *Love to Langston*. New York: Lee and Low, 2002.

Meltzer, Milton. *Langston Hughes: A Biography*. New York: Crowell, 1968.

Miller, R. Baxter. *The Art and Imagination of Langston Hughes*. Lexington: University Press of Kentucky, 1989.

———. "'Even after I Was Dead': The Big Sea-Paradox, Preservation, and Holistic Time." *Black American Literature Forum* 11:2 (Summer 1977): 39–45.

Moglen, Seth. "Modernism in the Black Diaspora: Langston Hughes and the Broken Cubes of Picasso." *Callalo* 25:4 (Fall 2002): 1189–1205.

Moore, David Chioni. "'Colored Dispatches from the Uzbek Border': Langston Hughes's Relevance, 1933–2002." *Callaloo* 25:4 (Fall 2002): 1115–35.

Mullen, Edward J., ed. *Langston Hughes in the Hispanic World and Haiti*. Hamden, Conn.: Archon, 1977.

Nichols, Charles H., ed. *Arna Bontemps–Langston Hughes Letters, 1925–1967*. New York: Paragon, 1990.

Nwankwo, Ifeoma. "Langston Hughes and the Translation of Nicolás Guillén's Afro-Cuban Culture and Language." *Langston Hughes Review* 16:1–2 (Fall 1999–Spring 2001): ii, 55–72.

O'Meally, Robert G. Afterword to *The Book of Rhythms*, by Langston Hughes, 50–55. New York: Oxford University Press, 1995.

Ostrom, Hans. *Langston Hughes: A Study of the Short Fiction*. New York: Twayne, 1993.

Presley, James. "Langston Hughes, War Correspondent." *Journal of Modern Literary History* 5:3 (September 1976): 481–91.

Rampersad, Arnold. *The Life of Langston Hughes, Volume I, 1902–1941: I, Too, Sing America*. New York: Oxford, 1986.

———. *The Life of Langston Hughes, Volume II, 1914–1967: I Dream a World*. New York: Oxford, 1988.

———. "The Origins of Poetry in Langston Hughes." *Southern Review* 21:3 (Summer 1985): 695–705.

Rollins, Charlemae Hill. *Black Troubadour: Langston Hughes*. New York: Rand McNally, 1970.

Rummel, Jack. *Langston Hughes: A Poet*. New York: Chelsea House, 1988.

Smethurst, James. "'Don't Say Goodbye to the Porkpie Hat': Langston Hughes, the Left, and the Black Arts Movement." *Callaloo* 25:4 (Fall 2002): 1225–36.

Spicer, Eloise Y. "The Blues and the Son: Reflections of Black Self-Assertion in the Poetry of Langston Hughes and Nicolás Guillén." *Langston Hughes Review* 3:1 (Spring 1984): 1–12.

Stewart, Donald Ogden. *Fighting Words*. New York: Harcourt, Brace, and Co., 1940.

Thurston, Michael. "Black Christ, Red Flag: Langston Hughes on Scottsboro." *College Literature* 22:3 (Fall 1995): 30–49.

Tracy, Steven C. *A Historical Guide to Langston Hughes*. New York: Oxford University Press, 2004.

———. *Langston Hughes and the Blues*. Urbana: University of Illinois Press, 1988.

———. "To the Tune of Those Weary Blues." *MELUS* 8:3 (Fall 1981): 73–98.

Trotman, James C., ed. *Langston Hughes: The Man, His Art, and His Continuing Influence*. New York: Garland, 1995.

Walker, Alice. *Langston Hughes, American Poet*. New York: Thomas Y. Crowell, 1974.

White, Jeannette S., and Clement A. White. "Two Nations, One Vision: America's Langston Hughes and Cuba's Nicolás Guillén: Poetry of Affirmation: A Revision." *Langston Hughes Review* 12:1 (Spring 1993): 42–50.

Westover, Jeff. "Africa/America: Fragmentation and Diaspora in the Work of Langston Hughes." *Callaloo* 25:4 (Fall 2002): 1207–23.

Whitlow, Roger. *Black American Literature: A Critical History*. Chicago: Nelson Hall, 1973.

Selected Secondary Sources

Abu-Jamal, Mumia. "Interview with Mumia Abu-Jamal." Interview with Sally O'Brien. In *In Defense of Mumia*, ed. S. E. Anderson and Tony Medina, 180–91. New York: Writers and Readers, 1996.

Ahmad, Aijaz. *In Theory: Classes, Nations, Literatures*. London and New York: Verso, 1992.

Allen, Theodore W. *The Invention of the White Race, Volume One: Racial Oppression and Social Control*. London and New York: Verso, 1994.

Anderson, Benedict. *Imagined Communities: Reflections on the Origin and Spread of Nationalism*. London: Verso, 1983.

Anderson, Perry. "Components of the National Culture." In *Student Power: Problems, Diagnosis, Action*, ed. Alexander Cockburn and Robin Blackburn, 214–84. Baltimore: Penguin, 1969.

Baker, Houston A., Jr. *Blues, Ideology, and Afro-American Literature*. Chicago: University of Chicago Press, 1984.

Baraka, Amiri. "Aimé Césaire." In *The LeRoi Jones/Amiri Baraka Reader,* ed. William J. Harris, 322–32. New York: Thunder's Mouth Press, 1991.

———. *The Autobiography of LeRoi Jones/Amiri Baraka.* New York: Freundlich, 1984.

———. *Blues People: Black Music in White America.* New York: Morrow, 1963.

———. "Expressive Language." In *Home: Social Essays,* 166–72. New York: Morrow, 1966.

———. "Heathens." In *Transbluesency: The Selected Poems of Amiri Baraka/ LeRoi Jones, 1961–1995,* ed. Paul Vangelisti, 213–16. New York: Marsilio, 1995.

———. "The Myth of a Negro Literature." In *Home: Social Essays,* 105–15. New York: Morrow, 1966.

———. "The Revolutionary Tradition in Afro-American Literature." In *The LeRoi Jones/Amiri Baraka Reader,* ed. William J. Harris, 311–22. New York: Thunder's Mouth Press, 1991.

———. "The Theater and the Coming Revolution." Interview with C. W. E. Bigsby. In *Conversations with Amiri Baraka,* ed. Charlie Reilly, 130–45. Jackson: University Press of Mississippi, 1994.

———. "Y's 18." In *Transbluesency: The Selected Poems of Amiri Baraka/LeRoi Jones, 1961–1995,* ed. Paul Vangelisti, 230. New York: Marsilio, 1995.

Barnouw, Erik, ed. *Radio Drama in Action.* New York: Rinehart and Co., 1945.

Baudrillard, Jean. "Continental Drift: Questions for Jean Baudrillard." Interview with Deborah Solomon. *New York Times Magazine,* November 20, 2005, p. 6.

———. *The Vital Illusion.* New York: Columbia University Press, 2000.

Belli, Gioconda. "The Blood of Others." In *Sandino's Daughters Revisited: Feminism in Nicaragua,* by Margaret Randall, 168. New Brunswick: Rutgers University Press, 1994.

Benjamin, Walter. "The Author as Producer." In *Reflections,* ed. Peter Demetz, trans. Edmund Jephcott, 220–28. New York: Schocken Books, 1986.

Bennett, Lerone, Jr. *The Shaping of Black America.* New York: Penguin, 1974.

Berger, John. *Ways of Seeing.* New York: Penguin, 1972.

Beverley, John, and Marc Zimmerman. *Literature and Politics in the Central American Revolutions.* Austin: University of Texas Press, 1990.

Blues in the Mississippi Night. 1946. Rykodisc, 1990.

Bone, Robert. *The Negro Novel in America*. New Haven: Yale University Press, 1958.

Boyd, Melba Joyce. "The Politics of Cherokee Spirituality in Alice Walker's *Meridian*." In *Minority Literatures of North America*, ed. Wolfgang Karrer and Hartmut Lutz, 115–27. Tübingen, Germany: Gunter Narr Verlag, 1990.

———. *Wrestling with the Muse: Dudley Randall and the Broadside Press.* 2003.

Brathwaite, Kamau. "History of the Voice." In *Roots*, 259–304. Ann Arbor: University of Michigan Press, 1993.

Brennan, Timothy. *At Home in the World: Cosmopolitanism Now.* Cambridge: Harvard University Press, 1997.

———. "The National Longing for Form." In *Nation and Narration*, ed. Homi K. Bhaba, 44–70. New York: Routledge, 1990.

———. "Places of Mind, Occupied Lands: Edward Said and Philology." In *Edward Said: A Critical Reader*, ed. Michael Sprinker, 74–95. Oxford: Blackwell, 1992.

———. *Salman Rushdie and the Third World: Myths of the Nation.* New York: St. Martin, 1989.

Breton, André. *Manifestoes of Surrealism*. Trans. Richard Seaver and Helen R. Lane. Ann Arbor: University of Michigan Press, 1969.

Brown, Deming. *Soviet Attitudes toward American Writing.* Princeton: Princeton University Press, 1962.

Brown, Sterling. "Arna Bontemps: Co-worker, Comrade." *Black World* 22:11 (September 1973): 92–98.

———. *Negro Poetry and Drama and The Negro in American Fiction.* New York: Atheneum, 1969.

Burns, Ben. *Nitty Gritty: A White Editor in Black Journalism.* Jackson: University Press of Mississippi, 1996.

Cabral, Amílcar. "The Weapon of Theory." In *Unity and Struggle: Speeches and Writings of Amílcar Cabral*, ed. PAIGC, trans. Michael Wolfers, 119–37. London and New York: Monthly Review Press, 1979.

Calverton, V. F. *The Liberation of American Literature.* New York: Charles Scribner's Sons, 1932.

Carew, Jan. *Fulcrums of Change: Origins of Racism in the Americas and Other Essays.* Trenton: Africa World Press, 1988.

Caute, David. *The Great Fear: The Anticommunist Purge under Truman and Eisenhower.* New York: Simon and Schuster, 1978.

Chuck D. *The Autobiography of MistaChuck: Report from the Commissioner.* Mercury Records, 1996.

Clarke, John Henrik, ed. *Marcus Garvey and the Vision of Africa.* New York: Vintage, 1974.

Cross, Brian. *It's Not about a Salary: Rap, Race, and Resistance.* London and New York: Verso, 1993.

Cruse, Harold. *The Crisis of the Negro Intellectual: A Historical Analysis of the Failure of Black Leadership.* New York: Quill, 1984.

Cudjoe, Selwyn R. *Resistance and Caribbean Literature.* Athens: Ohio University Press, 1980.

Davis, Arthur. *From the Dark Tower: Afro-American Writers, 1900–1960.* Washington, D.C.: Howard University Press, 1974.

Dorfman, Ariel. *The Empire's Old Clothes: What the Lone Ranger, Babar, and Other Innocent Heroes Do to Our Minds.* New York: Pantheon Books, 1983.

Du Bois, W. E. B. "Back to Africa" (1923). In *Marcus Garvey and the Vision of Africa,* ed. John Henrik Clarke, 105–18. New York: Vintage, 1974.

———. *Black Reconstruction: An Essay toward a History of the Part which Black Folk Played in the Attempt to Reconstruct Democracy in America, 1860–1880.* 1935. Reprint. New York: Atheneum, 1969.

———. "Closing Ranks Again." *Amsterdam News* (1942). In *W. E. B. Du Bois: A Reader,* ed. David Levering Lewis, 739–41. New York: Henry Holt, 1995.

———. "A Litany at Atlanta" (1921). In *The Poetry of the Negro, 1746–1949,* ed. Langston Hughes and Arna Bontemps, 18–21. Garden City: Doubleday, 1949.

———. "The Negro and Democracy" (1924). In *W. E. B. Du Bois: A Reader,* ed. Andrew G. Paschal, 74–78. New York: Macmillan, 1971.

———. *The Souls of Black Folk.* 1903. Reprint. New York: Penguin, 1969.

———. "Two Novels: Nella Larsen, *Quicksand,* and Claude McKay, *Home to Harlem.*" *Crisis* 35 (June 1928): 202.

———, ed. "Negro Editors on Communism: A Symposium of the American Negro Press." *Crisis* (April 1932): 117–19.

During, Simon. "Literature—Nationalism's Other? The Case for Revision." In *Nation and Narration,* ed. Homi K. Bhabha, 138–53. New York and London: Routledge, 1990.

Ellison, Ralph. *Shadow and Act.* New York: Random House, 1964.

Fanon, Frantz. *The Wretched of the Earth.* Trans. Constance Farrington. New York: Grove, 1968.

Franco, Jean. "Dependency Theory and Literary History: The Case of Latin America." *Minnesota Review* 1:5 (Fall 1975): 65–80.

Franklin, John Hope. "Ethnicity in American Life: The Historical Perspective." In his *Race and History: Selected Essays, 1938–1988,* 321–31. Baton Rouge: Louisiana State University Press, 1989.

Galassi, Peter, ed. *Roy DeCarava: A Retrospective.* New York: Museum of Modern Art, 1996.

Garon, Paul. *Blues and the Poetic Spirit.* London: Eddison Press, 1975.

Gates, Henry Louis, Jr. *The Signifying Monkey: A Theory of African-American Literary Criticism.* New York and Oxford: Oxford University Press, 1988.

Gayle, Addison. *Claude McKay: The Black Poet at War.* Detroit: Broadside Press, 1974.

Glissant, Edouard. *Caribbean Discourse.* Trans. J. Michael Dash. Charlottesville: University Press of Virginia, 1989.

Gramsci, Antonio. *History, Philosophy and Culture in the Young Gramsci.* Ed. Pedro Cavalcanti and Paul Piccone. St. Louis: Telos Press, 1975.

———. "On Education." In *Selections from the Prison Notebooks,* trans. and ed. Quintin Hoare and Geoffrey Nowell-Smith, 26–43. New York: International Publishers, 1971.

———. *Selections from Cultural Writings.* Trans. William Boelhower. Ed. David Forgacs and Geoffrey Nowell-Smith. Cambridge: Harvard University Press, 1985.

Guillén, Nicolás. *La paloma de vuelo popular—Elegías.* Buenos Aires: Editorial Losada, 1959.

———. *Prosa de Prisa: 1929–1972.* Vol. 1. Ed. Angel Augier. Havana: Editorial Arte y Literatura, 1975.

Guralnick, Peter. *Feel Like Going Home.* Boston: Little, Brown, 1999.

Gutiérrez, Gustavo. *The Power of the Poor in History.* Trans. Robert R. Barr. Maryknoll, N.Y.: Orbis, 1983.

Habiby, Emile. *The Secret Life of Saeed, the Ill-Fated Pessoptimist.* Trans. Salma Khadra Jayyusi and Trevor Le Gassick. Columbia, La.: Readers International, 1989.

Harlow, Barbara. *Resistance Literature.* New York: Methuen, 1987.

Harris, William H. *The Harder We Run: Black Workers since the Civil War.* New York: Oxford University Press, 1982.

Harris, Wilson. *Kas-Kas: Interviews with Three Caribbean Writers in Texas.* Ed. I. Munro and Reinhard Sander. Austin: African and Afro-American Research Institute, 1972.

Haywood, Harry. *Black Bolshevik: Autobiography of an Afro-American Communist.* Chicago: Liberator Press, 1978.

Hegel, G. W. F. *On Tragedy.* Ed. A. and H. Paolucci. New York: Doubleday, 1962.

Hobsbawm, Eric. *The Age of Extremes.* New York: Vintage, 1994.

Jacobs, Norman, ed. *Culture for the Millions? Mass Media in Modern Society.* New York: Beacon, 1964.

James, C. L. R. *American Civilization.* Ed. Anna Grimshaw and Keith Hart. 1950. Cambridge: Blackwell, 1993.

———. "The American Intellectuals of the Nineteenth Century." In *American Civilization,* ed. Anna Grimshaw and Keith Hart, 50–98. Cambridge: Blackwell, 1993.

———. *The Black Jacobins.* 1938. New York: Vintage, 1963.

———. "Black Power" (1970). In *The C. L. R. James Reader,* ed. Anna Grimshaw, 362–74. Oxford: Blackwell, 1992.

———. "An Interview: C. L. R. James and Pan-Africanism." Interview with Patrick Griffith. *Black World* (November 1971): 12–16.

Jameson, Fredric. *Brecht and Method.* London and New York: Verso, 1998.

———. "The Politics of Utopia." *New Left Review* 25:1 (January–February 2004): 35–54.

Jiménez, Mayra. *Poesía campesino de Solantiname.* Managua: Ministerio de Cultura, 1984.

Jiménez, Rafael Duharte. "The 19th Century Black Fear." In *AfroCuba: An Anthology of Cuban Writing on Race, Politics and Culture,* ed. Pedro Perez Sarduy and Jean Stubbs, 37–46. Melbourne, Australia: Ocean, 1993.

Jordan, June. "For the Sake of People's Poetry: Walt Whitman and the Rest of Us." In *On Call: Political Essays,* 5–15. Boston: South End Press, 1985.

Keil, Charles. *Urban Blues.* Chicago: University of Chicago Press, 1966.

Kelley, Robin D. G. *Hammer and Hoe: Alabama Communists during the Great Depression.* Chapel Hill: University of North Carolina Press, 1990.

———. *Race Rebels: Culture, Politics, and the Black Working Class.* New York: Free Press, 1994.

Kozol, Jonathan. *Savage Inequalities: Children in America's Schools.* New York: Crown, 1991.

Kubayanda, Josaphat B. *The Poet's Africa: Africanness in the Poetry of Nicolás Guillén and Aimé Césaire.* Westport, Conn.: Greenwood Press, 1990.

Kumar, Amitava. "Postcoloniality: Field Notes." *Minnesota Review* 41:2 (Spring 1995): 271–79.

Kunitz, Stanley J., and Howard Haycraft, eds. *Twentieth Century Authors.* New York: H. W. Wilson, 1942.

Laluah, Aquah. "The Souls of Black and White." In *The Poetry of the Negro,*

1746–1949, ed. Langston Hughes and Arna Bontemps, 385–86. Garden City: Doubleday, 1949.

Lamming, George. *The Pleasures of Exile.* Ann Arbor: University of Michigan Press, 1992.

———. "The West Indian People." *New World Quarterly* 2:2 (1966): 54–69.

Lasch, Christopher. *The Agony of the American Left.* New York: Alfred A. Knopf, 1969.

Latimer, Bettie Darcie. "For William Edward Burghardt DuBois on His Eightieth Birthday." In *Poetry of the Negro, 1746–1949,* ed. Langston Hughes and Arna Bontemps, 208–9. Garden City: Doubleday, 1949.

Lefebvre, Henri. *Critique of Everyday Life.* Trans. John Moore. London: Verso, 1991.

Lenin, V. I. "Preliminary Draft of Theses on the National and Colonial Questions." In *Lenin on the National and Colonial Questions: Three Articles,* 20–29. Peking: Foreign Language Press, 1975.

———. *Selected Works.* English Edition, vol. 2, part 2. Moscow: Foreign Languages Publishing House, 1952.

Livingstone, Dinah, trans. *Poets of the Nicaraguan Revolution.* London: Katabasis, 1993.

Lukács, Georg. "Reification and the Consciousness of the Proletariat." In *History and Class Consciousness,* 83–222. Trans. Rodney Livingstone. Cambridge: MIT Press, 1968.

MacDonald, Dwight. "A Theory of Mass Culture." In *Mass Culture: The Popular Arts in America,* ed. Bernard Rosenberg and David Manning White, 59–73. New York: Free Press, 1957.

Martí, José. "Our America." In *Our America: Writings on Latin America and the Struggle for Cuban Independence,* ed. Philip S. Foner, trans. Elinor Randall, 84–94. New York and London: Monthly Review Press, 1977.

Mattelart, Armand, and Michele Mattelart. *Rethinking Media Theory.* Trans. James A. Cohen and Marina Urquidi. Minneapolis: University of Minnesota Press, 1992.

McKay, Claude. *Banjo.* New York: Harper and Brothers, 1929.

———. *The Selected Poems of Claude McKay.* New York: Harcourt, Brace and World, 1953.

Minter, David. *William Faulkner: His Life and Work.* Baltimore: Johns Hopkins University Press, 1980.

Morejón, Nancy. *Nación y mestizaje en Nicolás Guillén.* Havana: UNEAC, 1982.

————. "Race and Nation." In *AfroCuba: An Anthology of Cuban Writing on Race, Politics and Culture,* ed. Pedro Perez Sarduy and Jean Stubbs, 227–37. Melbourne, Australia: Ocean, 1993.

————, ed. *Recopilación de textos sobre Nicolás Guillén.* Havana: CASA, 1972.

Morrison, Toni. *Playing in the Dark: Whiteness and the Literary Imagination.* Cambridge: Harvard University Press, 1992.

Naficy, Hamid. *The Making of Exile Cultures: Iranian Television in Los Angeles.* Minneapolis: University of Minnesota Press, 1993.

Naison, Mark. *Black Communists in Harlem during the Depression.* Urbana: University of Illinois Press, 1983.

A Nation of Poets: Writings from the Poetry Workshops of Nicaragua. Los Angeles: West End Press, 1985.

Newsome, Effie Lee. "Morning Light: The Dew Drier." In *The Poetry of the Negro, 1746–1949,* ed. Langston Hughes and Arna Bontemps, 55. Garden City: Doubleday, 1949.

Nixon, Rob. "London Calling: V. S. Naipaul and the License of Exile." *South Atlantic Quarterly* 87:1 (Winter 1988): 1–37.

Odum, Howard W., and Guy B. Johnson. *Negro Workaday Songs.* 1923. Reprint. New York: Negro Universities Press, 1969.

Randall, Margaret. *Sandino's Daughters Revisited: Feminism in Nicaragua.* New Brunswick: Rutgers University Press, 1994.

Reed, Ishmael. *Mumbo Jumbo.* New York: Atheneum, 1972.

————. *19 Necromancers from Now.* Garden City: Doubleday, 1970.

Retamar, Roberto Fernández. "Caliban: Notes toward a Discussion of Culture in Our America." In *Caliban and Other Essays,* trans. Edward Baker, 3–45. Minneapolis: University of Minnesota Press, 1989.

Robinson, Cedric J. *Black Marxism: The Making of the Black Radical Tradition.* London: Zed, 1983.

Rodney, Walter. *The Groundings with My Brothers.* London: Bogle L'Ouverture, 1969.

Rodríguez-Mourelo, Belén. "The Search for Identity in the Poetry of Langston Hughes and Nicolás Guillén." *Langston Hughes Review* 16:1–2 (Fall 1999–Spring 2001): ii, 39–54.

Rowe-Evans, Adrian. "V. S. Naipaul." *Transition* 40 (December 1971): 56–62.

Said, Edward W. *Beginnings: Intention and Method.* New York: Columbia University Press, 1975.

————. *Culture and Imperialism.* New York: Vintage, 1993.

————. "The Mind of Winter: Reflections on Life in Exile." *Harper's Magazine* 269 (September 1984): 47–55.

————. *Orientalism*. New York: Vintage, 1979.

Seibers, Tobin. *Cold War Criticism and the Politics of Skepticism*. New York and Oxford: Oxford University Press, 1993.

Sidran, Ben. *Black Talk*. New York: Holt, Rinehart and Winston, 1971.

Sivanandan, A. "All That Melts into Air Is Solid: The Hokum of New Times." In *Communities of Resistance: Writings on Black Struggles for Socialism*, 19–59. London: Verso, 1990.

Solomon, Mark I. *Red and Black: Communism and Afro-Americans, 1929–1935*. New York: Garland Press, 1988.

Smart, Ian Isidore. *Nicolás Guillén: Popular Poet of the Caribbean*. Columbia: University of Missouri Press, 1990.

Spady, James, and Joseph Eure. *Nation Conscious Rap*. Brooklyn: PC International Press, 1991.

Thiong'o, Ngũgĩ wa. *Writers in Politics*. London: Heinemann, 1981.

Thompson, Robert Farris. *Flash of the Spirit: African and Afro-American Art and Philosophy*. New York: Vintage, 1984.

Titon, Jeff Todd. *Downhome Blues Lyrics: An Anthology from the Post–World War II Era*. Boston: Twayne, 1981.

Toop, David. *The Rap Attack II: From African Rap to Global Hiphop*. London: Pluto Press. 1992.

Von Eschen, Penny M. *Race against Empire: Black Americans and Anticolonialism, 1937–1957*. Ithaca: Cornell University Press, 1997.

Walker, Margaret. "For My People" (1934). In her *This Is My Century: New and Selected Poems*, 7. Athens: University of Georgia Press, 1989.

————. *Richard Wright: Daemonic Genius*. New York: Warner, 1988.

Williams, Eric. *From Columbus to Castro: The History of the Caribbean, 1492–1969*. London: Andre Deutsch, 1970.

Wittner, Lawrence S. *Cold War America: From Hiroshima to Watergate*. New York: Praeger, 1974.

Woodson, Carter G. "The Negro Washerwomen: A Vanishing Figure." *Journal of Negro History* 15 (July 1930): 270–77.

Wright, Bruce. "Journey to a Parallel: Summer, 1947." In *The Poetry of the Negro, 1746–1949*, ed. Langston Hughes and Arna Bontemps, 200–201. Garden City: Doubleday, 1949.

Index

African American civil rights movement: beginning of, 10, 222; under attack by reactionaries, 21, 159; and anti-imperialism, 40; and the post-civil rights generation, 66; marginalization of, 86; and black culture, 130; and the American Communist Party, 139; effects of on U.S. society, 143; and Marxism, 145; as perceived by Hughes, 153–54, 181–83

African American working class: and party-building, 39; position of in the U.S. class struggle, 41, 82–91, 98–99, 103; of Harlem, 46, 149–54, 217; and Garveyism, 51; and the blues, 55, 113, 118–19, 124; and art, 68, 155, 160, 205; relationship of to the American Communist Party, 73–76, 80, 97, 189, 224–25; and class-consciousness, 112–17, 121; and popular culture, 125, 131–33, 136, 141, 164, 224

Ahmad, Aijaz, 26–27, 40–41

Allen, Theodore W., 21, 50–51, 84–86, 120, 143–44, 201, 224

American anticommunism, 2, 10, 107, 137–41, 157–62, 183–84, 190–92, 220–22, 224–25

American communist movement: relationship of to Hughes, 8–10, 87–97, 107–8, 131, 137–45, 154–57, 162, 220–21, 224–25; relationship of to black nationalism, 39, 74–77, 82, 100, 189, 226; position of on white supremacism, 51, 78; and "non-Americanism," 69, 73; and Afro-Caribbean politics, 70; in Harlem, 73, 78–79, 105; and the Popular Front, 80–81, 84–86; and W. E. B. Du Bois, 82; use of Lenin's self-determination thesis by, 100–102, 132; and African American intellectuals, 129

American socialist nationalism, 42, 154

American studies, 2–5, 26, 38, 46–49, 209, 219, 222

Anderson, Perry, 16–19

Anti-imperialism, 22, 40, 100

Bacon's Rebellion, 85

Baker, Houston A., Jr., 60, 65–66, 104, 129, 155

Baldwin, Kate, 98

Baraka, Amiri: aesthetic theory of, 8, 156, 210; view of on American studies, 27–29, 44, 49; and Marxism, 37–39; position of on cultural nationalism, 40, 57–58; embrace of anticolonial revolutionary nationalism by, 41, 201, 204; theory of the blues, 54, 72–74, 110–14, 221; on the African American

245